Grief and Powerlessness

Helping People Regain Control of Their Lives

of related interest

Storymaking in Bereavement
Dragons Fight in the Meadow
Alida Gersie
ISBN 1 85302 176 8 pb
ISBN 1 85302 065 6 hb

Interventions with Bereaved Children
Susan C Smith and Sister Margaret Pennells
ISBN 1 85302 285 3

Good Grief 2
Exploring Feelings, Loss and Death with Over Elevens and Adults
Barbara Ward and Associates
ISBN 1 85302 340 X

Good Grief 1
Exploring Feelings, Loss and Death with Under Elevens
Barbara Ward and Associates
ISBN 1 85302 324 8

Music Therapy in Health and Education
Edited by Margaret Heal and Tony Wigram
ISBN 1 85302 175 X

Grief and Powerlessness
Helping People Regain
Control of Their Lives

Ruth Bright

Jessica Kingsley Publishers
London and Bristol, Pennsylvania

The right of Ruth Bright to be identified as author of this work has been asserted by her in accordance with the Copyright, Designs and Patents Act 1988.

First published in the United Kingdom in 1996 by
Jessica Kingsley Publishers Ltd
116 Pentonville Road
London N1 9JB, England
and
1900 Frost Road, Suite 101
Bristol, PA 19007, U S A

Library of Congress Cataloging in Publication Data
A CIP catalogue record for this book is available from the Library of Congress

British Library Cataloguing in Publication Data
Bright, Ruth
Grief and Powerlessness : helping people to regain control of their lives
1.Grief 2.Bereavement 3.Loss (Psychology)
I.Title
152.4
ISBN 1853023868

Printed and Bound in Great Britain by
Biddles Ltd. Guildford and King's Lynn

Contents

A Personal Introduction

Definitions

Why Powerlessness?

Like Humpty Dumpty in Lewis Carroll's book *Through the Looking Glass* (Carroll 1933, p.114), we can make words mean whatever we choose them to mean, and some words have different agendas depending on who is using them! Powerlessness in the present book is used to mean loss of control over one's life as a whole, with all that this implies. Power for what purpose? The autocratic politician who treats the people of his country as objects to be manipulated for his own hunger for power and who loses his place in government or the exiled cruel dictator may resent their loss of power, but few of us would offer either of them any sympathy, except perhaps sadness that their lives were so grossly twisted.

But power is also the right to control at least part of one's own life (one cannot control all illness and disability), power to make decisions, and it includes being regarded as a person who has a right to personal relationships and privacy. Yet there are countless people throughout the world who either lose their power, their right to personal freedom and privacy, or who never gain it because of their skin colour, caste, poverty, political or religious creeds and so on. It is also true that none of us, even in a true democracy, has the right to make each decision on the basis of personal preference. The general good must be involved in the decisions of society. The person who scrawled on the wall of a shopping centre: 'F..k you and your laws,' clearly separated himself or herself from this concept!

No one book can deal with all humanity's needs, but I have strong feelings about the broader concepts of power and freedom and so am presenting here, necessarily in condensed form, some thoughts on the powerlessness of grief, and the grief of powerlessness.

What is Grief?

Throughout life we experience loss, an event or a circumstance which deprives us of something or someone. This may be a loved person, employment, prospects of health, hopes for the future. We experience change as we move from home to school, school to employment, the single life to marriage and partnership, and so on. Many of these changes are seen by outsiders as bringing unalloyed happiness and yet they involve major changes in lifestyle and, for this reason, they can be stressful (Paykel *et al.* 1969). Because such changes may be associated with loss of control, they can be a source of grief.

The child whose mother leaves him at school on that first day is going through a normal process, and yet, for that child, the sight of the mother walking away may elicit terrifying fears of abandonment. This might be because these fears are part of the child's normal response to change or because some previous experience, such as a time in hospital or the absence of his mother in some crisis situation, has taught him that life without her is scary.

All through life there are comparable situations of change and loss which *might* and many which, almost inevitably, *do* cause grief. But how do we experience grief? There can be:

- sadness, with crying, sighing
- constantly or frequently thinking and speaking of the loss
- fear
- anger
- disappointment
- guilt
- some changes in sleeping and appetite
- loss of interest in normal events, a wish for isolation
- loss of concentration on work and relationships because our focus is on our grief.

All these are normal responses to a significant loss, and (depending upon our personality, the nature of the loss and our previous experiences) there is an ongoing process of adaptation. We gradually experience a lessening of intensity. We do not forget, but our grieving over the loss and the loss itself cease to be the main focus of our lives.

To those who have not experienced a major loss, some of these (for example, anger and guilt) may seem surprising, but our language gives us some clues about the diversity of the experience. We speak of 'coming to grief', which can refer to a toddler running too fast for his own imperfect balance, a teenager driving recklessly, or a financier with doubtful ethics. But in each circumstance the phrase usually means risking trouble, and in the process causing physical or emotional pain, sadness and perhaps conflict to oneself and others. We refer to having a grievance, which usually encompasses anger, conflict and resentment, but may or may not include sadness. Staff in group homes or other establishments for handicapped people have, in the last few years, been required to keep a 'grievance book' in which residents can write down or ask to have written down complaints, comments and requests about problems they experience. Anger is often a strong component of entries in grievance books, and there may be sadness as well.

But anger is common in all forms of grief. It can be bewildering because people feel they should not be angry, whether with God for allowing the loss, with the person for dying, with oneself for feeling so lost and frightened, and yet they are angry. C.S. Lewis, in his book *A Grief Observed* (1962, pp.7, 29, 46), commented that he had not realised that grief was so close to fear, and fear is often linked with anger, as when a mother smacks her toddler for giving her a fright by running out on the road.

Manifestations of Grief

Anniversary Reactions

There are times when grief, apparently resolved, resurfaces. For example, it reappears on going to a significant place (the corner where the car accident occurred, the church where the marriage began which has now ended in divorce, and so on). Grief also re-emerges on anniversaries, not only of someone's death but perhaps of the date a diagnosis was made of a terminal illness, the last admission to hospital, the date a holiday had been planned, a birthday, wedding anniversary, and so on. There are the special times when we grieve someone's absence, whether from death or divorce: the wedding of a child, a graduation ceremony, one's own illness when one remembers past times of support and comfort.

Blocked Grief

We grieve when we see other people setting off for work when we ourselves are unemployed and longing for employment. This is a natural reaction, a normal grief. But there are also the grief responses we would usually describe as abnormal. These include the problems of those who find it difficult or impossible to cope with the loss, whose grief is blocked for a variety of reasons. Here we see chemical dependencies – abuse of alcohol, illegal drugs, prescription drugs. We may see depressive illness or other psychiatric disturbance, gross changes to appetite and sleep patterns, changes of relationships as when the person becomes strangely quarrelsome, alienating those who would otherwise be able to help, and so on. All such major changes in behaviour alert us to a potentially dangerous (perhaps lethal) situation, and we know that help is needed. (See also Chapter 11 on blocked grief.)

Perceptions of Grief

Grief has many faces and we must remember them all! Ideas on grief have developed over the last several years; *Grieving* (Bright 1986) was written at a time when most people thought of grief only in terms of death and dying, and as consisting of sadness. There was scant recognition of the many other aspects of grief and little general recognition of the diversity of our responses to loss, although that book did make reference to the broader view of grieving.

'Time is the great healer' is a truism responsible for much avoidable suffering, and one has to say, over and over again, that time does *not* heal unless one is able to use that time with insight and wisdom! Without this, time usually serves only to encapsulate the grief, as a time bomb which is likely to explode unexpectedly when some new experience hooks into the hidden memories.

Powerlessness

In the last decade, what has become more and more obvious is the powerlessness of those who grieve, a realisation that powerlessness is both a consequence of being in grief and is itself a cause for grief. This can be a two-way experience and may become a malevolent spiral downwards, when grief causes feelings of powerlessness which in turn cause us more grief, and so we go down, to what can become a living hell. When someone suffers a major loss, others often try to be helpful by making decisions for that person, and those decisions are frequently wrong yet cannot be reversed. A house is sold, someone is moved to live with a son in order to leave the house where so many memories of a relationship are centred, and so on. The powerlessness of those who are grieving is a major cause of subsequent unhappiness.

Being powerless is in itself a cause of grief, and we have seen a long-delayed expression of this in indigenous peoples who are only now able to express their anger and sadness over the destruction of their culture by settlers and conquerors. But private powerlessness is also a cause for grief, whether we consider the powerlessness of an abused wife to extract herself from an impossible marriage, the powerlessness of an abused child to prevent that abuse, or any other similar situation. The victim might not see this as being a grief, but it can justly be described as such, and the lifelong after-effects are indeed grief responses to the unhappy experiences and the powerlessness. And so this book discusses the linking of the two, the associations between grief and powerlessness. Clearly a single book cannot cover every detail of every experience, but I hope that enough has been included to suggest lines for further study and thought as well as giving an overview of the two linked topics.

Why Music Therapy? Is it a 'Must'? A Personal Comment

The reader will find many descriptions of music as a therapeutic tool, and, as a grief counsellor who entered the field through music therapy, I believe that music gives us an enormous advantage. Music does not make people unhappy, although it may appear to do so, as when an apparently cheerful individual starts to cry as a particular piece of music is played. What music does is to lift the lid off emotions which are already there, hidden below the surface. Within a therapeutic relationship, it helps to create an atmosphere of trust and openness which permits freedom of conversation, the giving of information and enhanced insight. This may lead on to resolution and change, and this too may include therapeutic use of music.

But although descriptions of the use of music permeate the book, the text is written for all the helping professions. The information about the use of music in therapy is intended only to illustrate and give additional clarity to the case histories described, it is no way a *sine qua non*.

Scope of the Book

The present book is written after 35 years of work with adults, so that case histories and references on the whole deal with adults. We also need, however, to understand about grief in children and adolescents (a) because many adults we meet need help because of childhood experiences which were left unresolved, and (b) because we also see some who are bewildered and frightened by the grief-related behaviour they observe in children for whom they have responsibility. There are therefore some reading lists and sections on grief in children. But I have worked also for many years with adults who suffer from mental retardation, whose responses are (because of their mental age) usually those of young children. Such people are not treated or perceived as children, but it is helpful to look at responses of children to loss and grief in order to understand their behaviour.

The material and ideas contained in this book are intended for a wide readership; for professional counsellors in hospital, clinic or community; for nurses and others who are not formally counsellors but whose work brings them in contact with those who are grieving; for those in related professions such as the clergy and funeral directors. Many hospitals use trained volunteers in personal work with relatives and patients, and (as in the Palliative Care Unit of the Royal Victoria Hospital in Montreal) for counselling intervention, bereavement follow-up, and other tasks which are far removed from the 'doing the flowers' routine to which volunteers have in the past been limited. The book will also be useful for the community in general, for volunteers in telephone support services, those who visit neighbours and friends, as well as those who, for no particular reason, want to find out more.

How the Book is Put Together

The chapter headings are self-explanatory, but there are many places where there is overlap in content. It is impossible, for example, to avoid discussing loss of expectation both in the section under that heading and in the section on the grief of chronic disability and handicap. I make no apology for this overlap because it demonstrates both the complexity of humanity, and the impossibility of neatly stacking emotions into numbered pigeon-holes! The book is empirical in nature. There are many areas in grief counselling which are not amenable to the extraction of hard data such as can be obtained in double blind trials of pharmaceutical drugs. The method adopted therefore is to describe observations and make deductions from those observations. This method has much in common with grounded theory (Glaser and Strauss 1968).

Over many years of work, I have been impressed with the capacity of people to look honestly into themselves (even if what they see is unpleasant or frightening), and to achieve change. I am continually amazed and heartened by people's willingness to speak about their lives; sometimes, it seems, telling themselves (rather than me) for the first time about what life has been like and how it has shaped them. Usually this leads to forgiveness rather than hate, and it is this forgiveness which empowers people to change, whether it is forgiveness of oneself or of others. Without the honesty and openness of my clients, neither my own work nor this book would have happened, and I offer them all my gratitude.

I am also grateful to colleagues who have accepted me as part of the team, even though my work has been on a part-time basis, and for their willingness to share their skills with me and talk about their own work. They have shared with me their hopes and fears, and honoured me by asking for help in times of their own professional and personal times of grief and loss. Last of all, my thanks to my husband, Desmond, for the help he has given by using his skills as an editor, as well as the many years since 1960 when he first encouraged me to work through music with disadvantaged people.

Terminology of 'Cognitive Impairment'

Many terms are used to describe a difficulty with cortical activity and intelligence; the oldest term I recall hearing is 'mental deficiency'. Unfortunately any word, if used in a disparaging manner, comes to have pejorative connotations, and for this reason we now see an array of descriptions such as:

- developmental disability (Australia)
- mental handicap (various)
- people with special needs (various)
- intellectually challenged (various)

But none of these gives a true picture of the person's real needs. Some parents, when told that their child is 'developmentally disabled', have thought that it meant only physical impairment. 'Mental handicap' could surely also apply to schizophrenia; the implications of 'intellectually challenged' are unclear, and even more confusion arises from 'special needs'.

We can see a parallel in 'death', which (to some) is so terrible a word that use 'passed away', 'gone over to the other side'.

But, in using euphemisms, we risk confusion.

In this book, therefore (at the risk of being criticised for using unfashionable terminology), the terms 'mental retardation' and 'mentally retarded' are used. These give a clear and definable picture of what is meant, and also conform to terminology used in the United Nations Classification system (World Health Organization 1980), in the Diagnostic and Statistical Manual of Mental Disorders edition IV (American Psychiatric Association 1994) and in international journals.

CHAPTER 1

Coping with Loss
The Context and the Response

Griefs of Adult Life

All through life we experience grief and loss, and one can in the present book only list some of the possible causes:

○ relationship breakdown

○ unemployment

○ death of significant persons

○ illness and/or disability which reduce independence and quality of life, in ourselves or significant others

○ loss of the mind and spirit of a significant person, through the processes of dementia, as in Alzheimer's disease

○ loss of contact with adult children because of quarrels or because they are moved away by work commitments

○ loss of relationship because the adult children lead a totally different life from that of their parents.

We deal with such losses in ways that reflect our own self-esteem and resilience, role models from the past or the present, support from those around us. Our ability to deal with loss also reflects our physical and mental health. We must not, however, neglect the difficulty of resolving even normal grief; the process is difficult and takes time. Bartrop described suppression of immune function during times of grief (Bartrop *et al.* 1977), and Parkes found significant variability to illness in the first year following the death of a spouse (Parkes 1975, p.101).

Not all losses are experienced by all people, and some of the 'non-universal' losses are dealt with elsewhere in this book. Death and dying are, however, necessarily part of the human experience, although there are wide variations in the age at which death occurs and in the trauma which it brings.

Death and Dying

Sudden death usually leaves us with a great deal of unfinished business, whether the death has been a natural one from a heart attack or similar abrupt incident, or the more traumatic death from suicide. Dealing with this is complex for anyone, and especially so if the relationship has been a difficult one. The long-term illness, whilst bringing its own distress, does give us the opportunity of saying 'good-bye' and of tying off the loose ends of life's relationships, even of discussing with the soon-to-be-survivor the possible plans for the future (important when the death is to occur at an early age and there are children to be considered).

The dying person himself or herself is often able to deal with the illness and its terminal nature, especially if cared for by a supportive palliative care team, with home care for as long as possible and (when it becomes necessary) admission to a unit where good palliative care is practised, including pain management and other techniques to control the distressing features of terminal illness. The relatives, too, benefit from the support given in the context of palliative care, and, when one attends clinical case conferences, it is interesting and heartening to see how much thought is expended on the needs of relatives, to ensure that they are given the maximum empathic support and comfort.

It is also true that, in coping with grief and loss, dysfunctional families cope poorly, and care is needed to prevent a maladaptive outcome (Kissane 1994). If such families can be identified and helped during the pre-death period, then we may assume that there is greater hope of successful processes of mourning than if maladaptive responses have already been established.

It is also important that patients and relatives are allowed to express their anger freely, without staff (who find this emotion hard to deal with) trying to talk them out of it! Most people who have received adequate support and appropriate counselling as they face the death of someone close to them do not go on to suffer psychiatric illness or chemical dependencies, although they are able to mourn and express their unhappiness.

Ideal situations are not, however, universal and staff of hospital units or free-standing palliative care hospices do meet difficulties which challenge their skills.

Problems with Death

One can imagine, for example, the sensitivity required in helping the young woman (mother of two small children and the wife of a man dying from melanoma) to cope with her anger because her husband had refused to seek treatment for the expanding black mole on his back because he expected divine intervention, and to look for surgical help would to him have been a failure of faith.

Anger made it difficult for a woman to adjust to or even fully to mourn the death of her middle-aged husband because he had refused to discuss the future or even allow her to say good-bye because such interchange symbolised a lack of faith in healing. She had needed to thank him for their many happy years together, talk with him about her future, ask forgiveness for the (minor) failures of empathy and so on. But this was all denied, to the detriment of her peace of mind in the years that lay ahead.

Empathy is also needed when there has been a mutual pretence (when both patient and relatives know that death is close but each pretends otherwise, in order to protect the other) or when there is denial, a total rejection of the possibility of death, for whatever reason. There is controversy as to whether the refusal described above, based on religious faith, should or should not be regarded as denial. The results, however, appear to be similar!

Attitudes of Dying People

It may be assumed that those who have an expectation of life after death will face death more comfortably than those who have no such expectation. However, this is not necessarily so. Hinton has remarked that, although a strong religious belief is supportive for those who are dying, a weak religious faith causes more fear of death than one sees in those who believe that death is the end, with no faith at all (Hinton 1967, p.84). It appears that some people of religious faith see God primarily as a being who punishes. They therefore look back over their lives, see their imperfections and dread eternity as being likely to bring eternal punishment and not eternal joy.

One case history which illustrates this well is as follows. The social worker asked that the music therapist visit a dying man because it seemed probable that he did know that death was near but his wife refused to permit him to be told.

On the therapist's arrival at the bedside, after some preliminary conversation on music and the patient's interests, the man was invited to select a piece of music he would like to hear played for him. He selected the metrical version of the 23rd Psalm, 'The Lord's my Shepherd', which includes a verse about passing through the valley of the shadow of death. As she was playing, the therapist thought about the man's reasons for selecting the psalm, and, deciding that it might be his way of leading to a conversation about death, said at the end, 'A lot of people ask me for that piece when they know that there is not a lot of life left for them.'

The remark was phrased in that way because if the man needed to deny his impending death, it was possible for him to reply non-committally, 'Oh really!', or with a similar remark which would probably bring the discussion to an end. But, if he wished to talk about death, then the way was open for him to continue. 'Yes, of course, that's why I asked for it' was the reply, the tone of voice suggesting that he was surprised that anyone needed to ask! After some further conversation about death, fear of hurting people, his own lack of fear about the future and so on, the conversation was drawn to a close.

The therapist was then able to return to the social worker and pass on the necessary information that the man did indeed know that he was to die soon. This in turn was passed on to the wife so that, for the past few days remaining to them, their relationship was able to be based upon openness and honesty, after the social worker had helped the wife to face her own need to deny the closeness of death for her husband.

This vignette provides a clear example of the occasional need for an outsider to facilitate communication when it has otherwise proved difficult for people to talk naturally to each other. It demonstrates the risks of the mutual pretence referred to above. Despite the possibility of difficult relationships during the final stages of living, those who work with dying people are continually heartened by the courage of patients and relatives alike, not in denying but in working through the suffering. Even when the loss is that of an untimely death, there are many who are able to acknowledge their grief, anger, disappointment over the premature nature of the death and their sadness over the dying process.

Euthanasia and Palliative Care

There are moves towards making chosen death – *euthanasia* (a good death) – freely available, but this topic is too wide to be dealt with adequately in the present book. Twycross's work on pain management should be required reading for all involved with palliative care and with the euthanasia lobby as offering scientifically sound and profoundly humane methods of dealing with this distressing problem (Twycross 1980, 1988).

The risks of making euthanasia *standard treatment* are that:

- depression will not be properly dealt with because a lethal injection will be given instead
- some will seek their own death to save the family money
- some will seek it to save their family distress
- some will be talked into it against their will, or over-persuaded by publicity in the media
- some will die because it suits someone else.

It is recognised that some people do truly seek death, and it is important not to allow the euthanasia debate to become confused with discussion of using or withholding methods which serve only to keep someone artificially alive when the natural outcome of a given condition is death.

A new fear about euthanasia has recently emerged in Australia where, in 1995, moves were made in the Northern Territory legislature to make voluntary euthanasia legal. This apprehension concerns Koori (indigenous Aboriginal) people who live a tribal or semi-tribal life, and who commonly fear hospitals as a place of possible death; it is believed that those fears will be heightened to an intolerable extent by a belief (however ill-founded) that Koori people suffering from what are deemed to be incurable conditions will be killed, and there is a very real expectation that, as a result, indigenous people will avoid seeking medical help. There were strong moves in mid-1995 to prevent the legislation being put into effect and to have the matter re-considered.

Many people who are suffering from a terminal illness wish to live it through to the end. Their wishes and philosophy must not be harmed by pressure or media coverage articles about an easy death. Pain and humiliation are often given as reasons for euthanasia, but we should be aware that there are reliable ways to give sufferers control over their own pain medication. This control is vitally important in reducing the feelings of powerlessness which affect some (though not all) of those dying from cancer.

Driver syringes which are fixed to the person's belt, operated by battery and delivering doses of medication directly under the skin, are one way of providing control and permitting the person to remain ambulant. For others, decisions about the amount of medication to be used, within predetermined limits to avoid toxicity, give control over pain to a remarkable degree. Not all people feel able or wish to be involved in their own medication in this way, but many people who are cared for by palliative care teams find comfort and power in making decisions on medication.

The fact that the oncologist and others take extended periods of time to talk with people about their pain, its severity, its timing, its quality, the bearable or unbearable nature of the pain and so on, is in itself a comfort in emphasising that one is still a person and not just a statistic!

Experienced physicians know that it is important always to *sit* for an interview, and if possible to sit at a lower level, so that the bed-fast person is looking downwards rather than upwards as the conversation continues (Pollard 1995).

For all of us who care for those who suffer, and who try to help their grief over that suffering, our gifts of empathy must take top priority. But we must use our brains too, to work out ways of dealing with particular situations so as to enhance the dignity of the grieving person!

Difficulties in Grieving

Despite the availability for many years of books and articles on grief and loss, we find misunderstandings about grief counselling such as those illustrated by these examples.

- ○ The psychiatric patient who stormed from the room saying 'I'm sad about my mother's death but I am *not* grieving!' (To him grief was a sign of weakness.)

- ○ The young woman who had given up her job to care for her dying mother said 'But how can I have grief counselling; my mother is not dead yet!'

- ○ A man of 35, suffering from chemical dependency following multiple relationship losses, said, 'How can grief counselling help, nobody has *died*!'

Community Attitudes

Community attitudes to grief and loss are changing, but some people still find it difficult to deal with grief and loss, and there are many possible reasons for this. Perhaps one reason is that our skills in finding cures for diseases have made us feel that even death itself should be curable by the right medicines or treatment. The powerlessness we feel when faced by incurable illness and death is a source of fear as well as grief.

Today's technology has another, different impact on our grieving. We are, in one sense, too strongly aware of the nature of disasters around the world.

So many scenes of violence and horror are shown daily on television that we may find it difficult to grieve in any personal sense; the whole thing becomes less rather than more real. The very extent of our awareness of modern disasters, whether natural or man-made, forces us to put our grief 'on hold' and we may end by never dealing with it. Perhaps we then transfer this blocking over world tragedies to our personal losses? Again we feel powerless; we can see on the screen, perhaps as a live telecast, all the tragedies which are taking place, but are totally unable to do anything about them.

Parents have always experienced the death of children, and, although in times past there must have been personal grief, there would also have been a fatalistic knowledge that several children in a large family would die before adulthood, and indeed a recognition that large families were necessary for survival for that very reason.

Disability too must always have occurred, and in the past it was less likely that the child would survive into adult life.

In some parts of the world even today infanticide is used to rid society of children who are perceived as a potential or actual burden on the community.

But it is probably only in a high-technology society, with advanced medical care, that parents experience that sense of astonished and horrified disbelief coupled with the frustration of helplessness when told that their child has a major disability, or a fatal condition and cannot live beyond a few weeks or months.

People have always died from the illnesses and disasters which afflict mankind, but in the past we did not have the possibility of maintaining existence by artificial means. Euthanasia, too, has probably long been a reality, and is still a topic of burning controversy as to the ethical and moral implications. Here we are seeing not powerlessness, but reluctance and ambivalence about using the powers we have for fear of doing harm instead of good.

Difficulties in dealing with loss arise in many instances because of difficulties in relationships from the past. The woman who has been the victim of marital abuse but has kept it secret finds it impossible to deal with the comments at the funeral about how wonderful her husband was and how much she will miss him. Sometimes the widow has cried bitterly at the funeral, and this has supported the on-lookers' beliefs that she was heartbroken over the death. In my work with such women I have found, however, that the grief was for the relationship that never was, sorrow that her hopes for shared love and companionship were never achieved. She may go on to develop a full-blown depressive illness or a chemical dependency or otherwise become submerged by her own pretence and unhappiness.

Parents whose son was addicted to hard drugs and caused great difficulties in the family, find it hard to cope with their feelings of peace when he eventually dies from an overdose.

Only rarely does one see someone who has the courage openly to express feelings of relief, as a mother did about her daughter, for many years a self-mutilator who had made many suicide attempts, when finally one of those attempts was completed.

Processes of Grief

Worden (Worden 1982) has described the four tasks of grieving as being:

- accepting the reality of the loss
- experiencing the pain of grief
- adjusting to an environment in which the loved person is no longer present
- withdrawing emotional energy from the lost relationship.

He sees the function of grief counselling as being the effecting of these tasks. But these processes also apply when the loss is not of a person but some other significant entity or relationship, in ourselves and in others.

There are risks in adopting the steps of a process too rigidly, and even in 1986 there was reference (in the present book's predecessor) to the stages outlined by Kubler Ross as not being intended as an exact prototype for dealing with the prospect of death (Bright 1986, p.49). But Worden's simple list of tasks provides us with a basis for understanding both normal and what we may decide to call abnormal grief.

Many people do accomplish the tasks alone, but there are also many who, for one reason or another, cannot cope without help. That assistance can consist only of facilitation, the empowering or enabling of the grieving person. Nobody else can grieve for us. There is no surgical procedure to remove the experience painlessly, nor does the prolonged use of sedatives achieve anything except an added risk of prolonging or blocking the grieving process, thereby harming the individual and the family.

When we are trying to facilitate the grieving process, we need to recognise that every individual and every family has a unique timetable and an agenda, which provide the context in which we mourn. We cannot, and we should not attempt to, either hurry the process along or delay it. Nor should we distort it because of our views on what constitutes normal grief. Instead, we should try to recognise the style of life and relationships of the grieving person(s) so that our facilitating may be the more effective.

The Reality of Loss

The first requirements in Worden's list, accepting the reality of the loss, followed by an experience of pain and adjustment to the loss, all vary with individuals, and our timetable strongly affects the rate at which we achieve acceptance. Mothers of children who have died will describe their searching behaviour, how, sometimes for years, they wonder whether a mistake was made, whether it is their baby in the pram outside the shop, their child going down the road to school, and so on. The elderly widow shocks her neighbour by saying, 'I must go in and cook the meal, my husband always likes it to be ready when he gets home.' The widower waits to hear his wife's key in the lock years after she has died, with an unconscious thought that she has been away again visiting her ailing mother.

Are these instances of abnormality? Or is it that the dead are so imprinted on us that they have a kind of continuing life within our hearts? Or is it a kind of occasional protection against intolerable pain? Whatever answer we give, it is certain that we must not label people as abnormal because they take a long time over the first and second steps. Sometimes they return to them after other steps seem to have been accomplished, and they seem to have adjusted to a new way of life and reinvested their energy in other aspects of living.

There are indeed responses to grief which are rightly called abnormal, such as the dependence upon chemicals in order to avoid dealing with the loss. But there are also minor variants to the process of relinquishment which we can accept as being within normal limits.

The Pain of Grief

We have seen that ideas on grief have developed over recent years, with greater understanding that there is work involved. Statements about time healing everything are still heard. These can be simply platitudes mouthed by an onlooker who does not know what else to say to a person in grief, but it can be an excuse or reason for that person to avoid painful memories, because 'They will eventually all go away anyway, won't they?' But do they? It seems more likely that, unless people are empowered to deal with them, the pain of the past remains like an unexploded bomb primed to go off when some new experience hooks into the hidden past. We must recognise this phenomenon if we are not to be puzzled by some instances of apparently inexplicable anger and sadness.

An elderly Jewish lady was referred to the physiotherapy department of a hospital for pain management, and staff members were surprised by the level of her anger. She revealed that she was the only one of her generation to survive the Holocaust, and her only grandson, the one hope for family continuity, had recently died (aged 12) from leukaemia. Her pain was perceived by the clinicians as being a manifestation of sadness, old and new, together with new anger with the medical profession for not being able to cure the condition, new anger with her son for allowing the boy to make his own decision about discontinuing treatment, and old anger at the genocide which had almost wiped out both families. One can guess that the concentration camp requirement, that emotions be hidden, was responsible for this lady's legacy of hidden anger, which was expressed only at the death of her grandson.

Adjusting an Environment

The unique agenda of each family and each individual also means that emphasis on particular losses may seem to be different from what we might expect, and we see displacement. A woman who appeared to have dealt fairly well with the death of her son in a motor-bike accident focused her loving attention upon his dog. When the dog died, she appeared more distressed about that than she had about her son, and brought the dog's collar and leash to hospital when she came in for surgery, hanging it beside her bed.

The father of a young man who had shot himself appeared to focus his grief on the fact that his son had borrowed his, the father's, gun in order to kill himself. It was, one assumes, actually the guilt and grief about the death itself which was at the basis of his distress, but on the surface it appeared to be the gun alone on which his thoughts were centred.

When looking into patterns of family relationships, as the context of grief resolution, we must recognise that the 'family' may indeed consist of blood relatives and relations by marriage. But for the socially isolated individual, the 'family' (whether or not so designated) may consist of workmates, golfing rivals, drinking companions, the handyman at a block of apartments, or fellow members of a religious congregation. For individuals in an institution, 'family' may consist of the staff who care for them.

Groups of people living together because of a shared attitude or commitment to an ideal may well regard themselves as a family, whether or not this concept is recognised legally. Even those who live in separate places, such as a church congregation, may perceive themselves as 'family' in a sharing of mutual concern and support.

In the 1990s the legal concept of family is changing so that same-sex couples (perhaps with adopted children or, for Lesbian couples, with a child born to one of them by artificial insemination), may be classified as a family. (The construct of the family – who is or is not accepted as part of it – affects mourning processes in AIDS-related illness and bereavement. See Chapter 8 on AIDS.)

Families (however we define that entity) vary greatly in their structure, intimacy and mode of living. The extremes may be seen thus:

○ some families are so closely knit as to be incapable of independent decisions and life

○ other families are so loosely knit that individual members may find it hard to gain support and comfort in times of stress

○ some families have rigidly structured modes of living, so that any change to those modes causes despair or other manifestation of disaster

○ other families have no structure and may be frankly dysfunctional; they therefore find it hard to cope with disaster or change because of their lack of organisation and/or constant conflict between members.

Olson and colleagues, in a helpful article, have discussed family patterns of response in terms of their existing structures and modes of operation, in terms similar to these (Olson, Russell and Sprenkle 1983). But these are extremes, and most families fall somewhere in between, with some traits of organisation and some of disorganisation, some traits of closeness and some of separateness. As long ago as 1967, Ellard wrote of the impossibility of helping a bereaved spouse without comprehending the type of relationship which had characterised the marriage (Ellard 1967), and this is only one more aspect of family life in general.

Withdrawing Emotional Energy

The balance of power may be crucial to family relationships, and disability, death and loss, grief and resolution all change that balance, subtly or grossly, depending upon the style of the family. Unless we have some understanding of family structures and group relationships, we shall experience difficulty in helping many of our clients to cope with their losses, because today we are working not so much with individuals alone, but in the context of the individual as part of his environment. Perhaps what is most difficult of all challenges, we also need to understand ourselves, since our own feelings about family relationships can influence our style of working.

There are some who appear to be without any family, either biologically or conceptually, and we must be aware of the implications of this too. The griefs may be different – disability, loss of employment, and so on; or the grief may be concerned with the lack of a supportive family. Some of those who appear to be without family are bearing a heavy burden of loss because the family broke up, or because many members were lost through war or other disaster. It is a rarity for someone to be totally self-contained, totally self-sufficient. People who describe themselves in that way are often found to be carrying a hidden anger and sadness over past relationship failures.

Abnormal Grief Responses in Psychiatric Illness

Someone with an established psychiatric illness finds it difficult to deal with a loss, and one commonly sees a new episode of the illness if the person has been in remission or, if the person is currently ill, an exacerbation of the present episode. It seems probable that some who have a first episode of psychiatric illness following a loss have been at-risk or dysthymic before- hand, but have not been identified as *a case* (Bright 1994). The nature of the illness may modify the abnormal response, but we are likely to see reactions which are stronger than what would be regarded as normal, or we may see an unusual, even a bizarre, response.

Such was the case with the young man of 24, whose 'difficult' father had died after a short illness. A month later the son presented himself at a local police station asking for help because he said that God had killed his father as a punishment for his, the son's, masturbation. He was highly agitated, depressed and obsessed with the delusional belief. He spent seven weeks in hospital, with a diagnosis of schizophrenia, still on the whole maintaining this belief, and was re-admitted some months later, again highly agitated and depressed with constant conversation and requests for reassurance about his beliefs regarding his father's death and his own behaviour as the cause of it. Eventually the illness yielded to treatment and the young man was discharged to return to the university. But, on the first anniversary of the death, he came to the out-patients department of a major teaching hospital seeking further reassurance and, shortly afterwards, required re-admission to an acute unit.

Those who are classified as forensic patients, having come into hospital after killing someone, and having been found 'guilty but insane' or the equivalent verdict, are a cause of staff dilemmas. As the illness yields to medication, we see the patient's growing awareness of what he or she did, often with a wish for death through suicide. Do we say or imply that there is no need for grief or guilt over the killing, and so cut off the grieving process, because the death was a consequence of illness? Do we encourage the expression of grief and risk the possibility of suicide? Or somewhere in between?

A helpful response in such situations has been to draw a middle line, saying, in various ways, 'It is very sad that it happened.' It is then all right to grieve, but the grief can be over the illness. It prevents blocking of grief processes, it prevents an unhealthy 'it really doesn't matter' approach, but it allows the person to survive without total loss of self-esteem because of guilt.

Meaning in Dying

We need to reassure ourselves that death is not in vain. Despite strong opposition, Australia supported the USA in the Vietnam war, and sent some conscripts. In 1995 reports quoted various Americans involved in that war saying it had been un-winnable and should never have been fought. Strong anger was felt in Australia at these reports; this responce illustrates our need to find meaning in death. It is bad enough to lose young men in war believing that their deaths achieved something. But when those in command say that it was useless and should never have happened, the sadness is deepened because the deaths are seen as useless (*Sydney Morning Herald* 1995). The wave of anger which arose is two-fold, felt by:

- those who need to retain a sense of meaning for that war, so that they can continue to believe that the sacrifices were indeed necessary
- those who believe that the war was useless and wrong, who are angry because the sacrifices were demanded at all.

The yearning for meaning may find its outlet in action. This does not diminish the sadness of the loss but perhaps deals with the anger; it is manifested in many ways:

- The striving of parents of a child killed on a dangerous stretch of road to get a pedestrian crossing placed there, to prevent further deaths and so that the death of their child is not utterly wasted.
- The wish of someone with a terminal illness to be involved in drug trials. (There are those who perceive this is a form of bargaining with death, but it is clear that, for many such volunteers, this is not the covert motive.)
- Activity to promote pacifism so that war would never happen again.

○ The search for a non-material dimension to death in finding a way to a greater reality on a spiritual level.

All of us who work with people who grieve need to look at our spiritual attitudes, and accept the right of others to have beliefs which are different from our own, so that those who do seek for a spiritual meaning in impending death, in the death of others or in other tragic events are helped and not hindered in that search. A video recording made in the palliative care unit of a major teaching hospital helps us to new thoughts on this, as we see and hear two patients, within days or hours of death, speak of their (different) spiritual attitudes at that time (Mount 1992).

Other Special Risks through Life

One observes that those who are themselves ill and in hospital at the time of a bereavement are especially at risk of a poor outcome because of feelings of guilt at not being there, not being able to prevent the death. Inability to attend the funeral, for whatever reason, further militates against adequate resolution; there may even be doubts as to whether the person truly is dead (Bright 1994).

Mutilating surgery is also a time of trauma for the patient, and we see all over the world the setting up of support groups, for those having mastectomy, laryngectomy, colostomy or ileostomy, and so on. But each person must cope personally with his or her grief, and we should recognise the period surrounding such surgery as being a time of high risk.

The elderly parent of a now-middle-aged handicapped 'child' is also at risk of depression at the time the parent is too frail to continue to care for that child and, for the first time, the child is moved into a group home or some other establishment.

Those who gave birth to a handicapped child at the time when parents were told, 'Put him into an institution, forget about him and get on with your life', describe how they now suffer from strong feelings of guilt when they read of encouragement to parents to keep their handicapped child at home. One such woman said, 'We only did what we were told and now we hear that we were all wrong. But how were we to know?'

Comparable difficulties are experienced from time to time when, in the emphasis on normalisation, parents are led to feel that they should not be involved in their adult child's welfare, that only professionals know what is best! Trends and fashions in the care of handicapped children are an ongoing source of bewilderment in some areas, so that new philosophies constitute times of special risk for parents of those who are disabled.

CHAPTER 2

Griefs of Children

Children experience many changes as a normal part of life, as was mentioned in the Introduction, and the way the child responds to this will depend upon many factors, including:

- stable relationships and trust which have been already established between the child and the family
- how much preparation for change has been done, assuming the child is at an appropriate age, for example, when starting school
- probably, the child's genetic armamentum, since it does seem that, for no obvious reason, some children are better able than others to cope with separation and change.

We see in the way adults speak to children about death an indication of their own attitudes, their own incredulity that modern medicine cannot cure everything, a confusion as to the immortality or destruction of the human spirit.

Children and Death

It had been thought that children had no concept of death in their early years. In the twentieth century and in Western society, it became common for children to be shielded from death, sent away at times of critical illness, prevented from attending funerals, told lies such as 'Grandma went on a long journey'. But such behaviour is not universal. It would, for example, be pointless in 1995 to tell a child in the Israel–Palestine border areas that so-and-so had gone on a journey when the child has seen that person dismembered by a bomb.

In the Elizabethan era, memorials were placed in churches (and are still to be seen), showing the mother kneeling at one side, her dead daughters lined up behind her, the dead sons behind their father. Under such conditions of child mortality there would have been no possibility that children would be unaware of death. Fatal illness and the facts of bereavement were a normal experience.

The attitudes of today, and the implicit expectation that medicine can cure everything, have already been mentioned. It does seem that the shielding of children from ideas of death is also part of our shielding of ourselves, an enactment of our own fears of the unknown future beyond the grave. We hear adults explain that they cannot grieve because it might upset their children. We are dismayed at the effect this blocking of natural responses must have on the children, but realise that this is probably an excuse by the adult to avoid the pain of doing their own grief-work.

It is not difficult to imagine the bewilderment of children who are grieving the death of their mother when they see their father apparently unmoved by the event or drinking himself into a stupor after the funeral. What do such children learn of death and grief, except to do the same?

In talking with children we are forced to look at ourselves. We have to answer questions and be ready to speak of what we ourselves truly believe. And, if for one reason or another we are unable to do this, it is easier to pretend than to talk. Hence the lies 'She has fallen asleep', 'He has gone away but will be back one day.' Some children have developed a terror of falling asleep because of that particular euphemism for death!

What do people in general and children in particular think and believe about death? Kastenbaum and Aisenburg have remarked that even very young children can recognise the difference between *dead* and *living*, and they describe the sorrow of an 18-month-old child on seeing a dead bird. It would seem, however, that it is some years before a child recognises that death of a person is different from the 'death' of a motor car, and that death, in its real sense, is permanent (Kastenbaum and Aisenburg 1972). Thus, a 4-year-old boy, on the way home from attending the funeral service for his grandfather, said, 'When Poppy comes back, we'll go and visit him, won't we Mum?' This inability to comprehend the permanence of death has implications when we are considering childhood suicide.

One young child, when she was 6, had an interesting concept that when a person died, it was the head which went to heaven, because she said that it was your head which made you the person you are. Thus, if the *person* survived, it must be the head that went to heaven. This idea also probably illustrates the confusion experienced by children because their use of words is often different from that of adults. We may speak of the body as the antithesis of the soul, whereas to a child the body is the main trunk and limbs as distinct from the head. Thus to speak of burying a dead body probably implied that the head was not buried. To avoid confusion, we must choose our words and concepts carefully when we talk to children, to fit in with their stage of development.

It is not difficult to bring up the subject of death. A dead bird on the side of the road, the death of a pet, the prolonged illness of an elderly relative, an ambulance speeding down the road to a motor vehicle accident, these and other situations can be the trigger for conversation at an appropriate level. A new development which has brought benefit to many children has been the setting-up of resources for schools, for children of all ages from kindergarten to the end of high school.

Dr Louise Rowling has done extensive work in schools in relation to the occurrence of fatal accidents to school children, either outside school activities or actually in the course of school programmes (Rowling 1994). Events which need to be dealt with include, for example, accidents in which a school child is killed whilst on a school expedition, or a bus accident in which several children are killed on their way to a special event.

The rate of accidental death in the community is such that one can take it for granted that deaths of pupils, deaths of parents or siblings will occur within a school community, and some of these may well be by suicide. There will also be divorce and separation in students' families. In all of these, the life of the child at school (his or her schoolwork, behaviour, relationships and so on) will be affected, and the staff need support and help in dealing with these situations. Working with school staff has been shown to be useful, both when a tragedy has actually taken place and in preparation for a possible tragedy.

There are now several useful books about death in children, and those recommended are listed in the 'Ideas for Reading' at the end of the book.

Fear of the Unknown

The child is dependent on security for optimum development (Kastenbaum and Aisenburg 1972, p.283). Death and ideas connected with death may symbolise for all of us the fear of the unknown, and for the child no less than for the adult. 'You'll come back again – not like my Mum?' This was the frantic plea of an adult mentally retarded man when told that someone was going overseas for a holiday. This same man asks at the end of every music session 'When you come back?' And it would appear that this constant questioning dates only from the death of his mother and the lie told him at that time.

The concept of death as falling asleep may destroy the peace of mind of children in that they may be afraid to go to sleep in case they too die in their sleep. Perhaps this childhood concept lies beneath the fears felt by many at the prospect of an anaesthetic? There are, of course, other aspects of fear of the unknown which we must consider in relation to children and death. The adult who is himself afraid and uncertain as to *where* and *what* death is will not cope well with the questions of children. Before entering into any such discussions one must make up one's own mind about what happens when life ends.

The Dying Child

Children are sometimes able to express symbolically things which they cannot put into words. One 5-year-old was dying from a cardiac condition but the family was uncertain as to whether or not the little girl knew that she was soon to die, until she did a drawing of her family. This showed a tree with six branches on it, each with a red heart drawn at the end of the branch, one branch for each member of the family – parents and four sisters – but she drew no branch for herself. Instead, she drew on the ground beneath the tree a large red heart to represent herself. What surprised her parents was that the child had not talked of the heart as being the seat of the illness, nor of her impending death, and yet through her symbolic drawing she was able to tell them that she knew the truth of her situation.

Because of the difficulty parents have in talking with a dying child in a realistic way about the future, or loss of future, one often observes what may be called a 'bogus jollity' from the visiting parent in a children's ward. One hears remarks such as 'When you get better and come home we will do so-and-so', but the child is aware, because of the experience he has of extreme illness, pain, fatigue, and so on, that he is not going to get better. This false bonhomie leads to isolation of the child, who usually colludes in the behaviour because, it is thought, he has the feeling 'My parents cannot bear to talk about what is going on, I had better protect them.' The consequence is that, unless there are understanding staff who can bear to talk honestly about the future, the child is utterly alone in coping with impending separation from life.

We should not delude ourselves. Children *do* need honesty at this time, at their own pace; they are often indeed aware of impending death and desperately need acceptance (Waechter 1971). Parents, too, need support in their fears and sadness, not least because support will enable them to maintain an honest relationship with their dying child. Honesty may also help to lessen the guilt experienced after death, when the knowledge that they were *not* able to say goodbye nor to finish unfinished transactions would be likely to lead to regrets or deep remorse.

Speaking in a lecture given in 1978 at the Rozelle Hospital in Sydney, Australia, Elizabeth Kubler Ross told the audience that mothers hold on to their dying children in a spiritual sense so that it is rare for a child to die when his mother is present. Rather, she said, the death occurs when the mother is away having a meal or a sleep, and unless the parents know this they may suffer deep remorse that they were not there when the death took place. This may apply just as much to adult children as to young children. Grown 'children' too may only be able to let go their hold on life when their parents are absent, and the parents of adult children who die in their absence also suffer grief and guilt because of this.

Grief of Separation

The long-lasting nature of scars from grief of separation, and the capacity of the adult to relive traumatic happenings long after the events when something triggers the memory, was clearly illustrated for me in 1982, on seeing the documentary films made by the Robertsons of children's grief and despair over separation from parents (chiefly from the mother). These films are referred to by several authors (Parkes 1975, p.271; Robertson and Robertson 1967).

At the age of 5 I spent some weeks in a London hospital. At this time visiting by parents was evidently perceived as creating a hazard for the child, and visiting was permitted for only one hour once a week. To see the Robertsons' films as an adult proved a highly stressful experience. Although several memories had been retained of the unhappiness, some had been forgotten and to see the films brought these too to the surface. Amongst the terrifying memories which returned was that of a staff nurse (her flashing silver belt is a clear picture) saying after visiting hour, 'I wish your mother didn't come to see you; she just upsets you', and of the fear that crying would lead to visiting being forbidden. So tears were held back, but (presumably as a displacement) frequent vomiting occurred, to the anger of the senior nursing staff. Strong memories also returned of an attachment to a particular nurse and a feeling of abandonment when she had her time off, a feeling that there was no longer a champion available. Even today a feeling of love and gratitude to that girl is retained!

If these were the feelings and the lasting scars for a 5-year-old who had as much as possible explained beforehand, how much worse must the grief be for younger children or those who have not had careful preparation and explanations. Fortunately today the situation is improving, and parents are encouraged to be present at times of crisis and and regarded as allies rather than as enemies. There will probably always be feelings of disquiet about the presence of some parents, because there are those whose own anxiety is a source of anxiety to the child. Here our aim should be to facilitate the parents' own peace of mind, but time constraints may make this impossible.

Although there are times when a child needs to be (metaphorically) taken away from present miseries by fun, shared activity and laughter, there is also a need, at appropriate times, to support a child as he or she looks at his or her own griefs and fears.

The work done by some music therapists in children's hospitals in Australia, especially in burns units and more particularly at the times of debridement, are especially valuable. In debridement the layers of dead burned skin are removed and the procedure is exceedingly painful, not only physically for the child but emotionally painful for the staff. The situation for the child is a mixture of pain, fear and grief, and the music therapist is able to facilitate for many children a feeling of being in control of the situation through songwriting and other music therapy techniques, as is taking place in work emanating from the University of Queensland music therapy course (Edwards 1994).

Fear of Loss and the Withdrawal of Love.

Guilt is a common experience for children. There are some parents who use fear (Bowlby 1975, p.271) as a way of getting their children's obedience, or who act in a punitive manner in a variety of ways.

> 'If you are naughty, I will go away and leave you.'
>
> 'Worrying over you will be the death of me.'
>
> 'Worrying over you will be the death of your mother.'
>
> 'You make me ill with worry.'

Several patients with whom I have worked have, from the experiences of childhood and young adult life, been able to uncover clear memories of such remarks. Therapy for them has included talking and activities which are designed to take away some of the pain of the memories as well as reducing the consequences of the destructive thinking. One young man, mentally retarded, whose mother had died not long before and who had been admitted to hospital with a depressive illness, said as, crying sadly, he walked into the room, 'I didn't kill my Mum. I loved my Mum!' His father had said frequently and, it seemed, spitefully, 'Worrying over you will be the death of your mother!' The man needed substantial work to build his self-esteem.

Sibling rivalry, even if it has been mild, can lead to guilt when the child of whom the sibling is jealous becomes ill or dies. The child who has grown up thinking that everything he does is wrong, and that anything that goes wrong is probably his fault, is not only at risk during childhood of guilt and grief when illness, death or disability affects a family member, but will probably retain that feeling of guilty responsibility for the whole of his life.

Even a very young child can suffer grief, although it may not be recognised as such. For example the 13-month-old sibling of a baby which died at age six weeks from Sudden Infant Death syndrome showed marked changes in behaviour, being tearful, and also irritable and aggressive to a cousin with whom he spent much time. It is possible that much of this response was because he sensed his mother's sadness and tensions, but this was not necessarily the whole explanation. His awareness of what had occurred was demonstrated when, some 13 months later, a new baby was born. He said to his mother as she arrived home from hospital 'Will this baby die too, Mummy?'

Grief in Illness

Children experience grief in many situations during illness; it is not restricted to the child who is terminally ill. The sense of loss may be temporary; by adult standards it may seem trivial. But to the young child to have an arm in a sling for weeks, to have long periods in traction following an accident, or a prolonged admission for specialised treatment may seem like a lifetime. Grief is compounded with fear and probably with anger also. Children to whom it has been emphasised that they must be good whilst in hospital may inhibit all of their natural responses, and we see this, too, in those who are extremely fearful of what is happening around them.

One boy of six years had refused to drink anything whilst in hospital, during an admission for an extremely high fever of unknown origin. Because he was becoming dangerously dehydrated, it had been decided to use intravenous fluids, but – as a last ditch idea – the music therapist was invited to become involved in work with the child. Some popular kindergarten songs were played to him, and he joined in.

He was then given a glass of dilute orange drink and a game was instituted in which, as long as he drank the juice, the music would be played. But, if he stopped drinking, the music would stop also. The result was almost miraculous to those looking on in the distance – laughter, drinking, occasional breaks in the music, more laughter, more drinking and so on until (over many minutes) a total of a litre of fluid had been consumed. What was more important still, once the cycle of fear and discomfort had been broken, there was no further problem; he drank fluids and ate in a normal manner for the rest of his time in the ward.

Anger at the hospital admission, even when the child is old enough to appreciate the need for the admission, can be strong. A very active boy of about nine years had one leg in traction, attached to a frame above the bed. He appeared to be very 'good', but it was suspected that this 'goodness' masked other feelings, since his mother was often heard to tell him to be a good boy while she was not there.

Thanks to the co-operation of the sister in charge of the ward, percussion instruments were used, and a pair of large cymbals was given to this child at a time his mother was sitting there. His face changed to an expression of anger and frustration, quite different from the smiling mask he had presented otherwise, and he banged the instruments together so hard that his mother told him to play more gently.

She was told that it was all right for him to be noisy, and a few comments were made about the frustrations an active child experiences when confined to bed, especially in a position of considerably restricted movement. She was able to understand this, and went on to describe how active he normally was, that she was always afraid he would have an accident on his bicycle, which was exactly what had happened. The permission given to the child to be angry about what had happened, to put his anger to work in contributing to the shared musical activities with the children in the group (beds and cots were pulled together for the occasion) helped him to be less restless in his enforced inactivity.

Was this grief? Perhaps not, in the adult sense, but certainly a sense of loss (of his normal mode of living) and anger, at the restricted movements. It is likely that the reassurance given to the mother also helped, that she became less anxious about him being good and was more relaxed with him.

Deformity and Grief

Children also grieve over deformity, when they are old enough to realise that they look different from their peers. One such child was to have surgery to correct a hand deformity, and the plastic surgeon was attempting to photograph the hand before the operation, to make a record of the 'before' and 'after' state. The child, aged about 5, was weeping bitterly and hiding the hand behind her in what appeared to be shame, until I suggested to her that it might be quite nice to have a picture of what her 'poor old hand' used to look like, so that when it was all fixed she could look at the picture and think, 'Yes it was worth it.' Whether these comments really meant anything to her one could not be certain, but she did permit the photograph to be taken without any further protest, and went on cheerfully to sing some of her favourite songs. Perhaps the feeling was a mixture of embarrassment and grief rather than grief alone, but it needed to be dealt with!

A teenager who was in hospital for some minor follow-up adjustments of plastic surgery around her eyes spoke openly of her feelings before and since the complete remodelling of her face. She described the cruelty of children at school, and even of adults who would either make derogatory remarks about her grotesque appearance, referring to her audibly as a monster, or hastily look away after their first shocked glance. She had suffered greatly from grief about her appearance despite a minor degree of intellectual handicap, and had a real sense of joy at the improvement which had been achieved.

She had the entire front of the face moved forward, including extensive orthodontic surgery to move her teeth forward also, an eye had been repositioned to look rather more normal, and various other repairs and improvements made to her appearance. The grief which she expressed did not, in retrospect, include any anger, but she described feelings which probably were anger as well as unhappiness, right through her childhood until it was considered that the time was appropriate in her growing cycle for the reconstruction to be done.

In some young children who have become disabled as the result of an accident, it is clear that initially there is no real comprehension as to the extent of the impairment they have sustained, either by the child or the parents. In such cases the grief of the losses will presumably take effect over a period of time, probably mostly after returning home, when the extent of the changes to normal living becomes obvious. Today we would hope that community support and domiciliary services will provide help for child and parents.

If, as does occur, the accident or illness is perceived by the parents as partly their fault (whether or not this is actually the case) one observes various constraints in the relationship between child and parent even while still in the hospital setting. There is a mixture of grief and guilt and one sees that the relationship can be extremely difficult and complex so that some intervention is required. The social work department of a hospital will be able to offer help in such a situation.

Mental Retardation

Children who are intellectually disadvantaged do show signs of grief when their intelligence level is such that they are aware of their deficits, aware that they are different from other people. This feeling of loss may appear most often as frustration and resentment, irritability, rivalry for attention, etc. It does not, however, seem to be over-extending the use of the term *grief* to use it to explain the underlying feelings which prompt such behaviour.

One observes the clinging behaviour of many handicapped people in asking for hugs and kisses from visitors or staff. We see attention-needing behaviour, such as always having a problem which requires sympathy, always having a special anecdote to recount which has to be told without interruption from other people nearby, always having a minor illness which needs care, and so on. (The term *attention-needing* is seen as preferable to the more usual *attention-seeking*, which carries with it a punitive overtone. Attention-needing expresses the reality of existence for most of the disadvantaged of our society, who do indeed need attention, and often have to resort to undesirable behaviour to get it.)

There is today a recognition of the sexual needs of all handicapped persons, and a strong emphasis on *rights*. Difficulties can arise if the handicapped person is totally unaware of his or her own problems, so that there is shock when his or her overtures with sexual overtones are unkindly rejected and yet he or she has learned that it is his or her right to enjoy the same intimacies as everyone else.

We must be thankful that today normalisation is the aim for people with cognitive disabilities, in order to minimise their handicaps and enable them to live in ordinary society. But even in the smaller family-size group homes in which most disadvantaged people now live, there are still times when the group living imposes a strain, when anti-social behaviour is seen. In one such house where weekly music therapy sessions are held, one man is so jealous of another that for him to participate fully in the music he enjoys, the work must be done in a separate room away from the man he clearly sees as a rival. Chronologically these men are not children, and yet their developmental age is probably less than two years, so that child-like responses must be regarded as normal despite their physical age.

Clearly this need for attention is a consequence of the loss, or failure to develop, of ordinary family love and care. It would seem reasonable to label this behaviour, inconvenient though it can be for staff of training centres and hospitals, that of grief. Many writers, for example Bowlby (1981, p.355) and Winnicott (1974), have described the behaviour of children who are separated from normal parental relationships because of illness or for other reasons. Some children respond by being excessively good, by adopting rituals which the child thinks may have magic powers to restore the missing parent, but some become extremely 'naughty' and difficult.

When there is a profound level of mental retardation, it is perhaps more likely that the behaviour will be 'bad' rather than 'good' because the persons concerned are not able to perceive the possible consequences of good behaviour and modify their behaviour accordingly. Einfeld (1992) has written of psychiatric problems in those who are retarded, of the failure of professionals to recognise grief and provide help to meet the grieving person's needs. Is it reasonable to categorise the difficult behaviour of some handicapped people as a form of grief at the loss of normal family relationships? Should we extend this to the behaviour of psychopathic young people who have never experienced love and bonding? It is worth considering even though it is outside the scope of this book.

Other Griefs of Children

Children grieve over many experiences and losses, not all of which are fully understood by adults. Many mothers have seen the distress of the child who has lost a transitional object such as a security blanket (often of highly disreputable appearance!) and, whilst doing their best to find the beloved blanket or rag, have found it hard to understand even on the basis of their own childhood memories, why this thing is so important to the child's peace of mind.

Loss of a pet, by death or by disappearance, is another grief-laden experience for a child, as it can be for an adult. There is the same searching behaviour (identical in essence with the searching behaviour of a widow or bereaved parent) seeking to replace the loved friend, so that animals of similar appearance are seen as being the lost animal: 'There's Meggie, she's come back!'; only to find that it was not the dead corgi but one which was rather similar, to quote a family experience with a four-year-old.

Whilst walking to the post-box one evening, I heard a sad wailing and found a boy of about seven years sitting on the ground at his garden gate, rocking to and fro.

'Can I sit down beside you for a bit?'

'mm...'

(*A few minutes later*) 'Do you want to talk?'

'mm....' (*pause...*)

'I'm dyslexic and so is my Dad. He's the only one who understands what it's like and my Mum has sent him away!'

We sat there for a few minutes, he cried and talked a little more, he told me his age, what class he was in and at which school. Eventually the sobs eased off a little and he was called indoors.

All that could be done was to write a note to the school principal (but asking that no reply be sent) describing what had happened, giving his age and class, hoping she would know who the child was. Then the staff could be asked to keep an eye open for unhappiness, because there is a possibility that parents do not tell the school of marital breakdown and the child is seen as naughty rather than unhappy. In this instance, the grief over parental splitting was complicated by grief over the loss of the person who understood the child's learning difficulties; the two losses were intermingled.

Children who live with violence and abuse are likely to carry into adult life memories of fear and powerlessness, especially boys who have not only suffered abuse themselves but have also seen their mother or sisters suffering. Men who have grown up in such a milieu recall wishing they could defend the victims against attack, and also remember feeling guilty that they were not strong enough to do so. Some remember having definite plans for dealing with the perpetrator (usually their father or their mother's partner) and preventing continuation of violence as soon as they were grown sufficiently to be able to do so. These may include plans to kill the perpetrator.

In adult life, some of those who were abused come to see that the abusive father was himself a victim of abuse in his childhood, who had lived out the same patterns of behaviour. The miracle to me is that some people with whom I have worked have come not merely to an intellectual understanding of the patterns but some degree of forgiveness.

Children who have been seriously bullied at school or on the way home from school may carry long-term emotional damage in low self-esteem and apprehension; today educationalists are starting to deal with the problem in a preventative manner, rather than – as sometimes in the past – perceiving the victim as somehow being the cause of the bullying. Such memories of childhood fear, frustration and anger are not easily dispersed, even after many years.

Understanding Children's Grief

Few adults can fully understand the grief of a child, but we may enter into some at least of the sadness by being attuned to apparently irrelevant behaviour, accepting naughtiness as a normal protest against loss of security, loss of affection, loss of a friend, loss of the house, loss of the parents' marriage relationship and all this implies in the child's life, and all the myriad losses which a child may experience.

There are some losses which are heavy for a child to bear but which to an adult may seem trivial (such as the beloved blanket), but if we try to be in empathy with how the child feels about the loss, then we shall be able to offer some help to children in coping with their griefs and losses.

Some children perceive changes, such as changing schools and finding new friends because of parental change of location or employment, as a challenge but others respond to them as grief-laden. The same pattern might continue through life, modified by later life experiences and relationships which may enhance personal security, making changes easier to cope with, or vice versa.

Loss of a parent either from death or marital break-up is a loss remembered usually for the remainder of life, and in times past (when such loss often sent a child to an institution) the loss itself and the subsequent experiences may be remembered not merely with sadness but with horror and fear.

Some losses and griefs seem to an adult observer (who has forgotten his or her own childhood!) to be merely trivial: not being chosen for a basket-ball team, not being invited to a party, not being included in a circle of girls whispering secrets to each other, dropping a catch in a cricket match and being labelled 'butter-fingers'. But to children who have doubts about self-esteem such events can shatter their world.

The fears, grief and losses of childhood may not present as unhappiness but as difficult behaviour, and information can help us to understand and help the unhappy child. (See Ideas for Reading.)

CHAPTER 3

The Griefs of Adulthood and Old Age

Adults can all recall times of humiliation, times of loss of self-esteem, times when relationships prove destructive rather than supportive. These events continue through life unless one attains a totally pre-eminent position in society. Even then, people experience (and sometimes admit to) private feelings of having erred, moments of self-doubt, times of sadness and loss of control over life. Illness and disability at any age affect us in this way. Loss of role, loss of expectation, loss of status are also causes for grief in adult life, each individual having different experiences through life.

Through the death of relatives, friends, colleagues and acquaintances we all experience bereavement. How well we cope with these deaths is determined (as with children) by our self-esteem, our capacity for adaptation and our personal life-history, by whether or not we feel guilty about the death, and – most importantly – by the quality of the relationship with the person. Paradoxically, it is easier to work through the processes of mourning and adaptation for someone close to us whom we loved than for someone we hated, orworse still – for someone about whom we were emotionally ambiguous or about whose death we bear a burden of real or imagined guilt.

Because, in the past, grieving was forbidden in many cultures as being a sign of weakness, many elderly people still carry sadness from past losses. They benefit from supportive counselling even though many years have elapsed. The grief of adults is discussed in various places, such as the grief of disability, loss of status and self-esteem and so on. But the latter years are unfortunately often characterised by multiple losses and continuing grief.

Grief and Powerlessness in Old Age

Anyone who goes shopping for food is familiar with the *use-by date*, the date at which the substance is deemed to be unusable, perhaps potentially harmful. There can be so much emphasis on youth that older people either feel themselves, or are seen by others, as having passed their use-by date. But do we necessarily become powerless in old age? Obviously the answer is 'No'. We can think of many private and public figures who demonstrate that old age can be a time of fruition and not failure. Yet many people do experience a feeling of being out-of-date, and this can arise from something as simple as hearing grandchildren using computer jargon, realising that children today learn about topics or learn in ways which, in the past, were perceived as being for adults only.

The newly-described classification in the *Diagnostic and Statistical Manual* (*DSM IV*) (American Psychiatric Association 1994a, p.684) of *age-related cognitive decline* may (because of its wide readership) have profound effects on the self-esteem of older people, by seeming to suggest that cognitive decline is universal, rather than acknowledging that there are those who do not suffer such decline but continue to be creative and productive into their ninth and even their tenth decade. Exceptional certainly, but not unknown and certainly not abnormal!

A study conducted to investigate the relationships between residential environments and old people (Russell 1995) describes the dread which many people have about old age, fear lest physical frailty leads to placement in a nursing home and that this in turn leads to powerlessness, loss of the right to make decisions over one's own daily life or in larger matters. Russell describes one such person, entirely housebound because of physical problems and dependent for survival on the help from neighbours, Meals-on-Wheels and other domiciliary services, who yet resists strongly any move to a nursing home. She is quoted as saying that in her own home, she can (if she wishes) watch television all night, organise her day's timetable according to her own preference in a way which would be impossible in a nursing home. Such fears are shared by many who fear that their minds will outlast their bodies. Older people whose health is poor can see themselves as financial burdens to their families, particularly in countries where costs of medical and hospital or nursing home care are high.

There are cultures in which old age has been regarded as the ideal and old age was equated with wisdom and dignity, so that older people are treated with extreme respect. Is this still so? From informal observations on suburban trains in Japan it seems that this attitude may be changing in some people. In Western society, opinions vary. A young man said that he had 'to believe in the value of old age because the alternative wasn't very attractive!', but several groups of younger nurses have said that they hope they die before reaching old age.

The possible griefs of old age are many. I discussed these throughout a book on geriatrics (Bright 1991) but list them here in concise form:

- feeling differently about ourselves (including being a sexual being)
- loss of health and capabilities
- loss of independence because of the above
- loss of dignity, because of community or family attitudes
- loss of friends because of death
- loss of contact because of difficulties with mobility and/or hearing
- feeling oneself to be out-of-date and perhaps stupid
- loss of contact with family, because of work-related moves
- loss of family members through death, especially if young relatives have died or been killed
- loss of pets (who have become 'family' for the lone individual), the loss can be by death or because of move to nursing home or retirement community where pets are forbidden
- loss of achievement because of health problems or community attitudes
- loss of previous niche in society from various causes, including attitudes of others
- loss of hope for the future
- fear of being a burden to others if one becomes sick, demented or handicapped
- loss of decision-making because one is alleged to be incapable, even when one is in fact in full possession of all one's faculties; powerlessness against the decisions of others.

These losses are echoed in life for persons born with disabilities, except that for them it is not so much that these attributes are lost as that they were never found, never developed. A person of any age who acquires a disability and becomes handicapped will probably have the same losses.

Community Concepts of Ageing

Retirement can be a cause of grief if it brings with it some feeling of uselessness. A person will grieve if leaving the workforce brings a loss of achievement and if the reduction in income is traumatic. Such responses to retirement are not universal. Some have longed for the day when they would leave work; they are content with their prospects of financial security and are confident that hobbies, social contacts and so on will provide all they need for future happiness.

But hopes are not always realised; people's planning is not always realistic. Illness may supervene, and there are some who find the loss of status more difficult than they anticipate, so that there is a grief over the loss of expectation.

The world is almost too aware of changes in usefulness and, as a consequence, negative stereotypes have developed about old age. Newspaper and magazine advertisements reveal society's attitude so that we see advertisements and articles telling us that we *must* try to look younger by tinting our hair, disguising or removing wrinkles and age spots, hiding thinning hair by wearing a toupee and so on. Many advertisements use fear to sell their products, fear of losing a job, a romance, status, and so on, and older people are often portrayed as in imminent danger of decrepitude.

It is interesting to see that advertisements aimed at men seem to concentrate on fears about employment and romance, whereas advertisements aimed at women seem to focus only on romance. Employment for women is now so much part of life that one would expect advertisements to use women's fears of being ousted by younger, more glamorous employees!

Ironically, one of the most admired and loved figures of our day, Mother Teresa of Calcutta, makes no attempts to hide her wrinkles nor to disguise the fact that she is an old woman. Is there any hope that one day we shall see advertisements telling us how to make ourselves look more mature, wiser, more experienced by looking older?

We are frightened and powerless if we share the negative views on old age, brain-washed into believing that we are like that, or actually feeling some loss of competence intellectually and physically even though we have no actual organic disease of mind or body. As a consequence we are afraid: of deterioration, of being sent to a hospital or nursing home, of the unknown. All these are part of the negative views of old age which we may be led to share.

Because illness is more common in old age, people carry additional fears such as a married couple's fear that they may end up in two separate nursing homes (this has been known to occur!), fear that medical expenses will overwhelm them (not unknown in places where medical care must be paid for), the fear of not being able to cope if one partner becomes frail, fear of feeling unwanted or of being actively rejected. A nursing home matron was instructed to tell a patient that her son had been transferred to another city so that he would not be able to visit her, although from the address to which accounts had to be sent the matron knew this to be untrue.

Stereotypes

Other misleading pictures of old age are that it starts at about 60, that all who are grandmothers are sweet old ladies who sit in rocking chairs knitting and waiting patiently for people to come and visit them so that they can offer comfort and a listening ear. In fact not all grandmothers are sweet. Some are isolative, some are chemically dependent, some are just plain difficult! Many grandparents are water-skiing and climbing mountains, travelling around the world, gaining university degrees, working creatively in the arts, doing important work in business and the professions, and generally finding life more satisfying than at any other period of their lives. They do not even have time to look after their grandchildren for a day a week!

A clergyman described the anger in older members of his congregation when it was suggested by the parish committee that the 'burden' of the annual fête should be taken from older people and given to younger ones. It was soon made clear that the fête was not a burden but a means of achievement!

Anger is a healthy response to adverse circumstances, and we should hope that what used to be called age-appropriate behaviour, meek acceptance by older people of gradual deterioration, will not continue. We must hope that older people, and their friends and relatives, will express their rage against discrimination, disadvantage, illness, disability. They must rage against the circumstances, so that everything possible will be done to treat the problem, find support services to meet their needs, find the money to pay for services and so on.

Genetics play a part in the quality of life in old age, so that the best recipe for a happy old age is to choose our ancestors wisely! Our early experiences, such as nutrition in childhood, happiness or abuse, chance happenings of health such as experiencing or avoiding war, accidental injuries, also have an influence for good or harm. And the attitudes on ageing of those we meet can have a profound effect upon our emotional outlook on life.

All these play a part in how we are in old age, and stereotypes are useless, whether we use the old one of a dismal old age or invent a modern one of an old age full of creativity and fun. Both are equally false because they are stereotypes, and thus fail to reflect human diversity. Even a positive stereotype can harm those whose life does *not* permit them to continue in employment, enjoy travel and study, etc.

An alcoholic client taking part in a separation session said, 'I don't mind telling you that when we first met I thought "what would this little old lady know about my problems" but I soon found you knew *all* about them and weren't shocked by anything!' It was a salutary experience to hear myself described as a *little old lady* and to note my own responses to his comments, even though the general drift of his remarks was complimentary!

We must also acknowledge that, although there is no certainty that we shall become frail or ill, it is simply more common in old age to have arthritis, to become deaf, to develop cancer, to suffer from one of the dementias. It is not true that these are actually part of the ageing process, but they are more likely to occur as we get older, and knowledge of this is undoubtedly discouraging. Thus we are vulnerable to derogatory remarks about old age, especially if such remarks reflect our own secret fears.

Powerlessness

Apart from the few who enjoy dependency, those whose dependency needs have never been met and who find old age a longed-for time of being cherished and protected, powerlessness – either actual or notional – is a source of loss and sadness. There are also griefs associated with losses in old age which are experienced by the spouse, adult children and friends of those who have become disabled, frail or ill in old age. These griefs include powerlessness to achieve change, to provide enough comfort, enough time, enough energy to give full support, and especially helplessness when the condition, such as Alzheimer's disease, entails a downward process of increasing deterioration.

Brody's (1978) article, 'Women in the Middle', is still relevant almost 20 years after its original publication. She spoke of the many roles women fill. Simultaneously a woman can be:

- someone's wife
- someone's mother
- someone's grandmother
- someone's daughter
- someone's sister
- someone's aunt
- someone's friend, and so on.

Today we would add:

- someone's employer
- someone's employee.

And somewhere in the middle, if she is lucky, she may be herself! The achievement of many women of the 1990s is enormous. And when to all the other tasks and challenges is added the care and protection of a dementing parent, with all the associated grief and powerlessness, it may become an almost unbearable burden.

The grief of loss is enormous when we see mental deterioration, the disappearance of the person we once knew in a dementing condition. A middle-aged woman, whose husband developed early-onset Alzheimer's disease in his mid-50s, described her bewilderment when he first started to behave oddly, and her anger when, for example, he used the corner of the living room to empty his bowels. She also described her present guilt as she came to understand that these changes in behaviour were not done in order to annoy her but occurred because her husband was ill.

It is common to wish that the sufferer would die, for his or her own sake, as release from deterioration and loss, and because the spouse is facing total exhaustion. But when a relationship has been an unhappy one, the difficulties faced by spouse and relatives are even more acute. It is common to have feelings such as:

'Serve you right if you are forgetting things, you always were a bully.'

'You used to beat me up, and now it's my turn to shove you around.'

'I wish you were dead because I have never loved you and you never loved me.'

Such difficulties arise in a parent–child as well as a husband–wife relationship. Is one more difficult than the other? There is no answer, but it is worth thinking about.

Support groups for relatives of those suffering from dementing conditions might now include telephone counselling services. Callers need tactful and supportive input from the telephone counsellor to be able to express such feelings, and yet imparting permission to express the inexpressible is a key part of grief counselling.

When the person dies, those who have had these secret feelings find it hard to cope with the grieving process. The referrals for many people suffering from depression and/or substance dependency have said something like: 'Please see Mrs X; she is heartbroken over the death of her husband from Alzheimer's disease.' Yet the truth is that Mrs X is trying to hide, sometimes even from herself, guilty feelings of relief.

Fear of developing dementia is common, and most who have reached middle age have occasionally thought, 'I can't think what I was planning to do, I wonder whether I'm going demented?' Reassurance lies in remembering schooldays, when everyone from time to time forgot to take homework to school, forgot to do an assignment, forgot to take a packed lunch to school, and so on, without anyone suggesting they were dementing. But when we pass middle age, every piece of forgetfulness is frightening and seems to presage an awful fate!

Dementia and Psychological Illness

There are, of course, instances of forgetfulness which are truly indicators of a dementing process, but we should never accept the signs or allow them to be accepted as indicating dementia without having expert advice. It is said that a percentage of dementing conditions are reversible. However, there is some controversy about this, some professionals believing that if it is reversible then it was not a true dementia but a depressive illness which mimics dementia. Nevertheless it is tragic if those conditions which are reversible, whether arising from true dementia due to nutritional inadequacy or from depressive illness, are not investigated because of fatalistic despair. Health Services normally include assessment units and we must make use of their facilities, whatever the outcome.

In her book *The Ageing Experience*, Cherry Russell (1981, p.119) draws to our attention the undervaluing of frail aged people in society. She describes, for example, a typical Frail Aged Club where the volunteer helpers sit at separate tables at lunchtime. The clients are segregated from them and treated in general as if they were socially and intellectually inferior to the helpers, being expected to adopt a suitably humble approach even when asking the helpers for coffee instead of tea.

Perhaps these attitudes have already changed, because older people are encouraged to participate in management decisions. Today attitudes are changing so that people no longer believe that accepting help indicates failure on their part. But as yet no research has been done to demonstrate whether these are mere chance observations or whether more fundamental changes of attitude are growing.

Psychiatric illness too must be dealt with. People who say 'I wish I was dead' may be suffering from a depressive illness. Unresolved grief and loss may be part of this (Bright 1994) and proper treatment is required. Neither platitudes nor punitive attitudes are a sufficient response to remarks such as that quoted above. Whatever the cause, personal needs have not been met!

When experts in grief counselling meet, there is frequent discussion as to how far grief responses should be equated with depression. Certainly some people do become depressed in bereavement. Are they people who were at risk already, dysthymic or an unidentified case of minor depressive illness? Or is depressive illness in grieving an entirely new disorder? Certainly the melancholic features delineated in *DSM IV* (American Psychiatric Association 1994b, pp.383–384), to be applied to a depressive disorder or episode (loss of interest, loss of reactivity to usually pleasurable stimuli and so on), do bear a strong resemblance to normal responses to bereavement. The answer is perhaps not crucial to the present discussion, except that we need to recognise depressive illness when we see it and ensure if possible that the person receives the right kind of treatment.

It is hard not to be irritated by the client for whom nothing is ever quite right, who cannot see that things are improving. This too can be part of the melancholic feature of a depressive illness for which professional help must be found. It must be recognised that merely being old does not change a difficult person into a plaster saint. People who have all their lives been difficult to live with, difficult to love, difficult to help, do not usually change by the mere passage of time, although there have been exceptions to this statement. It seems that, usually, we become more like ourselves as time goes by. There may have been very good reasons why one person found life easy and another found it difficult, and these differences affect their later life.

Strengths of the Aged

What are the strengths of the aged? Is it all disaster and sadness? Both written history and anecdote are full of stories of elderly people whose wisdom helped those around them, whose patience under suffering was an example to others, whose ability to learn new skills astonished those with whom they came into contact. One elderly woman especially comes to mind. She had diabetes of fairly late onset, and as a consequence had a diabetic retinopathy and was almost totally blind. She had one above-knee amputation and, at the age of about 85, was facing a second above-knee amputation. And yet her attitude remained one of hope. She sat up in bed straight and tall (no lolling back on the pillow for her, she said) as she knitted a variety of things for other people. She was able to talk to a far younger woman, with similar medical problems, although not so far advanced, and help her to face an amputation and the prospect of increasing visual loss with probable ultimate blindness.

Of such people are legends made. The factor which was obvious as one spoke with this elderly heroine was her high self-esteem, coupled with family love and support. It is much easier to cope with loss when one feels oneself to be a worthwhile person, and the fact that she was able to help someone else would also have contributed to her self-esteem.

Those who are working with older people know the fine edge which marks the balance point for life of the aged. It takes relatively little to disturb this balance and to cause unhappiness, illness, and general disaster. For example, younger people might feel sad but will generally adjust to a change of neighbours. But for the elderly person, a change of neighbours can bring with it loss of vital support systems for shopping, changing lightbulbs and general minor repairs, and – more important in many ways – friendship and emotional support.

For an aged person a respiratory infection, which a young adult would shrug off quickly, can cause complete loss of intellectual functioning with apparent psychotic behaviour. Even a sore toe can set in train a tragic series of events. The soreness leads to wearing loose footwear, which can lead to a fall. This can cause a fractured femur, perhaps lying for days helpless, resulting in death or (if found immediately) at least in physical and emotional shock. Then follow admission to hospital, surgery and prolonged rehabilitation. We may not see a sore toe or a change of neighbour as griefs but they have a potential for loss and grief.

Summary

Grotjahn's (1955) reminder is still valid, that those who work with elderly people should work out their own feelings about ageing, and about problems and attitudes connected with our own life experiences with the aged, with our parents and so on. Otherwise these unresolved feelings and conflicts will complicate our work. (The topic of transference and counter-transference will be treated in more detail in Chapter 13.) But given personal insight and the courage to face our own old age, working with older people who suffer grief and powerlessness is worthwhile and personally satisfying.

Younger people today are familiar with the ideas of openness and sharing, but, for those who are elderly in the 1990s, there is no such tradition of free expression. Our elderly friends and patients are the more in need of facilitation if they are to be able to gain comfort for their hidden fears and feelings. It is the role of the helper, whether a therapist or counsellor employed in a professional relationship, or a friend, acquaintance or neighbour, to allow the grieving elderly person to express his deepest thoughts without fear of judgement.

As we go through life we experience change and loss as well as positive and happy experiences. Most of us are able to cope with these, with both happiness and sadness, with satisfaction and with powerlessness, because the circumstances are not totally overwhelming. But a significant number of people throughout the world are either overwhelmed by the circumstances surrounding them, circumstances over which they have no power, no measure of control, or with which they cannot cope because their own resilience has been damaged by harmful events and relationships.

Fortunately today there is a possibility for change for those who are able to reach grief counsellors, specialists trained for grief resolution in a number of professions (psychiatry, psychology, social work), each of which has something to offer. The context of grief is a major factor in the extent to which people are able to benefit from the help which is available, whether Their grief arises from an isolated incident in an otherwise peaceful and positive life or from one more tragedy in a disaster-ridden existence. Rutter's concept of resilience in the face of adversity has been a profound influence upon my work and thinking (Rutter 1985).

The changes and losses we experience through life and the way we adapt to them will vary depending upon our circumstances, the country in which we live and the support which is available. The context of our lives is something over which we have usually little control and yet it may be the deciding factor in whether loss destroys us or whether we have the strength to move ahead.

CHAPTER 4

The Interweaving of Loss of Role, Status, Expectation

Life necessarily entails a series of events which bring change and adaptation, starting with birth itself as the newborn child moves from the secure (albeit crowded!) life of the womb to the less protected world outside. Those who cannot adapt to change will suffer and may never fully mature.

Loss of Expectation

As we look at losses, we are aware that many of them overlap, so that we see an interweaving of our feelings about loss of expectation, loss of status, loss of role. Each has its own characteristics, but there is also much in common between them. What they have in common is loss of expectation, if life turns out to be different from what one had hoped or planned. In some few instances, there can be a pleasurable change to expectations, as when a woman who had dreaded the menopause finds that, rather than lost sexuality or the sadness of the *empty nest*, the menopause brings undiminshed sexual satisfaction, perhaps even enhanced by removing the fear of unwanted pregnancy and a creative upsurge in areas away from parenting.

There can, however, be a causal link between change and grief. An illness or acquired disability changes one's expectation of the future, changes one's role and status in employment, in society and in one's own eyes, and we then experience grief and powerlessness. We know that our roles in life change and adaptation to such change is essential for maturity. We change from a dependent child to an adolescent who moves between dependence and independence, from a single person who deals primarily with his or her own needs to the responsibilities and co-operation of marriage or partnership, and so on.

Change of Status

But changes are not always easy even when they bring apparent increase of status, because they alter relationships. A worker who has been promoted from the floor of the factory to a supervisory or managerial position may wish that the promotion had never been achieved because relationships become difficult with the people who have previously been on the same rung of the status ladder, and friendships may be lost outside as well as inside the workplace. There are also potential difficulties in relating to those who are now colleagues when they have previously been *the bosses*, perhaps even *the enemy*, and this too exacerbates any difficulties which one experiences with those who were previously workmates on the factory floor.

In personal life too, an upward change in work status can complicate relationships, as when a marriage deteriorates and finally ends because one partner believes that the other's education and social skills are inadequate to match the new managerial role. Those who are promoted from one level to another in the professional world also experience difficulties, for the reasons set out above but also because promotion often involves becoming an administrator rather than a hands-on worker.

One psychiatrist, at the time he had been promoted to a senior management position, said, 'One of the sad things about moving up one's professional ladder is that the higher one goes, the less one does of the task which originally attracted one into that profession!' This could equally have been said by a newly-appointed school principal, an engineer or a scientist entering management for the first time, and others.

Some organisations accept that it is helpful to have a double ladder of promotion. Those who wish to remain 'hands-on' can do so without any loss of career prospects whist those who wish to enter management can do so, and there is thus a double path for professional work and advancement. But this is uncommon and, in most professions, there is a certainty that promotion will bring an end to direct involvement in the task, and this loss may well be a source of sadness. This is worsened if the task of management proves difficult or unattractive. Perhaps the principal or administrator of a school finds that he or she really dislikes managerial tasks and prefers teaching. Then there are difficulties in self-esteem by asking to step back to a hands-on position.

Selye's (1975) concept of good stress, *eustress*, as a stimulus to living is known, but stress also has its outcome in depression, as Paykel's thoughts on *entry* and *exit* life events reflect (Paykel *et al.* 1969). The apparently good events postulated above are good illustrations of the fact that progress can be painful!

Powerlessness in Status

Powerlessness and loss of status are inescapably associated with loss of self-esteem, and we know that reduced self-esteem is in turn linked with psychiatric disorders (Ingham *et al.* 1986). It is thus necessary to take a broad view of these topics rather than separating them rigidly into one group or the other.

There are many whose role and status are fixed for them at birth with little or no opportunity for upward movement. People whose skin colour, poverty, race, religious affiliations, disability, nationality, language, social class or formal caste are tied, with very rare exceptions, to an underdog life. The very powerlessness of their situation is a source of grief, which commonly includes strong elements of anger and despair as well as sadness — except for those whose spirit has been so damaged by life that they remain apathetic, exhausted simply by a battle to survive.

Psychiatric illness still imposes a stigma on both sufferer and relatives. Society sees an illness which affects thinking and behaviour as risky, and it may well alter the status of a family in, for example, marriage prospects. Deprivation of voting rights by people deemed 'insane' is still on the statute books in many places and organisations, and this underlines the powerlessness experienced in psychiatric illness.

There are even some who believe, or behave as if they believe, that psychiatric illness is somehow contagious, so that the social isolation of those concerned is severe. The grief over loss of status, loss of social networks and general friendship or support has profound effects on people at times when they are most in need of help and kindness. Psychiatric illness is thus in itself a cause of grief because of its effects upon self-esteem through stigmatisation, and upon our role, power and status in society.

Other circumstances which cause downward changes of role include family breakdown and poverty, economic recession, illness, crime, addiction, political strife and religious persecution, civil or international war, and many others.

Retirement

When someone is asked to take early retirement in middle age, or, more difficult still, when someone is 'sacked' for one reason or another at any age, there is grief about the loss of self-esteem and of role. The *unemployed role* is seldom happy and, because of their unresolved grief, unemployed and retired people may present to medical practitioners and therapists as suffering from depression.

Problems can arise in the home as a consequence of retirement. An efficient businessman may find himself irked by what he sees as inefficiency in the running of the home, and reorganises his wife's methods of doing things, much to her irritation, distress, anger and humiliation. He tries to compensate for the loss of his power and status in his employment by becoming super-efficient in household tasks, becoming an expert cook, expert shopper for bargains etc. This damages his wife's self-esteem and their general relationship.

Another potential hazard in retirement is the strain on a relationship which has been maintained during the working life of one or both partners with a degree of stability but with no real depth, and which then breaks down in retirement simply because of enforced propinquity, when the defects in the relationship are brought to the surface by the amount of time the partners spend together.

Financial worries too can have adverse effects and can symbolise powerlessness as a form of grief: the loss of expensive holidays, difficulties in house renovations or repairs, or an extravagant partner who can cause anger and anxiety to the more provident partner, and so on.

Disability and Status

An acquired disability also changes family relationships and the balance of power, and can lead to problems and disagreements, as when there is an exchange of roles between partners. In those relationships where power has been implicitly vested in one partner, often the male, that partner feels demeaned by the woman taking over that power because of his disability, and if (because of brain damage) he is unable to perceive his own difficulties, the situation can become explosive.

One such man became violent towards his partner when she failed to understand what he was saying. He suffered from jargon aphasia (Kertesz 1985), in which he was talking what sounded like a different language but was unable to monitor his own speech to realise that the words he spoke had no meaning. His frustration over powerlessness was clearly the cause of the violence.

If in the past their roles have previously been strongly stereotyped as the man being dominant, the wife dependent, the husband may find it hard to take over housekeeping, or the wife may find it hard to take over financial management of the partnership. One such woman constantly sought further rehabilitation for her husband in the hope that he would eventually return to the dominant role. Perhaps, too, she hoped to put off the day when she would be left in full responsibility for her husband's welfare, rather than (as during the time he was an out-patient of the hospital) being able to get professional help.

Depressed mood can also follow a cerebrovascular accident, and may have a twofold origin, of psychosocial losses together with biochemical changes as a result of altered vascular supply to the brain (Robinson, Book Starr, Lipsey, Rao *et al.* 1985). Depression in a person newly disabled by a stroke makes the exchange of role, and any changes in the power structure of the relationship, complex for both partners. (Similar situations are seen in any acquired disability.)

It is easy to concentrate on the practicalities of change in role and status, but the words of a volunteer grief counsellor when she spoke of the grief and the losses of expectation in an untimely death or an acquired disability, bring home to us the emotional losses as well. She spoke of 'the loss of the memories of tomorrow', because the hoped-for roles can never be fulfilled.

Family Breakdown and Role Change

When a relationship is lost or changed in a radical way, whether through death or for any other reason, there are emotional as well as practical consequences. Anger with the person who is lost or with whom a relationship is broken is very difficult to deal with, and yet acknowledging anger is essential if the grief is to be resolved in any way. For example, the parent of a young person whose risk-taking behaviour in drug use or reckless driving leads to death or major handicap will feel not only unhappy but also angry. Grief over the discreditable death, or one which the community perceives as discreditable, is difficult to resolve.

Ending of relationship by death is seldom simple, whether the relationship was good or bad. Status, role, expectations of the future – all of these change.

It has been said that families cope more easily with changes which involve only physical disability than with those which involve changes to the person's thinking and behaviour (Proctor 1973). This is not surprising in that the severely brain-damaged individual may seem to be no longer the same person, so different is the behaviour after the injury from the behaviour beforehand. (Gosling's (1980) comments on 'mourners without a death' and being 'not officially bereaved' are helpful.)

Family adjustment to role change in major disabilities is difficult and often impossible. Thus the counsellor's task may well include helping relatives to reach a decision on separation, facilitating their ability to cope with loss of expectation, change of role and status, and so on.

Those who are formally separated or divorced or who have brought an established relationship to an end, suffer from a range of difficulties. These include:

- change of role and status
- blame versus guilt about the ending of the relationship
- deciding who takes what from among their joint belongings
- financial and property arrangements
- where the children are cared for and by whom
- how each person will re-establish life alone, whether to seek actively for a new partner, and so on.

All of these have practical and emotional connotations. There are changes of role as well as grief. When there are children and one parent has, temporarily at least, to take over both parenting roles, this can be very difficult. When a woman has been essentially the gentle, nurturing figure in the family, it is difficult to become disciplinarian and decision-maker on major issues also. Conversely a man left alone may find it difficult to take over home-making tasks and attitudes, if this is entirely new to him.

Sexual stereotypes have already changed and will continue to do so. Single-parent families are today perceived as being families, and one hopes difficulties will not arise in the future about interchangeability of roles, but some individuals themselves have difficulty in making such adaptations. The divorced man who loses contact with his children because his ex-wife has custody of them experiences not only loss of his role as father but also a painful grief. He will also feel humiliated if he has been stigmatised as being a risk to the children's well-being. (In some countries, 'custody' and 'access' orders relating to children after divorce have been replaced by 'residence' and 'contact' orders, in order to move away from the concept of the child as the property of the parent(s) and to emphasise the crucial nature of the welfare of the child.)

Anecdotal evidence suggests that women who wish to prevent their children having contact with their erstwhile partner have spoken of possible risks of sexual harassment if he has access to the children. Legal authorities are usually unwilling to take the risk, even if there is no clear evidence of abusive behaviour before the marriage breakdown, so that the father is denied access to his children. A decision to exclude the man on these grounds when they are unfounded is destructive to his self-esteem and his reputation.

Loss of Childhood

Loss of expectation can refer to loss of hoped-for achievement or relationship, but it can also apply to something never experienced, such as loss of childhood. When we work with older people, we can see clearly which losses were the most damaging by the extent to which they are still remembered with pain. Our clients may speak, with varying emphasis on sadness, resentment and disappointment, of the loss of their childhood when a parent died and the child was told 'You must look after your mother now' or 'You must be the father of the family now that your mother is left alone.'

Children who are asked to bear the burden of acting as a parent are deprived of the normal childhood role, of opportunities for a relatively carefree existence, and creativity may be blocked as a consequence of not being allowed to play adequately (Winnicott 1974). Damaging loss of normal role may also be experienced when a child loses a sibling and the parents expect the surviving child to take over the role of the dead child (Cain 1964), or who compare the surviving child, to his or her detriment, with the dead sibling.

The survivor may then try to be a different type of person or try to develop skills which do not come naturally. The fact that the dead child had skills with his hands does not mean that the surviving sibling will have these skills too. Even without the loss of a sibling, a child may be expected to fill an inappropriate role if the parents are trying vicariously to live out their own unfulfilled hopes. The jokes about 'My son, the doctor!' are not at all funny for the young person if what he wants to be is a carpenter or a professional sportsman.

A young man, pushed into competetive swimming by his mother because her own ambitions had been unfulfilled, described his humiliation when he was never quite good enough, never met her expectations of vicarious success. A family which has a tradition of being *musical* can be an unhappy milieu for a child who dislikes music or who has no aptitude. Clients who tell the music therapist that they hate music or that it makes them feel unhappy are sometimes found to be carrying the scars from such childhood experiences.

Pain, Terminal Illness and Issues of Control

One wonders whether the yearning for legalised euthanasia represents the yearning for control in terminal illness or extreme disability. The decision whether to live or to die is, after all, the ultimate in empowerment, and this may, incorrectly, be perceived simply as a pain issue, as discussed in Chapter 1. There are in terminal care, however, other important connections with loss of role in life, loss of expectation and of status. The person who is unable to face these losses because of a prolonged and debilitating, perhaps humiliating, illness may seek death not so much because of pain but because of powerlessness over those other aspects of life or because of a depressive illness (Chochinov *et al.* 1995)

Depression in terminal illness appears to be, in part, due to loss of personal control and, as we have seen, to give the patient the right to make decisions on medication can help to deal with this particular aspect of depression. There is, however, a very real need for psychiatric services in a terminal care unit, and this was been recognised relatively early in the development of palliative care services (Stedeford and Bloch 1979). This need has not disappeared! We must deal with all the psychosocial aspects of dying, the ending of the ordinary role in life to be replaced by the *sick role*. Alternatively, since there can be plateaux and remissions even in terminal illness, we have to manage the uncertainty of the gradually-becoming-sick, the up-and-down periods of remission and exacerbation. All of these changes involve loss, sadness, anger, disappointment, and need to be dealt with vigorously.

Eric Cassell's article 'Being and becoming dead' is useful for those who seek to understand philosophical dilemmas of death and dying, as these impinge upon people's psycho-social needs (Cassell 1972).

Other Losses of Role

Sexual abuse and family violence also deprive a child of childhood. The abused child is forced into a spurious maturity, because the sexual activities which are experienced are well outside those appropriate for their age, because fear twists their relationships and their capacity for creativity and fun, and because contact with peers is made difficult by the secret. Planning how to avoid the abuser, how to lie convincingly, how to avoid telling school friends or teachers what life is really like at home; all these take up the child's energy and spontaneity.

When sexual abuse has been experienced as physical enjoyment, with pseudo-affection rather than cruelty and violence, this is itself a source of grief and a twisting of the role of normal childhood. The person may look back in adult life with feelings of shame that the experience should not have been but was a source of physical pleasure.

Anger and a feeling of betrayal of parental role are experienced by the adult. Some abused children are also able to describe such feelings. The adult wonders why the mother betrayed her responsibility, why she did not protect him or her from violence or sexual abuse, and either pretended not to know, because it seemed easier than facing a confrontation and possible violence, or was glad that the sexual abuse took her husband's sexual needs away from her body.

People lose their childhood in other ways too. An elderly woman, in hospital for treatment of rheumatoid arthritis, cried as she spoke of a childhood in which she was never allowed to be a child because her mother was always busy. She had to bottle up her feelings, never expect cuddles or caresses, and really, she said, only got attention if she was sick, when her mother was very prompt to get her to the doctor or to the local hospital. She found relief in being encouraged to talk of these experiences, in crying openly and finding acceptance of the sadness and resentment she had felt all her life. The lasting nature of her grief came from a loss of role, a role in fact never begun, of carefree and affection-filled childhood.

A few days later, her operation for joint replacement was delayed because the anaesthetist was not available. She was outwardly accepting of this, but when told that it was all right to say she was angry about it, she thumped the bed-table, her faced became flushed, and she swore loudly, all of which astonished nursing staff as being out of keeping with her usual quiet and ladylike behaviour! Some researchers suggested that the need for repression of emotion in childhood can be causal in the development of rheumatoid arthritis (Solomon and Moors 1965). Was this lady's illness an example of that mechanism?

Children lose their childhood if they live in areas of war, famine or natural disasters. Television news items remind us of this when they show small children digging in rubble after an earthquake, handling guns, scavenging for food, hurling rocks at the enemy with real intent to injure or kill, or themselves dying of injuries, starvation and disease. One cannot believe that normal development is available to those who survive such trauma.

Status and Loss of Expectation in Society

Each of us has a role in society because of our employment or lack of it, our position in the family, the status of our family in society, and so on. There are some who can readily relinquish power and control over others, as in retirement, but loss of power to control one's own life, health and place in society is more difficult. Some jobs or positions appear to have high status, others appear to have low status, but for some people there are factors which negate the public view. For example, one finds people in the religious life who feel fulfilled in their lowly role. At the other end of the scale, a person who either has, or is associated with, wealth or power in society may feel sadly estranged from those around him or her because of that association.

The wife of the managing director of a large international company was approached shyly by another mother at the local kindergarten, who said that her husband too worked for the same company. The second woman said later that she had felt diffident about making the approach lest it be seen as boot-licking. The wife of the senior executive replied sadly 'I wonder how many friendships I miss out on just because of John's job!'

But whether we enjoy our job because of money, because of prestige, because of the interest it holds for us or because our self-esteem is invested predominantly in our working life, we feel sad when unexpected circumstances take it away, and even a planned retirement can bring sadness if we have invested much of ourselves in the job and its role or status. Fortunately a new role is provided and retirement made more interesting for many by the establishment of organisations such as the University of the Third Age, School for Seniors, special mature age requirements which make it easier for older people to study for a university degree, social clubs for retired business and professional men and women, and so on.

There is also, in some places in the world, enhanced decision-making in society for older people through 'Grey Power', in which politicians are reminded of the increased voting power of older citizens. Through all these events – intellectual, creative, political – a new status in society is thus created. But there will be many who are not able to join in such programmes because of lack of money, poor health, or because a psychological isolation builds a wall around them, so that the loss of role in retirement is damaging to them.

In the late twentieth century, women have professional roles in business, commerce, politics, the professions and the arts. Although it is not yet universal, there is a growing recognition by society that woman are not limited to being 'barefoot, pregnant and in the kitchen'! Sadly, however, as a result of changes in status and role for women, older women who look back over their lives often say 'Oh, I was only a... (mother of children, street cleaner, shopgirl, etc.)', usually in a tone of apology or shame. At the time there would perhaps have been no disappointment about their role in life, but knowledge of what women are able to achieve today has caused a retrospective regret.

One needs to be aware of all these areas of possible difficulty when we work with older women who grieve that their lives were not worthwhile compared with women today. We must enhance the sense of value in past endeavours by reminding them of what it was like to be 'only' a housewife during the depression. Cutting down old clothes to make garments for their children, making a doll out of a clothes peg, inventing a game with jam tins and string for stilts, singing together, making up recipes for interesting dishes out of almost nothing, coping with constant financial anxiety. 'Only' a housewife!!?

Simone de Beauvoir, in her book *Old Age* (Beauvoir 1972, pp.213, 268), says that in general wives dread their husbands' retirement. They see the retired husband as being always underfoot, asking questions, causing more work and bringing in less money. This feeling is noticed by the husband, who feels devalued as a result. And although such feelings are not universal, they do exist.

Loss of role may follow loss of expectation, as when a mother's sadness is followed by loss of role after the death of a child. The sadness and loss of role in hands-on mothering are obvious. Less obvious but none the less real is her loss of belonging in groups to which she previously belonged – formal parent groups at school, the informal group of mothers who wait at the school gate each afternoon, the 'aren't kids awful' talk over coffee.

A young mother whose child had died described her loss of role as leading to thoughts of suicide because she felt that her little boy was lonely 'out there' without her and if she killed herself she would be able to go on taking care of him, thereby fulfilling her role as his mother. Rowling comments that teachers suffer loss and change of role when a school child under their care is killed or injured, perhaps on a school excursion (Rowling 1994). The teacher's role has been that of protector, and a critical incident causing harm to one of the children in her care destroys the validity of her holding that role.

Adults who await the birth of a child expect to fulfil the normal parental role, gradually relinquishing control and responsibility as the child grows to adulthood. The birth of a stillborn or an impaired child takes away all those expectations or drastically changes the hopes and expectations, and (with an impaired child) alters the role to one which will continue for the rest of life. In some cultures it is assumed that the mother is responsible for any impairment present at birth, and women from such cultures have been divorced because they gave birth to a child with an impairment. Thus they lose simultaneously their role in a marriage and in a family, their child, their emotional support at a time of sadness, and their self-esteem.

Infertility too is a grief linked with loss of expectations. It may be compounded by the insensitivity of those who assume that couples deliberately avoid having children, and who make adversely critical comments. 'Having a new car/interesting work isn't everything, you know; don't be so keen on getting things that you put off having a family for too long.' (I have clear memories, even after 35 years, of these actual remarks; they were not forgotten because children were later born to the marriage, although the remarks were forgiven!)

For those whose childlessness is a disappointment rather than a conscious decision, there are support groups to help them with fertility problems, and the *in vitro* fertilisation programmes offer help for some, but not all, and for them grief goes on.

The mother of a newly-qualified driver will say to her son or daughter, 'Drive carefully', but she might wince every time she hears the siren of a police car or ambulance, dreading a visit from the police to say that there has been an accident. But our normal expectations are that we and our children will go through life without being disabled by illness or accident, so that death or accidental injury brings profound shock, disbelief and anger when our expecations prove wrong.

Loss of expectation is also involved in grief over relationship breakdown and domestic violence. Although there are more people today going into relationships with the feeling 'We can always end the relationship if it does not work out' (and this has been portrayed in a 'proposal episode' in the comic strip 'Cathy' (Guisewhite 1995, p.65)), many people still have the expectation that the partnership is for life.

Untimely death causes anger and disappointment as well as sadness and loss. Diggory and Rothman, in a still-relevant study done in 1961, showed that high on the list of reasons for fearing death was the regret at plans left unfinished and hopes remaining unfulfilled. Presumably, this is why our response to the death of an old person is different from our reaction to the death of a young person. Death in old age is seen as timely, the person having completed his or her life. But a young person's death is untimely; he or she has died without fulfilling his or her role in life. We expect to die in old age but we do not expect to die in youth.

But the elderly person may not share this sense of timeliness; there may be a loss of expectation which is painful. A 91-year-old man in an Australian hospital expressed anger: 'I'm afraid this bloody operation [for extensive carcinoma of the bowel] may stop me making another trip to England to see my sister'!

Although the death of older people is generally viewed as less traumatic than the death of a younger person, there may be emotions left from earlier experiences which complicate matters, so that the death of a parent or spouse after an unhappy relationship leaves the survivor with guilty feelings of relief. These can affect behaviour after a bereavement. When the difficulties have been hidden from family and friends, their expectations that the survivor will be sad about the death can make matters difficult for the person who is actually relieved that the relationship is over! Funeral eulogies, letters of condolence, would-be comforting comments all show how different the onlookers' expectations are, and difficulties in dealing with this situation can lead to substance dependency or psychiatric illness.

Loss of expectation for some people represents loss of control. Emotional problems following a major loss are particularly common in those who have a life pattern of extreme control, manifested by obsessional tidiness, detailed planning and so on. An obsessively tidy and over-organised housewife attempted suicide when a bilateral above-knee amputation destroyed her personal command over her life. It may be that she had always had depressive tendencies, keeping her world safe by her excessive control, but she had not been identified as a *case*.

Even if there is no strong ideation of suicide, the anger experienced by the patient, expressed or unexpressed, may impede the rehabilitation process. Staff involved in rehabilitation will investigate patterns of life control when, rather than showing grief as such, a patient is angry and unco-operative rather than obviously depressed. The depression seen in post-stroke victims, probably includes psychosocial as well as biochemical components, so that we see grief over loss of role and loss of expectation.

Work in Music Therapy

From professional observations, it seems that grief over relationship breakdown is not forgotten, and music evokes expression of this grief because so many people have memories of music from their days of falling in love. When the music from that period of life is played, all the feelings from the past, the guilts and disappointments from the breakdown of the relationship or from bereavement, together with present loneliness, are brought to the surface in tears and sadness. It was in fact observations of this phenomenon which led to the development of my present work in music therapy for grief counselling. Given empathy and trust, expression of emotions can provide the milieu for catharsis and comfort so that the person can leave the past behind and move on.

Although the playing of significant music may occur by chance, the piece has often been requested by the person concerned. Sometimes this seems to be like lancing a boil, releasing long-felt pressures, and the therapeutic value of this will be discussed later.

Summary

It is obvious that, even though we may not spell out what we hope for in life, we do have unspoken and even unacknowledged expectations for the future, and the loss of these expectations demands from us minor or major adjustments. Adaptation to change is a crucial skill for survival. But because of circumstances, upbringing, inherited characteristics or other factors, there are many who are ill equipped to cope with the changes they experience in life, and who are greatly in need of assistance to enable them to compromise between the expectations and the reality.

CHAPTER 5

Loss of Material Possessions and Spiritual Pain
The Paradox

Why do people grieve over the loss of material objects? The answer may be linked to the circumstances in which the object was lost. As individuals, we lose material objects in a variety of ways:

- through theft

- through fire

- through carelessness, forgetfulness

- through the break-up of the home in divorce or separation

- through being forced to leave our home because of frailty in old age or because of disability at any age

- through being forced away from home or country because of natural disaster, political persecution, war, or similar circumstances over which we have no control.

Associations with the Past

Our loss is not only a cause of sadness but is often also linked with anger, with powerlessness, with fear, with regret and disappointment. Memories of the lost object are constant reminders of the emotions which accompanied the loss. Some people who mourn the death of someone close to them hide the objects associated with that person because they cannot deal with the memories that these bring to mind, and cannot cope with life alone.

Others cannot put the objects away, and Queen Victoria's obsession with objects associated with her dead husband, Albert, is well known. Her insistence that his shaving gear was to be set out each day as if he were still alive is an extreme example, probably of denial. But many widows and widowers have comparable ways of behaving, clinging to material objects and fearing their loss because they alone remain of the beloved person.

The timetable for relinquishment, if this does eventually take place, varies from person to person and cannot usually be changed by an outsider unless as part of a therapeutic intervention. Mention has already been made of the woman who kept the collar and leash of her dead son's dog after the dog died, fearing to lose them or even let them out of her sight lest she lost her last link with her son.

There are many other symbolic reasons for our sense of loss of a particular object.

- It can be a symbol of status or success, like an up-market motor vehicle, representing prosperity, or the certificate which states our professional qualifications.

- It may symbolise a relationship: a wedding ring, a bundle of letters, a baptism or marriage certificate.

- It may be all that remains of someone who has died or with whom we have lost touch: photographs, letters, a gift from the person.

Family photograph albums are an example of how the loss of a material object has emotional connotations. Many group sessions start with a questionnaire as to what objects one would wish to save from destruction by fire assuming that no life was at risk, and photograph albums are usually at the top of the list of priorities for those who live in a Western society in some degree of affluence.

It seems that photographs symbolise our past: the homes in which we lived, the people we knew, the ancestors who helped to make us what we are, the life events which shaped us. These are recalled with a vividness which can be shared, in a way which internal memories cannot. Thus their loss threatens our present as well as our past. We lose our roots and we may lose part of our sense of identity when we lose our photographs, because they have a spiritual dimension which is more important than simply the paper on which they were printed.

Loss of Security

Loss of an object can also represent loss of security, whether this is loss of the homeland in its entirety or, for example, the loss of our home through bush-fire, earthquake or other disaster. Loss of safety is well seen in the way children react to loss of a special object, such as a security blanket, a toy, a pet. In wider terms, safety is lost if their parents' relationship breaks down, when they move to another house when they are too young for this to be exciting, or when the move threatens their whole sense of well-being by symbolising loss of relationship (Bowlby 1971, pp. 368–373).

Religious and Other Icons

From time to time old churchyards are transformed to become parks for general use or to make way for new main roads, and there may be local feelings of desecration (Lord 1976). Traditional burial sites may be uncovered when foundations for modern buildings are excavated, and feelings may be intense for those whose ancestors were buried there. This is particularly so if the burial sites were those of indigenous peoples whose traditions were swept aside in the past by those who 'discovered' their land (Broome 1982, p.62; Stackhouse 1981). The material objects in such instances are more than mere tombstones or fragments of bone and clothing. They symbolise losses of emotional and spiritual significance.

Society, too, sustains the loss of material objects and may well grieve over this. Religious icons represent far more than the wood, stone, metal of which they are made. Australian Aboriginal and other indigenous peoples are today expressing anger about the past attitudes towards their religious icons, which include sacred sites in which a natural object such as a rock or a tree is endowed with spiritual significance.

The anger arises even today when roads or other developments for commerce or communication are planned in areas of special spiritual significance, because of the downgrading of importance of such objects or sites as being seen to be less necessary than roads or supermarkets. In the early days of settlement there was a total lack of understanding of the way of life being displaced, and the anger and powerlessness experienced by the original inhabitants have not yet been totally dealt with.

There is similar community rage about destruction of bushland and forest to build roads or holiday resorts. Not all of this is related to care of the environment. Some of the rage appears to be at what is perceived as symbolic desecration of nature. The two may, however, overlap.

War

As we look back on the effects of war, some people find that it is the destruction of great religious buildings which stays in the mind, because they are part of history and because they symbolise stability of religious life and spirituality. Others see the greatest sadness in the loss of ordinary homes, the focus of life for ordinary people. Some mourn chiefly the loss of important civic buildings, art galleries and so on. All of these have significance outside their strictly monetary value or their appearance.

Even when there is no official war in progress, we read of politically-motivated destruction of a mosque or a Hindu temple. There is great local or national outrage because the symbolism of the destruction far outweighs the material value of the buildings themselves.

Countries which have been developed relatively recently also mourn the destruction of their past: old buildings, old trees, old sand dunes, old ways of doing things. And yet we see in those same places the modernists who wish to sweep everything away in the name of progress, to achieve success in trade and commerce, new roads and new ways of living.

It sometimes seems that there is a hidden agenda for each way of thinking – fear of change, in those who cling excessively to the past, and fear of the past in those who must destroy the old to make way for the new! Which group has the greater need, and why?

Help for Those who Have Lost Belongings

What can we do for those individuals who mourn the loss of a 'thing'? Superficially it may seem trivial. The policeman who attended an accident, in which a brand new car was extensively damaged, said, 'If nobody is hurt, what do things matter?' And yet it may affect our inner being to lose something precious, something achieved after long planning and hoping.

A woman whose underclothes had been disturbed by a thief in his search for money and valuables, described her feelings of violation. She said that these were akin to a response to rape, that she felt she could no longer wear the garments but threw them away.

It is important to give the grieving person plenty of time to talk of the loss, even if one has heard the same story several times. Trying to talk someone out of their sadness makes the situation worse. 'But it was only..., you can replace it!' leads into further descriptions of why the object was so precious, why its loss is so devastating, why a replacement could never be the same. We also need to sense the symbolism which lies behind the words, even if we are never given the whole story. To grieve strongly over a material item commonly means that the object symbolised something far deeper than is described, with emotional and spiritual connotations which the mourner finds it difficult to disclose.

The link may be one of remorse: 'If only I hadn't... and now all that is left is...'. Or it may be one of symbiotic dependency for a person to whom total independence is impossible: 'I cannot go on without her, with this picture near me I can pretend she is still there and talk to her.' But whatever the reason, those who lose the significant objects are devastated in a way which parallels responses to death itself.

We must, of course, recognise that clinging to objects associated with the dead, and fearing or reacting strongly to their loss, is a normal transitional stage in mourning. Each person has his or her own timetable for grief so that to insist that an object really does not matter all that much is counter-productive to the grieving process.

Raphael, in discussion which followed a paper on response to disasters, described how a family who had lost their home and all their possessions in a bush-fire, and who found that a bulldozer had virtually eliminated all traces of where their home had once stood, were able to work through some of their grief by focusing upon a fragment of roof-tile (Raphael 1983). Small though the object was, it was possible to centre their grieving for all the other lost objects on this piece of tile, and gradually to come to terms with their losses.

Natural and Man-made Disasters

Major disasters such as a cyclone or a bush-fire, which involve loss of human life as well as of material objects, present a complex challenge to the grief counsellor. Grief over the loss of possessions (cattle, sheep, equipment, houses, farm buildings, vehicles, fishing boats and nets) is compounded by the powerlessness experienced at the time of the disaster when nobody could prevent or modify its progress. Grief is also made more complex by the fact that most of those affected are at the height of their productive years, so that the disaster affects hopes for the future as well as present losses.

Those who grieve the loss of objects may feel that they should not show their grief when others have lost relatives and friends in the same disaster (Raphael 1983). When someone involved in such a disaster suffers serious and long-term after-effects, this is normally classified as a post-traumatic stress disorder response. Rescuers too need to have their needs met.

Summary

Material objects are endowed with meaning far beyond their structure and colour. We associate things with people, with events, with beliefs, hopes, fears and so on. In mourning material objects we are mourning deeper losses and, for that reason, grief over mere things should never be disregarded or undervalued.

CHAPTER 6

Handicap and Frailty, Grief and Powerlessness

Introduction

Disability and resulting handicaps cause grief because they increase dependency, change our expectations of life. In 1980 the World Health Organisation's publication *International Classification of Impairments, Disabilities and
Handicaps* (World Health Organisation 1980) discussed the classification of
the entire range of problems, physical, intellectual, social and psychological,
which afflict mankind. In the introduction there is a useful analysis of the
relationships between these, and a linear model is set out:

DISEASE *leading to* IMPAIRMENT *leading to* DISABILITY *leading to* HANDICAP.

In this context *disease* includes congenital malformations and accidents as
well as *illnesses*. The nature of this analysis is important because there is
constant confusion as to which words mean what!

People experience handicap, a disadvantage in living, in different ways.
These depend on a variety of factors, such as the extent of the physical,
cognitive and social disadvantages, the individual's personality and outlook
on life, self-esteem, the genetic inheritance, the environment and circumstances in which the person lives, the emotional and practical support which
is available, and so on.

The Australian Bureau of Statistics, in publishing a summary of findings
the 1993 Census results on disability, ageing and carers (Australian Bureau
of Statistics 1993) also follows the usage which separates disability and
handicap, following the WHO publication. Their results showed that:

- 18 per cent of the Australian population had a disability (3,176,700
  persons)

- ° of that 18%, 78.7% had a disability which constituted a handicap (2,500,200 persons)

- ° 14.2% of the total population had a handicap, as follows:

    - 2.4% of total population (419,900 persons) *always* need help to perform one or more designated tasks; their handicap is *profound*

    - 1.7% of total population (301,100 persons) *sometimes* need help to perform one or more designated tasks; *severe* handicap

    - 2.6% of total population (455,500 persons) need no help but have difficulties with tasks; *moderate* handicap

    - 5.3% of total population (941,800 persons) did not need help or have major difficulty but used some aid; *mild* handicap

    - 2.2% of total population (382,000 persons) had some limitation, not classified (severity not determined).

The census revealed that disability (without handicap) and handicap increase with age, but disability without handicap decreased after age 70 to 74 because older persons with disabilities are more likely also to have a handicap resulting from that disability.

These statistics, although unique to Australia, are of general interest to all who work in grief counselling. Although the clear differentiation between *disability* and *handicap* is not in full general usage, this will probably happen eventually. The Census also revealed the extent to which persons of non-English-speaking background experienced disabilities and handicaps. These figures illustrate the importance for any country with a major migration programme of providing counsellors who are not only multi-lingual but also multi-cultural, who will understand the background and attitudes of the people concerned.

Perception of Handicap

We know that parents experience complex emotions when a child is born with an abnormality or when an impairment is observed during childhood. When a woman is pregnant, she has an expectation that the child will be born without an impairment, and will grow up to lead a satisfying life, using the gifts and capabilities which are his or hers. Women often describe moments of fear that the child will be stillborn or abnormal, that it will grow up to be a *delinquent* and so on, but such fears are normally transient.

This transience, however, means that the birth of a dead or impaired baby, an adolescent's chemical dependency or other waywardness, suicide or serious illness come as an enormous shock to the parents. Parents also experience feelings of powerlessness: 'I don't think I can cope with this', often with feelings of guilt: 'Was it something I did?' '... something I didn't do?' Associated with those feelings are often anger with the medical profession or with God for allowing it, and this makes the grieving process more difficult.

Parents whose child is abnormal may deflect their own feelings into blaming, wonder whether it was someone's fault, and, often, which partner is to blame if it is a genetic defect. This can lead to marital disharmony and breakdown. In one such situation, a woman spoke of her husband's anger when he found that their sons suffered from a progressive disease of genetic origin. He threatened to leave her because she was the carrier. She then described his disgust when he found that he too carried the faulty gene, so that the cause was shared between them and that the duplication of the defective gene was the cause of the extreme extent of the boys' disability.

Although the marriage was surviving, its future was precarious because of the loss of trust the woman felt towards her partner. One might imagine that there must have been something wrong with the marriage to start with for such a reaction to occur, but it does happen even in marriages which have previously appeared stable and happy. Statistical evidence shows the rate of marriage breakdown to be extremely high after a baby is born with an impairment (McNamara and Morrison 1982, p.125).

Uninformed comments can harm. For example, a man spoke of his grandson's disability, saying that it was caused by the adultery of the mother during pregnancy. He had no basis for believing that she had been unfaithful, but believed that disability is invariably caused by marital infidelity. Perhaps his anger was fuelled by the disappointment of a disabled grandson, and a longing to find a scapegoat.

When a pregnancy was unwanted, and more especially if there has been an attempt to abort the foetus, and the child is subsequently born with an impairment or suffers a life-threatening illness, parents suffer extreme feelings of guilt and need in coping with these feelings (Wolff, McCrae and Forfar 1973, p.1753).

Parents of children who are disabled, gravely ill or dying commonly suffer feelings of guilt about these events, even when that guilt is without logical foundation, but still worse is the guilt of adoptive parents, or foster parents, who feel deeply responsible for the welfare of the child whom they have 'chosen'. One such mother, whose adopted child had been injured in a motor vehicle accident, was unable to deal with her grief over another death in that same accident because of her sense of guilt that she should have been able to protect that child from harm, should not have permitted the children to be taken for a drive by someone other than herself.

Fortunately various organisations help parents to survive the death of a child, the birth of a child with an impairment, or to cope with long periods of illness of a terminal nature, so that it is less likely today that parents will be left alone with their grief and possible guilty feelings, as was so in the past. One such goup is Compassionate Friends, founded in the UK, but now with branches in 16 other countries as well.

Grief in Reaction to Disability

Those who are trying to help people cope with their grief and shock about a congenital or an acquired disability notice many and varied emotions. Immediately after an accident or a life-threatening illness, the initial response is usually one of thankfulness that the person is still alive. But gradually this changes to anger or despair as it becomes obvious that life will never be the same again, either for victim or family.

There is anger and sadness but also uncertainty, mingled with loss of expectation and loss of hope, about illness and disability, for observers as well as for relatives. Parents' hope for a miracle cure and restoration to normal function are lost as they go from place to place, from person to person, seeking help for their child. An orthopaedic patient is angry and sad as he or she realises that an amputation is inevitable, perhaps because lost circulation to the limb will not be restored. There is sadness and disappointment when the hopes for restoration to normality are finally lost, whether we are considering orthopaedic, stroke, accident, cancer or any other problems.

There is, of course, happiness and triumph when healing and rehabilitation are successful, but this can be a source of disappointment to those clients or patients in the rehabilitation unit or hospital ward, for whom things have not gone so well. It is difficult to rejoice that the person in the next bed is going home when one has just been told that nursing home care is the only option for oneself! Coping with such disappointments is difficult for staff, relatives and patient; anger, disappointment and sadness are mixed together.

Helpers need empathy too. A quadriplegic client, still in the rehabilitation phase of her care, discussed her feelings about disability, the horror she experienced when she first realised that she would always have to depend on enemas and manual evacuation of the bowel, and her dismay when an enema was administered by a young male nurse, of about the same age as her son. She felt that he had not thought sufficiently about her feelings of shock and her loss of modesty, of dignity, of independence, before he casually announced that it was time for her enema. She also commented on what she saw as defensiveness and lack of empathy from some staff members for the occasional times of sadness and irritability displayed by a person with a major disability.

Degrees of Disability

Research in the Head Injury Unit at Lidcombe Hospital, New South Wales (Tate, Lulham and Strettles 1982) showed that there can be greater difficulty from what are, to outward appearances, minor deficits than from the major ones. Someone might, for example, look quite normal at time of discharge, speak and walk normally, and yet be utterly incapable of normal family life. This can be caused by loss of concentration, so that he cannot maintain a simple task for more than a few seconds, by loss of memory, so that he cannot recall after a few seconds where household equipment is stored, or he may forget that he was asked to have a shower and go off to do something else. He might suffer from marked disinhibition so that he talks ceaselessly at great intensity, masturbates with no sense of social discretion, spends any available money without thought for the future, or other similar behaviours.

The brain-impaired person may expect to fulfil his or her previous role in society because he or she is not aware of the extent of the impairment. But the family members see that he or she is incapable of doing so, and there is difficulty about changing roles because of the difference in perceptions held by the impaired and by the unimpaired members of the family.

And yet a major physical disability such as paraplegia, without brain damage, may be easily accepted by the community and the family, probably because people can see what the problem is, and because the person is in full possession of critical and other faculties.

In both instances there is loss of expectation, when hoped-for life plans cannot be fulfilled. Further, there is change or loss of role in the alteration to employment and relationships.

Rehabilitation

When rehabilitation is a long-drawn-out process (two years is commonly stated as the length of time in which improvements can still take place following brain impairment) there are additional frustrations in not knowing the ultimate extent of the disability, whether the patient will ever return to home to look after the children or take up employment again, and so on.

Because of this uncertainty, the grief process itself has to be held in suspense. Although in some instances there is a gradual acceptance that improvement will not be as much as would be hoped for, a recognition that one should not hope for full return of functioning, this realisation does not always occur. Some relatives become increasingly angry and frustrated by the lack of certainty about the future. And, since planning for the future is partly determined by the outcome of rehabilitation, the delay in being able to make plans can be destructive for some people.

Some people cope well with unplanned loss of role, some people cope badly. The difference seems to lie in their personal self-esteem. The grief counsellor must find out how each client sees his role in life, how important to his emotional state the loss of role is. We must be flexible rather than arbitrary in how we respond so that we meet the actual need and not the need we consider should be there! We need the empathy which permits someone to be angry without ourselves feeling threatened or angry, recognising what is often a defence mechanism when the client's frustration reflects our own feelings of powerlessness to effect change in their condition.

Wright has written of the need for grieving over disability, of the risks of cutting short the grieving and adjustment (Wright 1960, p.114–5). Rehabilitation staff can be so enthusiastic over their tasks that the person has no time to work through feelings of grief about the losses sustained. Or staff may believe that grieving is incompatible with the atmosphere of optimism which is engendered in a rehabilitation unit. Each person has an individual way of coping with loss, and it appears that, for some clients, their extreme difficulties with adaptation to disability may have their origin in depression or dysthymia. Psychiatric intervention is a very real need in a rehabilitation unit, but one which is not always met (Holland and Whalley 1981).

The attitude of the individual towards a disability and whether or not people regard themselves as handicapped is of crucial importance in the grieving process. It varies from person to person, depending on the condition, the cultural ethos from which the individual and the family come, and on the personal attitude of the individual. Barker and colleagues (Barker, Wright and Gonick 1946) discussed this in a book which is still relevant to our understanding of attitude to handicap.

Family attitudes and culture can affect the outcome of rehabilitation. For example, an occupational therapist aims to help a client to gain some independence in daily living skills. But if the family and cultural attitude is that it is a family disgrace for a disabled older person to help with household tasks, then the therapist's hopes will come to nothing.

One person strives to overcome a handicap and in doing so is able to lead a satisfying and happy life. Another appears to use the handicap as a reason for opting out of life, whilst a third becomes an over-achiever, courting exhaustion by efforts to pretend, even to himself or herself, that there is no handicap. Striking a balance is not easy, and from time to time one may need to change from one position to another, because of fatigue or for other reasons. Throughout her book, Wright (1960) writes of *as if* behaviour, of the need some people have to behave as if there were no handicap, and of the toll this takes of the people concerned. The over-achiever described above exemplifies this type of behaviour.

Hearing Impairment

There is an ongoing controversy about the implanted bionic ear, because some people believe that deafness should be regarded as normal, that to accept a *gadget* is demeaning to personal pride. Is this an example of denial of handicap, *as if* behaviour, or is it the outcome of being treated as second-rate people over many years, of the paternalism and powerlessness of the past? Research into and evaluation of psychological problems of deaf people suggest that they are at risk, no matter what their age, of social isolation and its associated hazards because we depend more for perception of emotive content of speech on tone of voice than on facial expression (Stevens 1982).

More recently, Sloman and colleagues have discussed disordered communication and grieving in deaf-member families (Sloman, Springer, and Vachon 1993). They found that there are difficulties in communication which puzzle the observer. Why don't family members use sign language adequately? Why do the deaf family members avoid the gaze which is essential for adequate communication? And so on. The view presented by Sloman and colleagues is that this breakdown of communication arises out of unresolved grieving. This may include issues of rejection, childhood experiences of the parents of the deaf child, denial of the extent of the disability by parents and so on. It is also important to recognise the pride of deaf people and their right to be a cultural group with their own skills and joys, through which they are empowered to take their place in society. The article is strongly recommended to all who work with hearing-impaired people and dysfunctional families. Oliver Sacks' book *Seeing Voices* provides interesting insights into the development of language and communication skills (Sacks 1990).

It is of vital importance that we recognise the right of persons with any disabilities to decide for themselves whether they feel handicapped and to decide how much they wish to depend on technology, how much help they are willing to accept in daily activities.

The Sufferers' Own Perceptions

People who are intellectually disadvantaged show signs of grief when their intelligence level is such that they are aware of their deficits, aware that they are different from other people. This feeling of loss may appear most often as frustration and resentment, irritability, clinging behaviour, rivalry for attention etc. It does not, however, seem to be over-extending the use of the term *grief* to use it to explain the underlying feelings which prompt such behaviour.

Einfeld finds that persons categorised as *mentally retarded* frequently suffer from psychiatric illness, including manifestations of unresolved grief, without their need for help being recognised (Einfeld 1992). We must be aware that psychiatric illness and developmental disability are not mutually exclusive. We must respond appropriately and empathically if we suspect that unresolved grief is the cause of undesirable behaviour in our cognitively-impaired clients.

Society's Attitudes

In the 1980s and 1990s attitudes towards handicap have improved, so that we see mentally retarded people moving from large institutions to houses in suburban streets. We see people with various handicaps employed in the ordinary work force or in highly productive special workshops.

People in Western society who suffer from psychiatric illness are not necessarily made to stay in an institution unless the behaviour which results from their illness makes them a risk to themselves or to the community. And even those who, from time to time, do need to be cared for in a hospital are there for a minimum time with many safeguards as to the appropriateness of their stay.

But there are, even today, places in the world where disease, disabilities and resulting handicaps are not met with kindness and empathy. Infanticide may be used to rid society of burdensome disabled or unwanted children, and even in so-called civilised countries there are some who view disabilities with revulsion and who make their feelings plain.

Sexuality of Those Who are Handicapped

Society as a whole and individuals can experience problems over sexual behaviour. We are increasingly aware of the rights of handicapped persons to lead a normal life, and there is heightened awareness of sexuality in those who are handicapped. But some aspects of sexual needs can be difficult. Residents of group homes, for example, where there is an emphasis on normal living, have to be taught that masturbation *in public* is not acceptable, because this behaviour marks them out to observers as abnormal and so limits their acceptance by society, thereby limiting the activities in which they can take part.

When watching the loading and unloading of vehicles used to transport handicapped people, it is interesting to see the semi-flirtations and joking which take place between the disabled patients of any age and the drivers, whether this takes place at a day centre or at a suburban church. It is my belief that these relationships have a valuable part in normalising the life of disabled people, even though the relationships are probably of a limited nature only. One young woman with a marked degree of developmental disability refers each day to the 'cheek' of the driver, with glowing smile and delight in her own repartee, perhaps the one time in her life when she has felt sure of her own sexuality.

The emphasis on normalisation may lead a young man with only a moderate degree of intellectual handicap, who is attracted sexually to a girl he has met (such as a carer in a group home or someone he has met on the train going to a sheltered workshop), to expect that she will accept invitations or sexual overtures. But the girl herself may not wish to become involved in an intimate relationship with a handicapped person.

It is easy for the observer to understand how the problem has arisen. The handicapped young man has misinterpreted the friendly attitude of the young woman as indicating a personal attraction when she has only intended either *professional* kindness or the casual friendliness of a fellow train passenger. Anger, bewilderment, jealousy of others and suicide attempts are not unknown as a response to a rejection in such a situation. But in the context of normalisation, can such misunderstandings be prevented? Or are they to be expected as a hazard arising from an overall change in attitudes?

Is society truly committed to normalisation? Or are we saying, 'Normalisation is fine, so long as it does not involve me in personal relationships!'?

Anger as a Response to Disability

When a child with an impairment is born into a family or when one acquires a disability as a result of illness or accident, how much of our grief about this event is actually anger with the attitudes which we know some people will exhibit? In 1983, I gave a paper (unpublished) on anger, at a meeting of the (Australian) National Association for Loss and Grief, which focussed on 'The grief of chronic disability'. Two of the speakers were themselves sufferers from chronic disease (lupus and myasthenia gravis), and the audience was also largely made up of people who either had a chronic disease or were related to sufferers.

In the discussions which followed the papers, as well as in the papers themselves, there were repeated comments on feelings of anger as part of the grief of disability. Although this meeting took place over ten years ago, many of the complaints are still valid, and we still see the same sources of anger as were listed in 1983.

○ Anger with doctors who failed to make accurate diagnoses and instead labelled the person as neurotic, so that the eventual diagnosis of even multiple sclerosis came as a relief.

○ Anger at helplessness and humiliation.

○ Anger with those people who treat children, and especially their parents, with disapproval if the handicap causes behaviour which is socially unacceptable. Parents of autistic children describe many experiences in shopping centres when onlookers tell them they are bad parents for letting the child scream and shout.

○ There are still, in a few places, feelings of anger with some people in authority who continue to treat handicapped people as helpless, resisting plans for moving them into the community, continuing to regard them as *things* to be taken charge of, organised, treated as non-sexual beings, deprived of independence, deprived of their right to live messily if that is their chosen way, and generally cared for paternalistically and *en masse* whether they like it or not.

But such attitudes are yielding to change, more and more people with handicaps are living in the community with varying degrees of support, and (a personal observation) neighbours are today often highly supportive. In one house where people with severe-to-profound mental retardation live, the neighbours frequently bring in cakes and cookies. In another group home for young persons with intellectual and social difficulties, the neighbours invite the residents to share their family swimming pool. Things are changing!

It is also heartening to see improvements in facilities for people with mobility problems so that street directories usually include maps showing wheelchair access to railway stations, toilets, shopping centres and so on. Design of new buildings is not approved if wheelchair access is not provided. But older buildings are often poorly equipped.

We see today businesses and factories encouraged to employ handicapped people in a serious way, not merely as token philanthropic gestures. The recessions which affect world economy affect such employment; when so many people are out of work it is not surprising that people with handicaps are similarly unemployed. But this does not remove the grief of those who are out of work and who feel that, if they were not handicapped, employment might be easier.

Genetic Defects

Disabilities which are caused by genetic defects demand special attention because of the effects on family relationships. Guilt and anger are predominant in the expression of grief, and marital conflict is common.

It is useful to consider Huntington's disease as providing a quasi-paradigm for issues relating to inherited genetic disease. Huntington's disease, in which 50 per cent of the children of a person with the condition will later develop the disease, provides a clear picture of the possible difficulties.

- Should we try to find out which child is vulnerable?
- If one child (now adult) knows that he or she will develop the disease, will he or she provide the same level of care to the parent from whom the gene has come than if there was no such knowledge?
- Should children of sufferers of the disease have children?
- Does each person have the right to have children, running the risk that a child will inherit a defective gene?
- How do unaffected siblings of Huntington's disease sufferers feel? Relieved? Guilty? Responsible for future care? All of these?
- How does a parent feel when a child develops the condition? Angry? Guilty? Responsible for future care?

Similar questions arise with all genetic disease and grief is involved in the answers, no matter which decision is made. In some conditions there is the option for abortion if a genetic abnormality is found at amniocentesis during pregnancy, and the parents of the unborn child have to make a decision which is fraught with difficulty. Can the family cope with a handicapped member financially or emotionally? What are the ethical and moral views on abortion? And so on. Fortunately, major teaching hospitals now have genetic counsellors trained in this work, and their expertise lies in the medical, religious and cultural implications of the dilemma.

The Hazards and Grief Associated with Medical Technology

There may be differences in attitude to a disability which was present at birth and one which is acquired through life as a consequence of illness or trauma. No real separation can be made as to which is the more traumatic, whether for family or disabled person. Each person is uniquely an individual and no responses are standard.

Today we have skills undreamt of even 50 years ago: capabilities to save lives, assist with rehabilitation and reshape modes of living to take account of disabilities. But these same capabilities bring with them hitherto undreamt-of problems of decision making.

- Which person on the waiting list for transplants will receive the kidney from the accident victim, the cornea, the heart?

- Should we implant an artificial heart? Do a heart or lung transplant?

- Should a person with cardiac arrest be revived if there has been so much brain damage that future life will lack all quality?

- Should we continue with rehabilitation when it is quite clear that the patient is making only very small gains?

- And (in countries where medical costs can be crippling) can the family afford for rehabilitation and other treatment to be continued? (Woolley 1983)

Gosling (1980), in a letter to the *British Journal of Psychiatry*, drew attention to a further problem which arises out of our present-day skills – the grief of the mourners without a death, the 'not officially bereaved'.

When a death occurs, however sad the survivors may be, they have a finite event to cope with, in so far as any event in our lives can be said to have a beginning and an end. The death has occurred, the active relationship has come to an end. There will be grief-work to be done, guilts to work through, anger to express, but these are assisted by the fact that death is final and also by the ritualising of farewell in the funeral proceedings.

Chronic Disability

For friends and relatives of chronically disabled people, and for the people themselves, particularly when the disability results from a catastrophic event or degenerative disease such as Alzheimer's disease, there is no such finality, until death eventually takes place, often many years later. When the disability has resulted from an accident or an illness, there may be great difficulty for those who are emotionally close to disabled people in making the transition from the acute rehabilitation phase to the long-term chronic condition.

Some members of the family may be unable, for one reason or another, to accept that the damage is permanent, and they may get stuck in an intermediary stage of grief and anger for a long time, perhaps for years or even permanently. They might continue to hope for full recovery when this is totally impossible because of the brain damage sustained, still deceiving themselves as to the progress of the damaged person (Lezak 1982).

Even those who do finally accept the permanence of the damage suffer deeply in the transition period. A woman grieved for her adult son, apparently destined for a brilliant career, when a cerebral haemorrhage reduced him to quadriparesis and, it appeared, total loss of cognitive function. He was moved from a rehabilitation unit to a long-stay unit, and this change symbolised for her the recognition that he would not get significantly better and that her hopes for him, for his role as professional man and perhaps as the father of her future grandchildren, would never be realised. His status and role in society had been decided for him by the accident of a cerebral haemorrhage. She had been able to keep this recognition at arm's length as long as he was undergoing rehabilitation and investigative procedures. The changes in her own role too were difficult, with a need to 're-invent the wheel' and to return to the role of supportive nurturing mother of a child instead of her more recent role of loving parent-at-a-distance.

Friends and relatives have to cope with what they often call a *living death*, the survival of the body, often in a grossly damaged or handicapped form, with the mind and the personality imprisoned in that body, and changed so much that the individual has ceased to be the person they once knew and loved. There is no ritual in our society for saying farewell to the person they once knew because, technically at least, he is still alive, and even to admit to themselves privately that leave-taking is necessary is to many people a quasi-sacrilegious denial of hope and an acceptance of despair.

When the loss of the person is part of a decremental process, in which the relatives have to see someone gradually deteriorate in body or mind, it is almost impossible to offer any comfort except that of allowing grief to be expressed over the lost person, despite his remaining 'alive'. How can we help their grief? How can we give grieving relatives and friends permission to express the inexpressible, to say, perhaps, 'This person is not the man I married. I have to say "goodbye" to all that our marriage meant to me and the children, and try to adapt to a new relationship. I can only love the memories of him as he once was, I cannot truly love the person he has become.'

Problems related to sexual relationships and marriage are also strongly associated with grief and loss in chronic disability, and extensive counselling is commonly needed in order to help people cope with the new situation, whether this involves a life without sexual relationship or changes to previous ways of expressing sexual needs. We must be prepared to offer help and to find appropriately qualified helpers for partners whose relationships are altered by chronic disability. Spinal injury rehabilitation specialists have given particular attention to sexual adaptation, and sources of help are usually available through services associated with spinal injury. But adjustment is not easy, and is complicated not only by feelings of sadness and loss, but it may also include guilt and anger about the circumstances of the disability, as well as things from the past, such as previously-identified difficulties of the relationship.

Change of role, loss of expectation, grief, anger, sadness, all these are results of chronic disability, and some relationships survive whilst others do not. A nursing unit manager in a head injury unit gave the opinion that the parent–child relationship is more likely to survive severe brain impairment than is the marriage relationship. She believed that parents are better able than spouses are to adapt to changes of personality, probably because a parent is able to re-establish the parental nurturing role whereas the marriage partner has been one of an equal partnership.

It seems that every advance in medical science and technology brings with it a dilemma as to what course of action should be followed, and, with it, a conflict and a grief for someone!

Degenerative Neurological Disease

A somewhat different picture emerges for the grief of chronic disability when the condition is degenerative. There is increasing disability, continuing downhill progress with an almost continuing grieving process. An American gerontologist, speaking on geriatric psychiatry in New York at a conference on gerontology in 1985, commented that incremental downhill progress appears to be more productive of depression than a disability which remains stable. Examples of this are seen in multiple sclerosis, Parkinson's disease, Huntington's disease, the various muscular dystrophies, motor neurone disease, myasthenia gravis, Alzheimer's disease and so on.

A disabling illness leads to feelings of powerlessness for both sufferer and carer or observer. Parkinson's disease is a chronic and progressive condition characterised by difficulties of movement (tremor and rigidity) which include facial expression and expressivity of speech, and although medication may ameliorate the difficulties, the outcome is not always good and the effects of medication may diminish. It is true that dementia may develop in advanced Parkinson's disease (Ebmeier *et al.* 1990; Rabins 1982), but even then we must not assume that the sufferer is free from grief over the loss of control and decision-making.

Those suffering from the disease have described feelings of frustration and powerlessness, because of the difficulties of movement and because the impassivity of face and voice give an impression of being uninterested, bored, even vague or *retarded*, when inwardly there is actually a feeling of interest in what is going on and an emotional involvement in events which the superficial appearance belies.

In many instances of multi-infarct dementia (in which the sufferer has several small strokes affecting some but not all areas of competence) we see frustration and depression because the sufferer is to some extent aware of what is happening to him or her, but is powerless to do anything about it. Grief and depression may overlap and merge one with the other.

A patient with multiple sclerosis, being cared for in a ward for severe spinal injuries because of his particular nursing needs, said, 'When I first came here I was not too bad and I used to feel sorry for the quads because they had to have everything done for them. But then I realised that they were getting little bits of function back as time went on, while I just got worse and worse.' Sufferers from multiple sclerosis often show signs of a masked depression and not the euphoria which used to be listed in textbooks, and a significant percentage also suffer from cognitive impairment (Ron and Feinstein 1992). Is it easier or more difficult to cope with a condition such as MS in which one has some forewarning of deterioration which lies ahead? The answer may lie in the pre-morbid strengths of the relationship rather than in the circumstances of the disability.

Family Relationships

Loss of privacy is one of the sources of grief experienced by handicapped people and our aim must be to enhance the pre-existing relationships and not to intrude upon these. It is not surprising that relationships, especially marital relationships, are placed under such strain and indeed may break down, when one considers the circumstances in which they have to be lived out, in hostel, hospital or nursing home. Curtains may be drawn around the bed when the wife or husband is visiting, but there is the possibility that even this will be misinterpreted as standoffishness by those around.

Some hospitals and nursing homes do provide a room in which families may have private conversations, but when the patient is extremely disabled it may be impossible to make the move to a private meeting room, and in any case there are not enough rooms for each couple or family to be provided with privacy simultaneously. Thus all relationships have to be lived out within earshot of others and possibly even in the sight of others.

Other conditions too can present as encroaching disability: rheumatoid arthritis, vascular disease, cancer, a series of small strokes, all cause continuing disability and continuing disruption of normal family relationships. They all cause continuing humiliation to the sufferer because of powerlessness.

So the list goes on, each condition with its own disease pattern and expectation, and each bringing with it a prolonged period of grief and loss.

Summary

Our responses to long-term disability and handicap vary enormously. Some of us adapt, not happily but willingly and philosophically, to disability and handicap. At the other extreme are those who have such unmet needs for 'special-ness' and attention that, sadly, they find satisfaction in pain and disability. (This may, I believe, be an explanation for the Facticious Illness Syndrome, varient of Munchausen's syndrome.) Such persons require large resources for counselling because their patterns of living are probably long-held.

Those who work with them also need support because such people are not easy to help, and the psychiatrist has a valuable role in a rehabilitation unit (Holland and Whalley 1981), to cope with difficulties so severe that they are outside the competence of most helpers.

With developments and changes in the training of health-related disciplines, there is growing awareness of the importance of emotional responses to disability and loss. It is therefore less likely today that the nurse who sits to talk with a patient will hear 'Haven't you got something more important to do, Nurse, than just sitting talking?'!

There are too many particular causes of disability and handicap for them to be discussed here specifically, but the empathic helper will be able to transfer ideas presented here as concerning a particular condition to other situations, whether we are dealing loss of control over life through poorly controlled epilepsy, personal conflict through chromosomal abnormality and gender uncertainty.

Chronic disability and handicap may seem less obvious causes for grieving than death and dying, but the complexities which many people encounter make handicap, and the effects on our lives and relationships which are caused by handicap, a major source of difficult grief.

CHAPTER 7

Cultural Aspects of Loss
Migrants and Refugees

As we consider cultural loss, there are several directions for thought. These include:

- responses, customs and beliefs about death which are determined or influenced by cultural factors

- responses, customs and beliefs about other loss (such as the birth of an impaired child) which are determined or influenced by cultural factors

- loss of specific culturally-determined customs for migrants, such as changes experienced because of admission to hospital and experience of rehabilitation, changes to funerary practice

- loss and changes of general culture for migrants and political refugees;

- loss of culture of the host country if the migrants and refugees arrive in sufficient numbers to change that culture

- loss of culture of the indigenous peoples because of the settlement or invasion of their land.

Responses to Death

People do not all respond in the same way to tragedy, to the fear or prospect of death, nor to bereavement itself. Some of these differences result from micro-culture of families; some seem to have their origin in national patterns of behaviour. How do we interpret the behaviour of those who are newcomers when they do things differently? It is not easy to comprehend fully people's emotional and cognitive responses to loss even when one shares a common background of ethnicity. It is even harder to try to understand and help a person whose beliefs and customs differ widely from those of the would-be helper. For example, we may wonder whether those who keen and wail in a grieving response (as in many Middle Eastern countries) really do better than the person from, for example, British-style upbringing, with its attitude of restraint. Religious ritual alone may not be enough; one must have the faith which goes with the ritual if it is to help us deal with loss, and emotions must be congruent with the behaviour if there is to be any true catharsis.

There are reports of difficulties regarding funeral rites and customs when the practices from the homeland conflict with laws regarding hygiene and health of the host country. (I am grateful to Professor Eric Sharpe, of the University of Sydney's Department of Studies in Religion, for discussing these matters with me.) For example, it is the practice in some parts of Asia to place a dead body on a platform so that vultures can pick the bones clean. This would not be permitted under most legal systems in Western countries, and yet this prohibition may not have been understood at the time of migration so that grief over a death is compounded by being unable or forbidden to carry out traditional ways of dealing with that death.

Eisenbruch (1984a, 1984b) too has commented on difficulties over funerary practices. He has discussed at length the cultural differences in response to loss and grief, and the enormous difficulties faced by migrants or refugees when, for example, funerary practices in their new country differ widely from those of their homeland, and are totally unacceptable in their new country. One can imagine, for example, how funeral practices from Bali would be regarded in Australia or America, what the reactions there would be to the idea of burying a body temporarily until an auspicious day arrived for a ceremonial public cremation, with all the customary activities and behaviour which accompany the procession and rites. His two linked articles are essential reading for all who are involved in cross-cultural and trans-cultural counselling in grief.

Responses to Illness and Hospitals

Migrants and refugees often experience shock and bewilderment when they encounter major illness, trauma or bereavement, and realise how different practices are in their new homeland. Mention has just been made of the problems when funerary practices are different and their earlier customs forbidden, but differences in medical practice, hospital admissions and so on can bring equal dismay.

Some cultural differences may appear trivial and yet they can affect people's confidence or lack of confidence in treatment methods. For example, some European migrants expect medication to be given by suppository and so tend to distrust medication by tablets. Some expect that doctors will always wear white coats. Some believe that only doctors can be involved in healing, so that occupational therapy, for example, is seen as mere time-filling and music therapy as entertainment. Migrants who have suffered torture, on the other hand, might dread the appearance of someone in a white coat, and be uneasy in the clinical atmosphere of a modern teaching hospital.

Cultural influences on behaviour are seen also in less-than-tragic situations. The nurse in charge of a children's ward in a district hospital described her dismay on returning from her lunch break to hear loud crying and wailing coming from a group of relatives standing around the cot of a young child who had been operated on for a minor problem that morning. When she left at noon the child was doing very well and was expected to go home in a day or two. Had there been a major set back in the child's progress? Was the child expected to die?

To her surprise she found that the child was still doing well, alert and cheerful, apparently free from any real pain beyond discomfort. There appeared to be no reason for the mourning which was being expressed by the adults, except that they were southern European people, whose emotional reactions (the nurse commented) are more noticeable than those of the local people. Discussion arose amongst the staff. Were these relatives showing a greater love for the child than the calmer relatives around the other beds? Was this simply custom without real grief, or did it represent a deep fear of hospitals and surgical procedures, perhaps a dread because hospitals are somehow equated with death?

Even in rehabilitation one finds that attitudes to disability and handicap are affected by cultural factors, so that people vary from group to group in how they perceive the tasks of treatment and rehabilitation. Is the person to be encouraged towards a measure of independence or is it shameful in their particular culture to allow an older person, disabled for example by a stroke, to do anything for himself? Occupational therapists, in particular, need to find out about cultural attitudes towards disability. Otherwise they might be disappointed that their best efforts lead to success in the hospital's retraining kitchen but total failure to encourage the person actually to cook a meal at home!

A further difficulty, bordering upon grief, which is experienced by persons from other cultures who enter hospital, or who become disabled, is that men who are strongly the dominating figure in the family are distressed to find themselves in the charge of women, often young women (doctors, nurses and therapists). There may be rejection of instructions given in rehabilitation or other aspects of care simply because it is culturally unacceptable to be told what to do by women.

When this is further complicated by perceptual difficulties caused by brain damage, which make it difficult for anyone of any ethnic background to understand what is happening, the difficulty is even greater. Women staff, with thoughts of today's development of the role of women as leaders and decision-makers, might find it hard to comprehend the ethnic background which causes rejection of themselves because of their female status. One does sometimes see an initial anger and rejection by staff as a consequence.

Yet another difficulty, analogous to grief, is experienced as the result of strong religious taboos about physical contact. A young Sydney doctor found that a teenage girl of Muslim origin, wearing traditional Muslim woman's garb, became distressed when the doctor needed to examine her chest, despite the doctor being also a woman, and the girl's father had to be persuaded that this was a necessary process.

There may also be strong fear of treatment when there is insufficient understanding of Western medicine. An elderly eastern European woman totally rejected surgery for a crisis situation, thereby placing her life in jeopardy, and this fear, too, is not far removed from grief. Such failure to understand the need for treatment causes conflict for the helper too, in itself a form of grief, since it may lead to death or extension of disability because of the refusal or delays in instituting urgent treatment.

Attitude to Impending Death

Information about terminal illness or impending death is fraught with many cultural taboos, in addition to the fear and sorrow which is a universal experience. Is it acceptable to speak of cancer or must one always speak of *a growth* or *a cyst*? Is it acceptable to speak of the probability of dying and if so to whom? The patient? First degree relatives only? The priest?

In the migrant populations which originated around the Mediterranean (Italian, Greek, Spanish, Arab, and some others) one finds that there is a refusal to tell a dying person of his impending death. This causes conflict for the health worker who is

1. committed to an attitude of openness and honesty when working with those who are terminally ill, and

2. aware of common law which, theoretically at any rate, rules that information is the property of the patient, and that the information between patient and medical personnel is protected by privilege, unless it relates to various matters which must by law be notified,

such as venereal and other diseases, child abuse and some others.
(Health Commission of NSW 1981)

In their book on grounded theory in research, Glaser and Strauss (1967)
refer to death awareness and the attitudes which influence this. People's
awareness of their probable or certain death will depend upon the culture in
which they are living, varying from complete awareness of reality to those
who maintain a mutual pretence so that each person knows what is happening but nobody acknowledges it. They quote prison hospitals as being
strongly open in information and attitude in this respect.

I have discussed (Bright 1986) the inability of a man with severe
alcohol-related brain damage to interpret the signs of nearing death which
would have been obvious to a person whose capacity for insight was not
impaired. These signs included increasing frequency of pain-killing injec-
tions, increasing weight loss and frailty, dependency and so on. Although
alcohol dependency would not normally be described as a culture, there are
some similarities in the present context. Persons with alcohol dependency
may constitute a social grouping, a subculture with its own attitudes and
responses of either denial or failure to recognise such signs. One sees similar
responses in some family cultures.

Those who work in grief counselling and terminal care with persons from
varying cultural backgrounds must make themselves fully aware of custom,
conventions and beliefs of each ethnic group with whom they work. Mount's
video *Meaning in Dying* (Mount 1990) demonstrates this clearly, allowing us,
through interviews with women who were within days or hours of their
death, to sense the differences in attitude towards death based upon individual spirituality and ethnic origin. Yet the two women interviewed might have
appeared to the casual observer to share a very similar cultural background.

Response to Losses

Responses to tragic loss of expectation in the birth of an impaired child are
also affected by cultural factors such as beliefs in the evil eye as a cause of
birth defects, belief that the birth defect is caused by the mother's sin during
pregnancy, shame that an impaired child is born so that family honour is
impugned and marriage prospects of other family members diminished, and
other culture-based behaviour.

There are, even today, groups of primitive peoples who discard an
impaired child as being a hazard to a tribe on the move. From a historical
point of view it must be acknowledged that accepting responsibility for
disabled people is of comparatively recent origin. Did a mother in a nomadic

tribe experience grief when her abnormal child was abandoned and the tribe moved on, or was her belief in the tribe's culture so profound that she too saw this as a correct decision without connotations of sadness?

Neighbours and professionals alike need to gain as much knowledge as possible about cultural *mores* so that they will be able to deal empathically with the responses they meet, whether in ordinary social contacts or in a professional care-giving relationship. Sometimes we have to come to terms with refusal of some migrant or refugee people to allow proper assessment of a handicapped child. As a therapist, one seeks to know what is wrong, and why, in order to provide the best possible management and help the child grow up to make the most of his or her potential. But to the family there may be a dread lest the discovery of a genetic fault leads to family dishonour and damage to marriage prospects of other relatives. Thus it is safer for the family to refuse proper investigations and to leave the child as he is.

It is inevitable that health workers feel both sad and angry when they see, for example, a child with hydrocephalus who has suffered irreparable brain damage as a consequence of the pressure. They know that if the family had acknowledged the problem earlier and allowed it to be dealt with, the child would have had better prospects in life, and life would have been easier for the family. One would also like to be able to help the family deal with their griefs and fears. But language and cultural barriers often make this impossible, which is distressing to the therapist! We need the support of colleagues to deal with our own feelings about this.

Statistics provided by the Australian Bureau of Statistics (1993) indicate the large number of people living in Australia, having come from elsewhere, who suffer from a disability or handicap. The same is, one assumes, true for any country with a programme for migrants and refugees. Many such people have come from English-speaking countries, but many have not. Almost 200 different languages are spoken in Australia, so that the provision of professional interpreter services has been a high priority for government funding.

But, despite the operation of face-to-face and telephone interpreter services, such professionals are not available all the time. Those who work with people of different cultural origin need to make themselves familiar with differences in attitude towards death, dying, disability and handicap in order to fulfil the role of helper (Jamrozik and Hobbs 1989; Murphy 1977). It is helpful to work through a knowledgeable interpreter or to speak someone else's language, but we must also try to understand the stirring of the heart and the soul of each individual.

Assimilation or Cultural Identity?

In addition to cultural aspects of grief in response to death and bereavement, there are griefs over cultural losses themselves. How far can old traditions be maintained in the face of increasing urbanisation and the opening up of travel networks so that remote areas are remote no longer and modern technology changes patterns of living?

- Should migrants and refugees be encouraged to keep their old traditions and language or be encouraged to assimilate?

- Does the idea of separate cultural identity contribute to conflict with the population of the host country?

- How much do we lose of cultural diversity in world terms if we insist upon assimilation and the adoption of the culture of the new homeland? And, anyway, can we insist on assimilation? Will it happen?

- How will people ever adapt to their new way of life if they strictly maintain their original tongue, their old customs, old ways of thinking? Does it matter if they do not adapt at all?

- If the parents and grandparents maintain the old ways, will this cause conflict with their children who, because of school life and contacts with their local peers, adapt to the new language, the new customs?

Discussion seems endless without any clear answer to the question emerging. Either extreme has its own risks to human happiness. There is indeed conflict, actual or potential, between generations when parents and grandparents want to keep to the old ways and their children and grandchildren want the greater freedom generally open to their schoolfriends and contemporaries who were born in the new country. Conflict can arise even for those children of migrants who were born in the new country if the family adheres closely to the ways of the past.

It has been said that restaurants are the way to achieve a balance between assimilation and cultural uniqueness, that people enjoy food of their migrant neighbours and thereby come to accept those neighbours as being ordinary people who have something new and worthwhile to offer to the host country!

So far cultural diversity has been discussed in general terms, as applying to a society or nation as a whole, but there are also the micro-cultures of a family or group of families, whose customs, beliefs and responses may or may not match that of the population amongst whom they live, even though they have very similar cultural background. This is seen for example in those who say with pride 'In *our* family we don't show our feelings!' ThIs 'stiff upper lip' attitude is usually attributed to upper-class Britain, in which there is traditionally more suppression of emotion than in other groups. But it is not unique to Britain; there are many other examples of micro-culture, not necessarily restricted to English-speaking peoples.

Problems of Relocation

The shocks of relocation can be, apparently, trivial and yet can have profound effects in a sense of strangeness. Cultural and migration loss and grief can vary in scale. A person from the north of England, with its characteristic speech patterns, may – because of speech differences – feel nearly as strange if moved to the south western counties as the migrant who has moved from Italy to America feels. A family from Scotland moves to London and finds differences in speech, differences in vocabulary, differences in custom. Hogmanay is now New Year's Eve; Christmas is celebrated more than Hogmanay; words are pronounced differently; and so on. English-speaking people who move to another English-speaking country may be astonished at the differences they hear around them in the speech and vocabulary of their new homeland. In Australia, for instance, if one hears someone say, 'I was really crook last week!' it does not mean that he robbed a bank but that he was really unwell!

It may be that distress over such differences is a reflection of distress over an unwanted relocation, but it can also occur because the differences are unexpected. We cannot assume that relocation, with changes to ways of living from stress to security, is necessarily matched by changes in thinking and behaviour (Sigal, Weinfeld and Eaton 1985).

As Eisenbruch commented (personal communication), the large number of publications on grief which has appeared in recent years is actually dealing only with the various grieving processes of a very small part of the total world population. Three broadcasts in October 1985 by the Australian Broadcasting Corporation covered some of Eisenbruch's work with Cambodian parentless children who have been adopted into USA families. These children suffer enormous difficulties and emotional trauma if their adopting family has failed to recognise the sense of religious and cultural loss, their very real guilt and grief over (as they see it) abandoning the faith of their homeland.

In this same conversation, Eisenbruch described to me his use of traditional music in helping young Indochinese refugees to work through their cultural loss and grief, and gradually to adapt to the culture of their new homeland. This is similar to some work that I have done with young adults from Vietnam and Timor.

Other Aspects of Cultural Dislocation

We need to recognise that responses to grief which can be described as cultural may persist for a long time. Sigal and colleagues have investigated the coping style of persons who were in 'underground' resistance movements during World War Two or in Nazi concentration camps some 33 years previously. They found that the traits developed in order to cope with the difficult life situations had persisted to the present day and modified their responses to current life-situations (Sigal *et al.* 1985).

As described above, migration issues of cultural complexity arise from movements within a particular country. But most migration is trans-national, between places widely different in cultural background. In earlier migrations numbers were usually not large, the world population at the time being far less than at present. But in the latter half of the twentieth century we have seen huge numbers of people, travelling great distances, either as migrants or as refugees.

Inevitably, these movements have caused difficulties both for those who move and for their willing or unwilling hosts. The very large numbers of people involved today can lead to losses and changes to the culture of the host country. Many citizens of the host country welcome the diversity of face shapes and colours of skin to be seen in the shops, the different languages spoken in the streets, accepting cheerfully the need to provide classes in early schooldays for children who have spoken only their parents' tongue at home for the first few years of life.

Some, however, resent the changes and either write letters to the paper, telephone talk-back radio programmes or use spray-cans to paint angry xenophobic slogans on walls, protesting at the changes to their original culture or the perceived unemployment caused by the influx of large numbers of 'foreigners'.

One may speculate that the arrival of migrants and refugees comes as a shock and a source of uneasiness to some people of the host country, as they realise, perhaps for the first time, that their attitudes and ways of living are not universal, that other people live together happily in different ways. One may also speculate that this unease is more common in the non-professional classes than in those people who, because of education or travel, are more aware of the cultural diversity of the world as a whole, so that resentment of migrants may well become a class issue.

Today in Australia there is still a large number of migrants and refugees from Indochina, some of whom have arrived after horrific journeys in small boats, preyed upon by pirates and with fear of natural disasters. Many of them have been victims of cruelty and torture, and in Canada in 1991 I was able to discuss their special difficulties, comparing their needs with identical needs of those who have come to Canada from repressive and cruel regimes in South America (Reid, Siloh and Tarn 1990; Reid and Strong 1988).

In New South Wales (my home state) it has been estimated that, of a total population of over four million, there are more than 200,000 persons, migrants or refugees, who have been victims of physical and mental cruelty either in torture or in cruel imprisonment (Jamrozik and Hobbs 1989). The griefs and terrors of these experiences are seldom resolved without help, and possibly not even then, despite the establishment of special government-funded programmes for such people.

The experiences may also affect people who come into hospital in their new homeland, because of the practice (common in some places) of having a doctor assess fitness to withstand torture, so that a white coat or its equivalent has associations of fear and horror rather than help. This compounds fears of illness and possible death.

This situation is found in every place where refugees and migrants are resettled. In the UK, Professor Isaac Marks of the Institute of Psychiatry has worked extensively with post-torture victims (Basoglu and Marks 1988). In a letter to the *British Journal of Psychiatry*, Kohen (1991) wrote of the plight of those who have been forced to become torturers. Although it is common to vilify them as the perpetrators of cruelty, it is also necessary to consider the impact upon them of being forced to act in that way, for fear of themselves becoming the victims.

Even less dramatic factors can bring a feeling of strangeness amounting almost to grief to those who move from primitive to city conditions. One such young man, a few years after arrival, so that he was able to converse without an interpreter, described the difficulty of changing from life in a remote Indo-chinese village, where fresh meat was obtained by shooting monkeys with bow and arrow, to city life where meat was readily purchased in shops.

Griefs of Indigenous Peoples

Throughout history people have travelled, either as nomads, with no permanent home, as settlers or as conquerors. Some incursions which were regarded as settling by those who did it were seen as conquest by the indigenous peoples whom they displaced or whose way of life their arrival altered. We are seeing in the twentieth century an upsurge of anger and grief in various groups of the remaining indigenous peoples. This occurs because of the damage done to their ancestors and to traditional culture by the conquerors, and the powerlessness which was experienced is a major part of the grief over those losses.

Australian Aborigines have suffered loss of self-esteem as a consequence of the loss of their sacred sites, and the tribal person (and, to a lesser extent the urbanised Aborigine, too) commonly believes in the power of magic to cause disease and to cure it. This magic may have strong territorial connections. There are elaborate funeral rites involving music (Moyle 1980), and these are helpful in ritualising grieving processes. Health workers who are involved in helping traditional Aborigines, Laplanders, Canadian and American Indians and other indigenous peoples need to be well informed about their belief systems and customs. Even in the cities, these traditions are not forgotten. Indeed, in the growing pride of indigenous peoples, there is also a growing awareness of cultural heritage.

Today there are still some cultural groups of people who maintain a semi-nomadic way of living. The Lapps of northern Scandinavia follow the reindeer herds. Australian Aborigines follow the hunter-gatherer mode of living or go walkabout, not in search of food but to fulfil religious obligations by visiting the sacred sites of their tribal ancestors and sites associated with the myths of the Dreamtime.

Such ways of life have disadvantages in making it more difficult for children's education to proceed in such a way that, if the children later decide to leave that way of life, they are able to fit into a technological society. One church-based organisation attempts to deal with this challenge by providing education in Alice Springs, in Central Australia, for children of tribal families, returning the children to their families during school holidays. Because of their semi-nomadic way of life, locating the families can be another challenge, but usually the Royal Flying Doctor Service's two-way radio network is able to provide information as to where the family is at any given time.

This network provides two-way radio communication so that people in isolated outlying areas (where neighbours are separated by hundreds of miles rather than a few yards!) can talk to base for advice on medical needs, summon the flying doctor or get help for any other problems as well as talking with their neighbours. This rural population can be regarded as a separate cultural group, distinct from their suburban counterparts.

Culture-Bound Illness

Because there may be associations between blocked grief and psychiatric illness, we need to have some understanding of cultural influences on grieving, and the concept of culture-bound disorders (Eisenbruch 1984a, 1984b). By *culture-bound* we mean an illness which is unique to a particular culture. The superseded manual of disorders, *DSM IIIR* (American Psychiatric Association 1987), included no such classification, and the *International Classification of Mental and Behavioral Disorders 10* (World Health Organisation 1992) also lacks such a classification. However *DSM IV* (American Psychiatric Association 1994, pp. xxiv, 843–849) does include an appendix on culture-bound disorders and also (in the preface) reminds users that cultural and ethnic considerations must be borne in mind whenever making a diagnosis.

A culture-bound psychiatric disorder, unique to a particular culture, is regarded as different from a disorder which is well known throughout the world but which is coloured by the culture to take a particular form of presentation. Controversy continues as to whether there is such an entity as a disorder unique to a particular culture (Low 1985). We must, nevertheless, be aware that cultural diversity does cause diversity in the presentation of bereavement and of psychiatric illness, and this is further complicated when one has to work though interpreters.

One woman described herself in words which were translated by the interpreter as meaning 'feeling very nervous' when she thought of the death of her husband. But her behaviour suggested that she was not so much feeling 'nervous' as experiencing sorrow and guilt at having murdered him whilst suffering from a psychiatric disorder.

A refugee from East Timor perceived his hallucinatory voices as being those of the spirits who lived in the trees in his remote village, who castigated him for having left the village. Was this a culture-bound illness or a culturally-coloured description of recognisable paranoid schizophrenia?

As professionals involved in grief counselling we probably need not become involved in arguments as to whether diseases are indeed culture-bound or culturally-coloured. But we must recognise that cultural diversity of response is important.

Other Sources of Grief

We must note that some angry and unhappy people blame cultural differences for their problems when this is only actually a small part of the cause. Three older women, for example, said independently that the reason their daughters did not want them was because the culture in Australia is different, and old people are not valued. In each case it became very clear that the real difficulty arose from lifelong conflicts in relationships between mother and daughter, that rejection would have occurred no matter where they had lived, unless it had been in a culture which forced the daughter, however unwillingly, to care for her mother in old age and disability. This may be described as a quasi- or a pseudo-cultural grief.

The feelings of rejection, anger, sadness and isolation are no less real than those which arise only from cultural adaptation, but our approaches and intervention will almost certainly have to be different. We shall be trying to achieve some change in the fundamental relationships (which is usually difficult when the destructive patterns are long established), in order to prevent a perpetuation of the destructive triangle of blame, anger and guilt, rather than trying to assist adaptation to cultural change as such.

Dangerous Customs

Female genital mutilation, by excision of the clitoris in so-called circumcision or stitching of the vagina in infibulation, is a source of strong emotion in host countries such as Australia where the practice is illegal and generally repugnant. In order to avoid 'backyard' operations, educational programmes have been instituted. These programmes seek to explain that such customs are forbidden in the host country, because they denigrate the status of women as well as causing grave risks for happiness, sexual fulfilment and health of the girls thus mutilated.

The Australian Aboriginal traditions of initiation and other rites, which involve blood-letting, provide another clear example of the dangers of cultural rites. Should we today, with the knowledge we have about risks of transmission of AIDS and of Hepatitis C, try to stamp out such practices? Should we try to sanitise them? Should we insist that tradition must continue unchanged even if by so doing we risk the deaths of many people if one of the participants suffers from AIDS or Hepatitis C? What is the outcome if we bring these and other cultural rites to an end? There is no easy answer to these or other cultural dilemmas.

It was interesting, during a broadcast from the Australian Broadcasting Corporation's National network to hear an Aboriginal physician (specialising in sexually transmitted diseases) being questioned about this, and to realise that, because of traditional secrecy, he could not discuss the practices on radio except to say that the problem was being addressed (Australian Broadcasting Corporation 1995). It underlined the difficulties experienced by indigenous peoples in adjusting to problems of today and striking a balance between demands of hygiene and health with traditions laid down in an age which knew not AIDS!

In an attempt to equip professional health workers with the necessary cultural background, the (then) Health Commission of New South Wales published a loose-leaf folder on cultural diversity. This helped staff to deal with their clients and also their own sense of being 'at sea' with the attitudes and fears they met in those who were newcomers to Australia (NSW Health Commission).

Summary

In summary, then, we may see that cultural aspects of grief are three-fold: the sense of grief and loss over migration as such; the difference in philosophy and beliefs over life events such as disability, illness, dying and death; the varying responses and behaviours of different cultures in time of grief and loss, mourning rituals and so on. Although we can see links between these, it is also important that we learn about each separately if we are truly to help those whose cultural background is different from our own.

CHAPTER 8

The Grief of Being HIV Positive and of AIDS

Today there is discussion about the likelihood of progression from being HIV positive to having AIDS, and research as to what factors influence this (Easterbrook 1994). But the matter is still so unclear that a finding of HIV positivity brings anxiety and a form of grief to individuals and their significant others, and for this reason HIV and AIDS are dealt with together here.

The topics are dealt with in a separate chapter because the disease itself and responses to it are probably unique.

1. The disease itself entails suffering, but there are also many additional causes of distress in the opportunist infections which result from reduced immunity.

2. In the psychosocial ramifications of the disease the consequent grief and loss rivals the physical suffering which is experienced.

The factors which distinguish grief over AIDS from other griefs are several:

- Original causal link with male homosexual practices has led to major stigmatisation of sufferers.

- In turn this has led to fear and stigmatisation of those who have acquired the disease through inept clinical procedures such as transfusions using blood from inadequately screened donors (or transfusions which took place before there was full protection for recipients by screening of donors).

- Stigmatisation is seen affecting drug-users who become infected, with little regard to their life experiences and pressures which lead to drug-dependence.

- ○ Stigmatisation also afflicts the families of sufferers, to the extent that the true diagnosis is often hidden from others and grief is made more complicated and is disenfranchised. The implications for the family are extensive (Lippman, James and Frierson 1993).

- ○ Much fear attaches to the fact that, at the time of writing, there is much research but no certain cure for the disease once the status of HIV positive has occurred, nor any immunisation procedures available which will give advance immunity or confer certain immunity in those who suffer, for example, a needle-stick injury in the course of their work, and who are at risk of infection from infected blood.

- ○ The length of time between a possible infection, whether through sexual intercourse, blood transfusion, intravenous drug-use or by a needle-stick, and the confirmation through blood tests of either infection or freedom from infection is itself an enormous cause of stress.

- ○ There are ethical dilemmas for the professional as to whether or not HIV status is disclosed to those who may be affected.

- ○ The progressive nature of the disease and the distressing nature of its manifestations are a source of grief and fear to those who are infected as well as to their families and friends.

- ○ Last, there is fear, grief and anger over the inevitability of death if the full-blown disease developes.

In the predecessor of the present book, there was some discussion of the extreme fear in which AIDS was held, which led to people exhibiting an irrational AIDS phobia, and the moral judgements which were passed so readily (Bright 1986, pp. 51, 175). Today the disease is still feared, but there is a greater bank of knowledge so that fear is, in general, of the known rather than the unknown. There is, for example, greater knowledge about how the virus is contracted, how hygienic measures can be taken to prevent contracting the condition, and greater understanding of the life-history of the virus itself. Needle exchanges are set up in suburban pharmacies in such a way that no questions are asked and no derogatory comments made when people come in to get fresh supplies, so that intravenous drug-users do not need to share needles. The sex industry has set up requirements that condoms be used in brothels, many gaols provide condoms so that homosexual prisoners are spared the risks of contracting AIDS.

Whilst a narrowly moral viewpoint may condemn such preventive tactics as seeming to condone homosexual practices, illicit drug use and prostitution, it is nevertheless appears likely that those countries where preventive medicine takes precedence over moral judgements have had less spread of the epidemic than those places where moral judgements are the key issue. It is tragic if politics are allowed to influence decisions on such a critical health issue. We must bear in mind that when moral judgements forbid the dissemination of knowledge about hygiene and other preventive measures, those who suffer are often the innocent. Wives become infected because their husbands or partners have been infected, either from intercourse with opposite-sex prostitutes who are themselves infected, or because they are bisexual and have had sex with homosexual partners as well as within the formal partnership. The children born to those who become infected as a result of the pretence of that infected spouse suffer, as do children who are orphaned when parents die from the disease.

Children whose parents die from AIDS present a challenge to the grief counsellor. The topic is currently being investigated to identify any special problems and strategies (Siegel and Gorey 1994). What is vital is that a possible stigma attached to the death of the parent does not attach itself to the child.

We need to be reminded that we are not only seeing an epidemic of a disease but also an epidemic of fear, of discrimination, of scapegoating, and of stigmatisation. The extent of these epidemics will vary from place to place, depending upon the attitudes of the ordinary people, political pressures and the ways matters are presented in the media. As Gilmore and others comment, we must be intensely aware of the vocabulary which is used and the various other tools by which public attitudes are established (Gilmore and Somerville 1994). The words we use indicate at many levels our opinions of the topics we discuss.

The vulnerability of minority groups is seen in many issues such as freedom of speech and religious observance, especially in places where governments are oppressive. But what is especially notable about AIDS is that prejudice and vulnerability to opinion occur in places where governments are not generally perceived as repressive.

If we are to cope with the AIDS epidemic, we must deal with what Gilmore and Somerville refer to as the *them and us* approach. It is not uncommon to refer to an infected person as a *PLWA* (Person Living With AIDS), as distinct from a person dying from AIDS. But in fact we are all living with the disease, whether infected or not, because the whole of society is affected by the existence of the disease (Gilmore and Somerville 1994).

This applies whether we look at changed practices of disposal of hospital waste and blood products, changes in sex practices or changes in attitude towards sexual preference and behaviour.

Unfortunately, this positive change in understanding is not widely held. The *them and us* syndrome is still strong, and is a major issue in considering the grief, loss and powerlessness associated with AIDS. Sufferers and their families and carers are very much at the mercy of public opinion and it is frightening to realise how much that opinion is swayed by political pressures, attitudes of editors and broadcasters on radio and television, and other sources of influence who may abuse their power and influence to advance their own private agendas.

In an article on the politics of AIDS, Singer has drawn our attention to the manner in which an entire nation can be scapegoated. This has happened to Haiti, which, for a variety of reasons, has been identified so strongly as a heartland of AIDS that anyone of that nationality is marginalised (Singer 1994).

In discussing AIDS, it is important to recognise that it has been a highly politicised disease from its early days when it was perceived as and was labelled 'a gay plague'. Dealing with the epidemic has challenged all the established standards of public health, and we are forced to consider the ways in which society has influenced approaches to health (Singer 1994).

We know that the disease has a profound social impact not only in the cities of the developed nations but also in developing countries. Work done at the London School of Hygiene and Tropical Medicine, in its department of Public Health and Policy, demonstrates that this impact must be seen in personal, social and economic terms as involving labour productivity, development and production in agriculture, as well as the more obvious strains on the provision of health care and the personal stigmatisation of the sufferer (Danziger 1994).

Such knowledge and discussion have wide implications for grief and powerlessness in the people thus affected, whether directly or indirectly, by AIDS. Economic difficulties caused by widespread disease have their impact on the ordinary people, and, although they themselves may not be aware of the causal link, it is there to be seen by those who try to make improvements in living standards and human happiness in those parts of the world which are still in the developing stage.

Stigmatisation

There is, to many people, a great sense of shock in finding that a close relative or friend is HIV positive or has developed AIDS. This may be the first indication one has that the person is homosexual or is involved in the use of intravenous illegal drugs, which is still a source of enormous distress to those who see such sexual preference and the use of illegal drugs only as evil and abnormal. Thus parents and relatives are simultaneously attempting to come to terms with the person's sexual preference and drug use, the fact that he has an illness which may eventually kill him after an unknown period of time, and that the interim will be characterised by pain, humiliation, change and loss.

One elderly lady, referred to me for grief therapy following the death of her son who was known to have died from AIDS, was not able to disclose any of her feelings. Her shame at her son's condition, and the inferences which could be drawn about his lifestyle from the nature of his illness, were such that she needed to keep the nature of that final illness secret. Perhaps she kept it secret even from herself. She insisted that he had died from cancer, and the need to maintain this position defeated all attempts to help her to work through her grief. She could not let her guard down and be open for even a few seconds, so that facilitating her grief-work proved to be impossible.

Stresses of Carers and Friends

In the AIDS epidemic of which we have learned so much since the late 1980s, young adults may attend a constant series of funerals, knowing that there is no cure once HIV positivity has changed to AIDS, with death being only a matter of time, so that they may also carry to the funerals many fears about their own health. There is no chance to grieve adequately before the next loss occurs, and each mourner knows that there is more to come. Friends of those who have died, themselves possibly HIV positive, know too that the pre-death period is marked by pain, deterioration of every function and, for some, rejection by families and others. Grief for their dead friends is thus, for many of the mourners, coloured by the fears about their own future health.

One young woman, herself moving out of a life of prostitution and drug-dependency, described how she goes to funerals, not merely grieving for those who have died and for those who are ill, but looking round at her fellow-mourners with a furtive curiosity which both shocks and frightens her, to see whether anyone of her circle is showing early signs of the disease, of having moved from being HIV positive to having full-blown AIDS (anonymous personal communication).

Fortunately, despite the attitudes of some, not all religious groups turn their backs on sufferers, and many Christian churches or church-based organisations have established support groups with hands-on carers to provide practical help and comfort to sufferers, and support for those who are at risk and for the families or friends of sufferers. One Anglican parish in central Sydney provides support for people who are otherwise marginalised and scapegoated by society, and the funerals held there are often unusual, for example in having balloons and fireworks to symbolise the freeing of the spirit of the deceased. Yet the rituals of farewell bring comfort to those who are left, those who may be next. Not all churches condemn the sufferers and those at risk; all over the world Christian and other religious groups are giving care and support to those in need.

Care of those who are dying or suffering from a major illness has traditionally been given by parents, usually the mother, or by other women. But in the UK and USA a high percentage of carers for those suffering from AIDS are men from their own generation, many of whom are the sufferers' lovers, who may themselves affected by the disease (Folkman, Chesney and Christopher-Richards 1994). There is an approximate parallel in the life in the past of persons infected with leprosy, who were so ostracised and marginalised that sufferer cared for sufferer. The analogy is not perfect because AIDS sufferers often choose to be cared for by their intimate friends, spending their last months at home, dying at home, rather than in institutions however loving.

Such carers do not have the professional sense of distance, non-involvement with the people they care for, so that there is exhaustion not only with the physical task of caring for someone who is gravely ill, using one's out-of-work-hours time, but also in the emotional stress of seeing the deterioration of a person whom one loves. One young man is quoted as saying: 'I'm losing him in bits and pieces. It's not like he was hit by a car and then gone. I lose him a little at a time. It's excruciating' (Folkman *et al. 1994).*

To this is added what has been called disenfranchisement of grief, the denial of access to the dying lover by a family which seeks to hide the truth of their son's lifestyle. The lover is not allowed to visit his dying friend, often not told of the date of the funeral, not permitted to attend that rite of separation, treated as if he had no rights and indeed no relationship with the sufferer (Doka 1989). Doka has pointed out that leave from work is legally available only to those in conventional or de facto heterosexual relationships. There is no provision of so many days off to care for a homosexual partner as there is provision for leave to care for a heterosexual spouse, no allowance of compassionate leave for grief over the death of a homosexual partner. Stigmatisation even includes the denial of the right to care, the right to grieve.

When to this we add possible anxiety about one's own health, seeing in the downhill progress of a friend or lover a portent of one's own future, the strains are almost intolerable. There are many dilemmas which the carer is emotionally ill-equipped to solve. Dementia may be seen as associated only with old age or with the Alzheimer's disease, so that to think of a young person, one's son, friend or lover, suffering from dementia is difficult to accept, a source of disbelief and, subsequently, of grief. But dementia is a common feature of the disease itself, not simply the result of medical complications, and 50 per cent of persons with frank AIDS have mild cognitive impairment (Atkinson and Grant 1994).

For many sufferers, dementia is a major feature of the syndrome. Today with the effective use of medication, the incidence of HIV-associated dementia (HAD) appears to be diminishing, with estimates which are quoted as varying between 7 per cent and 14 per cent annually (Atkinson and Grant 1994). This decrease offers some lessening of anticipatory grief for sufferers and those who care for them, but none the less leaves a large number of people who are affected by a dementing process. It is important that carers are aware of the effects of this process on the sufferer, aware that slowed reactions or difficulties of comprehension are not mere obstinacy but part of the syndrome and thus outside the person's control. They must realise that it is not helpful to deny the effects because of the emotional links between carer and sufferer.

Many difficulties can arise for carers when dementia develops. For example, driving a car is hazardous for the dementia sufferer because responses to traffic situations or crises are slowed, decision-making is diminished or severely impaired, there is impairment of spatial sense, the sufferer is highly distractible, and it is safest for driving to be given up. And yet the carer may perceive that to be free to drive is the last bastion of independent living for the sufferer; it represents being a normal person and to suggest that it is no longer safe to drive may seem the acme of unkindness as well as a source of grief to the carer who has to make the decision.

Balanced against this are the ethics of safety on the road, not only for the AIDS sufferer but for pedestrians and other drivers. The only solution ultimately is to take the car keys away or put a steering lock in place, but the decision to act so powerfully is difficult in the context of a close loving relationship. We deprive the sufferer of an important function, and the prohibition is thus a source of deep grief to both people (Boccellari and Zeifert 1994).

All these dilemmas are well known in the context of Alzheimer's-type dementia, especially when the sufferer is of emotional significance to the carer, but are even more difficult to accept when the person concerned is young. In addition to the practicalities of caring, one has also to cope with AIDS phobia in the community, and there is a need for support groups for carers in which they can share experiences with those in a similar position.

Extra difficulties which bring grief and a sense of powerlessness arise for the carer in being unable to pursue a career with any measure of dedication. This in turn can lead to feelings of anger with the sufferer for making demands, either implicitly or explicitly, which require a career to be jeopardised or sacrificed. One cannot, for example, undertake business travel away from home, overseas assignments must be rejected unless temporary admission to a hospice can be arranged, and the inevitable distractions of continuing crises have adverse effects upon the carer's concentration. Employment, unless with an understanding and helpful employer, can be almost impossible. The dilemma for the carer of deciding whether to pursue one's own career, knowing that death will end the relationship and the carer will need to re-enter his world again, or whether to devote every available moment to the dying friend is not easily solved.

Most people try to effect a compromise by sharing energy between the tasks of employment and caring, but such a balancing act is achieved only with dedication and frustration. Women with children, who try to balance the different loyalties of family and children against employment and advancement in their career, provide a fair parallel!

Professional people, too, are subject to burn-out caused by continuing stress, even though the professional role provides a clearly defined relationship which gives some protective limits. (See Chapter 13.) A willingness to acknowledge the possibility of burn-out as well as an ability to recognise signs that it is happening provide a powerful protection against the condition becoming overwhelming!

The powerlessness of the sufferer may well be mirrored in the powerlessness of the carer, and this is true whether we consider the professional or the non-professional carer. As with those who care for older people suffering from Alzheimer's disease, it is not surprising that carers find themselves thinking, from time to time, 'I wish he would hurry up and die', followed by guilty feelings that such thoughts could arise about a loved person. Again the support group for mutual help is needed, in which such thoughts can be ventilated without incurring disapproval.

Summary

Is it all death and disaster? Can one find any meaning in the suffering associated with AIDS and HIV? The trite saying that suffering is good for us, ennobling the soul, may be true for some but for others suffering destroys the spirit. Nevertheless, to acquire the disease of AIDS has brought a new dimension of life to some.

In the late 1980s it was expected that there would be an increasingly high number of suicides in response to a diagnosis of HIV disease. This has not eventuated so that there is a marked difference in the reports of distress and despair in the papers published then and now (Chesney and Folkman 1994). This has resulted, one assumes, from the greater knowledge which has been disseminated, and the increasing range of medication available. Although they do not prevent death at the end, these medications do make the disease itself slightly easier to bear and deal more adequately with the opportunist infections which arise as a result of reduced immunity.

There are now some hopes that the immune system may, in some instances, reject the HIV organism. Bryson and colleagues have reported the apparent eradication of AIDS in a child, born to a mother with HIV infection, who was HIV positive at birth but who, at age 5, had cleared the virus and become HIV negative (Bryson *et al.* 1995). It is too early to build up sustained hopes on the basis of this report, but even one case helps researchers to find out what human response may prove to be effective against the virus.

Community attitudes too have, in many places, become somewhat less condemnatory, and the support groups available from both inside and outside the homosexual community have somewhat reduced the sense of isolation. One young man with a moderately advanced stage of the disease, who has been helped in the parish referred to above, visits various organisations, when he is well enough, to speak of his experiences. He has described his early life.

In childhood he was abused and was forced out of home whilst still a child because his mother had a new partner who did not want someone else's sons around. He spent his teenage years, ignorant of the possible avenues of support for children like himself, earning money by prostitution. Becoming HIV positive and progressing to the AIDS condition, he came into the loving care of a group of church people. He has described, in moving terms, how it was only after getting AIDS that he came to know what it means to love and be loved, to be accepted for himself without question or criticism for what his way of life had been but rather an understanding of the pressures and fear which led him into it. He has come to a deep Christian faith because of the love he has received, an experience which made him realise the travesty of the 'love-making' involved in the prostitution of his young body, which used him as an object rather than treating him as a person. He has found, through being HIV positive, a new meaning to life which has made even such a terrible disease as AIDS worthwhile.

As an onlooker, one must mourn the loss of childhood and the abuse suffered, so that it has taken AIDS to bring him happiness. But one must also rejoice that such a transformation of meaning is possible! People do manage to find meaning in even the stressful existence of terminal AIDS, seizing the moment to find fulfilment in the processes of caring, the shared moments of intimacy even if it is only in watching a sunset, listening to music or playing a board game such as Scrabble or cards.

Professionals from disciplines outside the strictly medical are working to help people find life worthwhile. They are:

- working out management methods to diminish the ill-effects of processes of the disease itself and of other infections
- recruiting volunteers for support of carers and sufferers
- mobilising and organising community support services
- arranging for the provision of psychiatric consult services
- working with community health teams
- working on links between HIV disease and substance abuse.

These measures all help to maximise health and diminish the impact of ill health (Boccellari and Zeifert 1994; Dilley 1994). The grief which accompanies HIV positivity and AIDS is made slightly more bearable by these and other strategies, because they denote a measure of empowerment, through knowledge, through medical improvements in treatment, through improved methods of management, through raised self-esteem and through solidarity.

CHAPTER 9

The Grief, Anger and Powerlessness of Suicide

Community Attitudes to Suicide

In the past suicide has been labelled a sin, a crime against oneself and against society. Those who had killed themselves were denied religious rites at their funeral, buried outside holy ground, perhaps at the crossroads with a wooden stake through their hearts. It was common until relatively recently for inquests on people who had killed themselves to end with the verdict 'Suicide, while the balance of the mind was disturbed', so that relatives were perhaps spared any stigma, and so that burial in consecrated ground could take place.

Today suicide has, in most places in the world, been decriminalised, although assisting someone to commit suicide generally remains a criminal offence. One assumes that this is a safeguard against murder being disguised as helping someone to kill themselves. But even now, when one attends a funeral in church of a person who died as a result of completed suicide, one may well hear the minister say something like, 'This death is as much the consequence of illness as if she had died from cancer, so that no sin was therefore involved in the ending of her life.' (This was said at the funeral of a woman with long-term severe depressive illness who had taken an overdose of medication and died.) Or 'He died because he suffered from schizophrenia, and it is this terrible illness which alone is responsible for his death.' (This was said of a young man with command hallucinations who had killed himself violently after many years of illness.)

On the whole, society is now less judgemental about self-killing than in the past, seeing it as a tragic response to an insoluble problem or to an intractable illness, and professional papers have been published which discuss *rational suicide* (Siegel 1982). Suicide can, however, become entangled in discussion about euthanasia, so that there may be a hidden agenda of which the casual listener is not aware. Nevertheless there is generally still a burden for those who are left behind, a stigma attached to being the close relative of a person who brought his or her own life to an end.

There is a paradox, in that those who speak of their own wish for death often say 'I wish I could kill myself but I haven't got the guts to do it', and yet at the same time there is a general perception in the community that suicide is the coward's way out of life. Thus the adult child of a person dead through suicide often feels that the parent was a wimp to take the easy way out rather than face up to coping with problems.

Reasons for Suicide

Why do people kill themselves? Reasons include:

- revenge and anger
- depression
- powerlessness
- loss of self-esteem
- psychotic delusional beliefs, hallucinations
- apparently rational decisions based on life prospects and the loss of these
- pain (physical, emotional or spiritual).

Revenge and anger as a source of self-killing may not be recognised for what it is if the suicide is completed. A young man jumped from a high roadway onto another road beneath, not primarily to kill himself but to see how many people he could kill in the accident his jump into the traffic would cause. Had he died it would have been assumed that his motive was self-killing because of despair or hopelessness but, because he survived, it was known that his motive was to kill others. A research study (Wahl 1971) showed that those who survived a genuine attempt at self-killing had believed, before the event, that they would be able to see the remorse of those whom the death was intended to punish.

Psychiatric Illness and Suicide

The risks

There may be some controversy as to whether a death was the result of true suicidal ideation. Does a young child, whose concepts of death are limited, really intend to kill himself, or does he assume that he will return to life afterwards? Young children do, however, die from what appears to be suicide. One should not assume that age alone is a preventive if one works with a depressed and psychiatrically disturbed child.

There may have been no intention of death in what appears to be an attempted self-killing, as with the schizophrenic young man who leapt from a considerable height because he believed he could fly. He became quadriplegic but, if he had died, it would have been believed that his death was intentional rather than a consequence of psychotic delusional belief.

Major depressive illness, with feelings of hopelessness and powerlessness, is a major cause of suicide, and can occur when relatives least expect it, perhaps when the person is beginning to have some energy and is beginning to exercise some control over life. This is not so surprising when one remembers that a severely depressed person has barely enough energy to eat, and certainly not enough to plan his or her own death. As the illness begins to recede, however, the energy begins to return but possibly before the feelings of hopelessness have dissipated, and the outcome is death.

Command hallucinations are a frequent incentive to suicide for those who are psychotic. Whilst professionals perceive that the voices can have their origin only in either remembered words of others ('You are useless, I wish you would kill yourself'), or in the inner thoughts of the sufferer, those same words are transformed by the patient's illness into the voices of outsiders or evil spirits with power to command. There are some reports of success with cognitive approaches in dealing with command hallucinations (Chadwick and Birchwood 1994) but nevertheless such voices remain a common cause of self-killing.

Loss of self-esteem

Loss of self-esteem as a reason for suicide is seen in the traditional Japanese Samurai practice of hara-kiri (disembowelment) following 'loss of face' at humiliation or a proven major error. But suicide through loss of self-esteem is known in many other instances outside Japan, such as occasions in which someone feels such shame over events that life is no longer tolerable.

Because grieving is often associated with depression, and is closely connected for many people with powerlessness and loss of self-esteem, those who care for grieving people need to be alert to possible indications of suicide. And, since loss of self-esteem is associated strongly with depressive illness, (Ingham et al. 1986) it may not be reasonable to separate too formally the loss of self-esteem and depressive illness as causes of suicide.

A highly intelligent mathematician who suffered from schizophrenia, grieving over personal losses, came eventually to acknowledge that the long-time relationship with his woman friend (conducted on an on-again, off-again basis for some years) had finally come to an end. This time she meant what she said and could not, as in the past, be persuaded to return to him. His self-esteem could not survive this ultimate rejection and his total powerlessness to change the situation. He became seriously depressed, his schizophrenia made it difficult to deal with changes in his life, and his suicide followed a few days later.

There is some discussion as to whether suicide occurs more often in some families than others, and, although opinions are divided, the carer needs to be especially alert if it is known that other family members have killed themselves (Khin-Maung-Zaw 1981).

Parasuicide

In death following drug overdose there is often controversy as to whether the death was intentional, whether the drug was impure or of an unexpected concentration, or whether it occurred because the person was for some reason more vulnerable than usual in the response to the drug. The death of a person who has frequently carried out suicidal gestures or parasuicides is also a source of discussion amongst those involved either personally or professionally.

Was this simply another *gesture* but one which, unintentionally, went too far? Perhaps the timing was wrong so that the person was found less soon than he or she had expected? Were the previous incidents, categorised as gestures, in fact botched genuine attempts at death? Was it the final decisive act for which all the others had been rehearsals?

Staff and relatives find it difficult to cope with a completed suicide when the action was different from previous parasuicides, such as death by hanging when the person had previously slashed his or her wrists or taken drug overdoses. Did the mode of death show that this time it was not a gesture but truly a desire for death? Or was it because the previous gestures did not meet with the desired response so a new method was employed, one which proved unintentionally fatal? Because there is no way of knowing the answer, it is exceptionally difficult to reach resolution of one's feelings after a death in which there is doubt as to intention.

It is also difficult to cope with the death of a person who has made many gestures, often of small potential for death, because these are a source of anger and frustration, so that the death of the individual brings strong feelings of both guilt and relief. (See Chapter 13.) It is a rare relative who can say, as one mother did, that it was a relief that her daughter's suicide had been completed. Her daughter's unhappiness and the frequent emergency calls for the parents to come urgently to the hospital had been so exhausting that she could feel only relief that the young woman was finally at peace.

Prevention

Expressions of wish for death

There seem to be various levels of death-wish, and it can be seen as within normal limits for someone to think, a few times in a lifetime, that it would be easier to be dead. But there are various levels of intention. These are:

- those who say (perhaps quite often) that they wish they were dead but who have no intention of doing anything about it or who may not truly wish for death; what they are asking is for someone to help them feel happier

- those who wish they were dead and really mean it, but do not seem to have definite plans

- those who wish they were dead and reveal definite plans when asked about it

- nihilistic comments, created artworks such as paintings or songs, which can, without verbalising a wish for death, reveal a death-wish and serious suicidal ideation.

Identifying the person at risk

Preventing the completed act of suicide, and, ideally, to deal with the feelings which lead to self-killing before plans are formulated, demands skills of empathy from all staff. It is now known that the old saying, 'Those who talk about it don't do it', is wrong. We know that people who attempt or succeed in self-killing have discussed it beforehand or have spoken in terms which indicate to the trained listener that suicide is intended (World Health Organisation 1981, p. 35).

We meet those who are so disabled that suicide is not a possibility, and staff may therefore relax on this issue. But we cannot ignore the despair which causes people to say with real feeling that they wish they were dead and that they would kill themselves if they could. Hopelessness is recognised as a prime cause of suicide (Beck *et al.* 1985). The links between hopelessness and powerlessness are obvious, so that we should be alerted to possible suicide in those who speak frequently about loss of power, and those who say that loss of control makes life not worth living.

We know that there are a number of predictors of suicidal behaviour (Petrie Chamberlain and Clarke 1988). Such predictors include:

- having no family or significant person
- depressive illness, especially at the time when depression is starting to ease and the person regains some degree of autonomy and energy
- previous attempts at suicide or suspicious 'accidents'
- Nihilistic comments such as 'No point in eating now', 'No point in planning ahead any more' and so on
- patients involved in creative arts therapies who reveal suicidal ideation through their art works - painting, poems, words of songs
- suspicions that certain potentially lethal tablets are not being ingested but perhaps stored secretly
- comments which suggest that definite plans have been made.

We must not believe that prevention is unnecessary for older people. In fact the rate for persons over 80 years of age is higher than for other age groups (Ross and Kreitman 1975).

It is encouraging to realise that asking whether someone has plans for suicide does not increase the likelihood of death occurring; we do not put the idea into their heads (Kennedy 1977, p. 245). If people truly have no such thoughts, they will deny it; but if they do have plans, almost invariably they will say so. Paradoxically, perhaps, this defuses the situation by bringing it into the open as something which can be discussed, and reduces the risk by restoring some measure of control to the sufferer.

Even when a suicide has occurred in a ward, a patient who is known to be suicidal may say, 'I find myself thinking about suicide but I don't really want to die. How will you stop me when so-and-so managed it?', and strong reassurance from staff is needed to dispel the patient's anxiety (Bartels 1987).

Most important of all in preventing suicide is the joint work of the therapeutic team. Adequate medication must be prescribed in adequate dosage, personal problems must be uncovered and, to whatever extent is possible, dealt with. An atmosphere must be maintained in which people can always find someone appropriate with whom to discuss anxieties and fears.

This is a team effort in which the client is included, so that he or she does not feel increasingly powerless as others take over control of events. However, it is commonly necessary for others to intervene at first in order to deal with impossible situations of relationship, finance, accommodation and so on. Gradually, perhaps over many weeks, the needed control is given back to the client, control which has so often been lost as a result of illness. For those living at home the community team will normally be involved, and for the person who has been in hospital during a crisis or an acute illness, it is normal to involve the community team in the discharge planning for future support.

An important aspect of therapy is that the presence of command hallucinations is recognised. One young man, schizophrenic since his adolescence and suffering from malignant neuroleptic syndrome, so that the provision of medication to ease the suffering caused by voices and other distortions of reality was fraught with difficulty, learned not to speak of his voices. He said that the only way he attained any freedom from close observation was to keep quiet about the voices which told him to kill himself.

This decision was respected by staff, and he was living in relatively normal surroundings in a halfway cottage within the campus of a psychiatric hospital. But he was kept under careful observation by staff of the unit so that, if possible, suicide would be avoided. Sometimes, but not always, it was possible to know that the voices were affecting him because of failure of eye contact, loss of concentration or other indications. Eventually, however, at age 34, he did kill himself in response to his voices; his skills in hiding the phenomenon led to his death. (For discussion of the debriefing which followed, see Chapter 13.)

There is research showing effective cognitive work with people suffering from command hallucinations (Birchwood 1992) but unfortunately suicide or other anti-social and destructive behaviour does still result from this phenomenon.

Effective work with a disturbed and suicidal client is not easy, whether we work in the community, in private practice or in a hospital; the availability of fellow-clinicians is of enormous support. Our 'antennae' must always be raised, to be aware of changes in vocal timbre, in choice of words, in eye contact, changes of posture, changes in restlessness or quietness, and so on. This may seem like what is commonly described as *intuition*, but what we really do is assess with the utmost speed the significance of these minute alterations in behaviour and, based on our general understanding of the illness and the particular knowledge of the client, reach the right conclusion.

Having a contract with the client

It may be helpful to have a contract with a person known to have strong suicidal ideation, provided that it is clear that the end of that contract is not the equivalent of permission for self-killing. It might seem to be effective to say, 'If you kill yourself you will make me deeply hurt and unhappy.' But this is an invitation to the client to take command of the relationship by giving or withholding approval from the therapist, which is ultimately unproductive since every therapeutic relationship must eventually come to an end. It also opens up the possibility of the patient committing suicide in order to punish the 'unempathic' therapist, or playing games by bargaining. There is also a very real possibility that the absence of that staff member because of vacations or change of employment will be perceived as betrayal and thus justification for self-harm.

'Promise that you will still be alive next week so that we can continue this discussion! But I do *not* mean that, after the discussion, you can go ahead and kill yourself!' This jocular style of establishing a contract has proved successful on many occasions because it is *real*, but the humour takes away the option for the bargaining mentioned above, which can mar a therapeutic relationship ('I'll only promise to stay alive if you are kind to me, promise to..., etc.'). Nor is this humorous contract likely to reinforce dependency. It can be renewed after each session, and, as the client's state of mind improves, can be used as a measure of this improvement. 'Do we need our usual contract this week?'

Areas of special risk

It has been noted that there are certain areas which are of special risk, such as the bathroom and bedroom in hospital (Bartels 1987) and at home. At home there are many suicides, usually of men, in the garage, perhaps because it is not in the normal family living area and it is common for people to spend fairly long periods of time in the garage or workshop without anyone checking to see what they are doing. Thus there is time for the suicide to be completed before discovery takes place.

But no precautions can entirely eliminate the risk. One patient who had become aware of his own dementing process managed to open a fire door on to the roof of the hospital and leapt off to his death because he was not willing to live through the future.

Confidentiality and Client Safety

For someone who is truly the prey of suicidal ideation with definite plans, it is essential that preservation of client safety overrides confidentiality. The Tarassoff decision originally concerned only risks from the client to others and the duty to warn others if a client intended violence (Tarassoff v Regents of University of California 1976; Treadway 1990; Wulsin Bursztajn and Gutheil 1983). Decisions on professional ethics have now extended this duty of care to include the safety of the client himself or herself, and this protection from harm, as overriding confidentiality, is included in codes of ethics and professional conduct of professional therapy and health-related associations.

Although the client may say that the therapist who *blows the whistle* will not be trusted again, this must not sway us from our intentions. It is found that the extreme suicidal urge may last only a very brief time, and the person whose plans for self-killing were thwarted is frequently grateful afterwards. It is, of course, essential that the client knows what we intend to do, and for us to explain (even if the client is too disturbed fully to understand our explanation) that this is not a personal decision but a professional requirement. Such an explanation is not simply to get ourselves 'off the hook' with the client, but to avoid (if possible) a perception by the client that we are seeking revenge or acting out of anger.

Professional Support for Those Who Have Survived a Suicide Attempt

This section is not for relatives of those who have completed suicide but for relatives of those who have survived or were revived after an attempt. The precise approach to support of a survivor must be tailored to the needs of the individual and the circumstances which led to the attempt. But there are two aspects of our care which are always necessary:

- ○ to find out whether this was a once-only attempt, or part of a series of attempts, which may continue in the future
- ○ to find out, if possible, whether there was a true search for death or whether this was a cry for help.

It may not be possible to determine the answers to these questions at the first interview, if ever, and if so one must act on the assumption that there is an ongoing risk, and act accordingly.

Preventive measures will depend upon the philosophy of the establishment concerned, whether there will be immediate intravenous medication, institution of a regime of medication by mouth, a temporary requirement for care in an open unit but with someone at no more than arm's length, care within a locked unit, and so on.

When providing help immediately after a suicide attempt, it was interesting to observe the relative calm of two such people, one of whom had been the subject of stomach-pumping only three hours before, and the other who had been returned to hospital after being rescued from the water under the bridge from which she had jumped earlier in the day. It seemed possible that the attempt had, for the time being anyway, laid guilt to rest and this

explained the atmosphere of peace in the people concerned. This direction
was followed up in therapy and proved useful.

Whilst it would be unwise to extrapolate these comments to all incomplete suicides, it is worth considering as a direction for counselling. Counselling in the acute phase for those who have survived an attempt on their
own lives requires highly professional skills, but volunteers in telephone
support services may find themselves dealing with the situation in later
weeks. For both situations, a non-judgemental attitude is important. At the
same time we must avoid colluding with any plans the person may have for
further attempts. We must advocate finding face-to-face help from a support
group, a trusted friend, a pastor or a therapist, avoiding isolation, avoiding
substance dependence, and so on.

Helping Those Whose Relatives Have Killed Themselves

There are heavy burdens to be borne by those who are left. This is true
whether we are considering suicide in a hospital unit or suicide at home. The
burden is especially heavy when, as happens frequently, the self-killing is the
act of ultimate anger against particular people who are perceived as having
betrayed or failed the person concerned, and when the deceased person has
left a note blaming those whom they believe 'drove' them to their death.

The sad feelings of loss, often tinged with relief, are compounded by
guilty feelings, whether justified or not, and by remorse, regret, the multitude
of 'if only's' which lie heavily on the hearts of those who are left. Today in
most parts of the world there are support groups for survivors of suicide, as
there are also for relatives of murder victims, victims of crime and so on. Such
groups provide a deeper level of understanding than is available from the
ordinary friend or neighbour because of the shared similar experiences.
Telephone books often list support groups. Even if the only lists are for
telephone counselling and support, such services normally have directories
of resources so that callers can be directed to the group best for them.

But we may meet such people either in a debriefing after the death or
because they themselves come into care for a related or apparently unrelated
illness. Their needs are for freedom to talk, reassurance that it is normal to
feel: totally numb (for the time being, anyway), angry with the person who
has died, guilty as to what more we could have done, lost and lonely without
the person, that the person is still there, and so on.

For some people, who have been avoiding the place where the suicide
took place, a visit to that place can be useful if it is assisted by someone who
is able to provide support and facilitate separation, so that the visit does not
become part of a series of ritualistic visits which attempt to keep the person

alive. These arrangements are similar to visits to the Cemetery, and Hill's (1993) thoughts on confronting the avoided spot are appropriate to such visits.

There is also a need to make relatives alert to anniversary reactions, for they may find themselves dreading the arrival of the time of year or the precise date of the suicide, suffer emotional turmoil on that day, or (surprisingly to most people) find themselves feeling unhappy for no apparent reason until the date is recalled. One such woman was admitted to a psychiatric unit at the time of her daughter's suicide without any conscious memory of the significance of the date, until music/grief therapy brought the memory to the surface.

Staff Needs Following Suicide

Staff members' emotional needs are discussed at some length in Chapter 13, but we should note here that there are also practical measures to be taken.

Debriefing is essential after any critical incident, and nowhere more so than after the completed suicide of a patient in a hospital or a close-knit treatment group. This debriefing immediately follows the suicide, and is a separate event from a post-suicide analysis of how it occurred. The latter can too easily degenerate into a witch-hunt, particularly if a senior member of staff is defensive and seeks a scapegoat. Whilst such degeneration is to be avoided at all times, it is probably less likely to occur if the emotional crisis is past, when all staff can look dispassionately at the events surrounding the death.

Fellow-patients and fellow-clients need debriefing and there may be discussion or argument as to whether they should be told the truth or whether the nature of the death should be disguised. Hiding the truth is useless. The absence of a fellow patient is noticed. All institutions are well-equipped with 'grapevines' for information and the truth is commonly less horrifying than the rumours (Kayton and Freed 1967).

This debriefing of fellow patients may well happen immediately after the death, before rumours have been able to circulate. At one such debriefing that I conducted, three fellow-residents of the hospital cottage expressed very different views.

- One was angry with the dead young man for killing himself and causing a 'lot of hassles' to the others.

- One was envious that he did not have the same courage to kill himself. (This person was placed in a unit where observation and special help would be available.)

- The third was frightened lest the dead man would go to Hell. She too needed strong support and, later that day, discussion with the Chaplain.

On another occasion, a patient who had been regarded as an extreme suicide risk (about whom there had been substantial discussion as to whether or not he should be told what had happened to his roommate) was actually less suicidal after the meeting than he had been before. The matter had been thoroughly ventilated and thus brought under his conscious control. Thus he gained some sense of power over suicide instead of feeling helpless in the face of his own urges.

Nevertheless, the fears of staff lest there be a suicide epidemic must be addressed and not dismissed as groundless. Staff members may have strongly differing views and opinions on the suicide.

- It is common (and normal!) to feel a sense of relief when the dead person has been a source of anxiety to staff over a long period of time.

- One can feel rejected that one's help was not sufficient, that the person did not say 'Good-bye'.

- One can feel angry for the same reason, one can feel guilty, as discussed above.

Many hospitals employ a person whose task it is to counsel staff following a traumatic event or other critical incident. The pattern for a staff debriefing is usually as follows:

1. Arrangements are made for a debriefing, usually for the day following the suicide, but possibly on the same day.

2. The group which gathers consists of all those who worked with the dead person, at all levels of the institution's hierarchy.

3. But it is of utmost importance that no hierarchical considerations affect the meeting that no one individual is perceived as being more important that another. At one such meeting, when the number of participants unexpectedly exceeded the number of chairs in the sitting room where the meeting took place, the head of clinical services (the medical superintendent) of a large state

hospital sat on the floor whilst one of the cleaning staff sat on a chair.

4. Rules of procedure, normally the matters 5, 6 and 7 below, are set up at the time of the meeting.

5. Confidentiality is complete. Anyone can say or do anything but all participants guarantee that nothing is disclosed to outsiders. This sets people free to cry, shout, express any emotion without fear of this becoming public knowledge.

6. A time limit is set, usually one or two hours.

7. Anyone is free to leave if they wish but all are encouraged to share the openness of grief, disappointment, anger or whatever.

The outcome of such a meeting is usually good, but participants feel free to seek further counselling or open conversation without fear that this will affect prospects for promotion or other career matters.

A memorial service may well be held. At the establishment best known to me, this will include relatives of the deceased, staff and fellow-patients and other residents. The service is followed by a cup of tea or coffee, so that informal conversation can take place. Such a service gives closure to what have often been long-term relationships, and gives opportunities for talking with relatives and sharing their sorrow, guilt, relief, anger.

Suicide offers the extreme in terms of separation from a client, but every separation, whether by normal death or by the person leaving hospital, can leave us with unresolved feelings. The therapist too may need to visit *the avoided spot*. For example, I found that separation from a dead patient was finally possible only by visiting the room in which he had stabbed himself, and where I had been one of the two people who found him. I sat on his bed, saying 'Goodbye', thanking him for the depth of a long-term therapeutic alliance, asking forgiveness if I had failed him, and so on, and recalling the music he had requested for the session which had never taken place, the 'Peace after the Storm' movement from Beethoven's Pastoral Symphony. Although the events are not forgotten, the separation was thus achieved.

The Need for a 'Suicide Autopsy'

As was stated above, the post-suicide analysis is separated in time from the emotional debriefing session. It may take place several days or even a week or two after the death. Its purpose is to determine how suicides may be prevented in future, and discussion of the past event, how and why it occurred, is in those terms only (Cotton *et al.* 1983). Given such an atmosphere of trust, with absence of recrimination and fault-finding, the autopsy is helpful and productive. Guilty feelings can be harnessed to finding strategies for the future!

It is improbable that, if adequate debriefing has taken place of emotional needs, a practical discussion such as is described above needs to take place in a family setting, since one assumes that suicide is usually a one-off event. But it may be that family members need to analyse what has taken place some time afterwards. With proper support from community workers, this could be helpful to survivors by allaying their guilt and enabling them to put the past behind them.

Summary

Suicide is amongst the most difficult crises we meet, whether the suicide has been completed or not. If the suicide was successful, the de-briefing of ourselves, relatives and friends, and fellow-staff will be the main function. (See Chapter 13.) For the incomplete, the 'failed' suicide, the needs of the therapists include coming to grips with our own inner feelings about death and self-killing in order to help others. Only then can we find ways of reaching the inner needs of the client, dealing with those needs if possible and, if we are not able to do this, referring the person on to those who have special skills. Above all, our aims must include helping him or her to find sufficient reasons for continuing to live that suicide risks are reduced.

CHAPTER 10

Volunteering, Neighbourliness and Helping

Volunteering is an established part of modern Western society. Volunteers deliver meals to those who are house-bound, stand behind cake stalls at school festivals and church fairs, visit people in hospitals and prison, raise money for charities, drive people to hospital for treatment when those people cannot afford a taxi-cab, become foster-grandparents for children with special needs, and so on.

Professionals give their skills for significant periods of time to under-developed areas of the world as physicians, surgeons, engineers or architects, helping to build new roads or water supply reservoirs, encouraging local governments into building better resources, teaching children in free schools and so on. We also see, in those who cannot actually travel or who are unable to give their skills on the job, a feeling of responsibility to provide funds for famine relief, medical care, new wells for dry villages – volunteering at one remove! Volunteering is probably one of the marks of an affluent society, but it is also a mark of a society which knows it is lucky and wants to hand on some of that luck by doing things for people who are not so fortunate.

Neighbours

Being neighbours may seem to be just a matter of sharing a back fence, living in adjacent apartments. But self-isolation seems just as common in those who live in blocks of apartments as in those who live in suburbs. It may even be that, when we live very close to each other, we protect our rights to privacy more carefully and tend to be less neighbourly because of contiguity than when we can easily escape unwanted intimacy because there is plenty of space available in the gardens that surround us. It is also true that disputes between suburban neighbours are common, over barking dogs, tree roots that wreck drains, loud music, smoke from garden fires, destructive children, etc.

Language difference, too, can cause difficulties in communication. Some migrants and refugees prefer to live in areas where their mother tongue is spoken so that there is neighbourliness within that enclave. But, for the same reason, language boundaries separate it from the community as a whole so that neighbourly relationships are difficult with those outside. Separation by racial or other prejudice can also cut across neighbourliness and a sense of the wider community. Such prejudice might be formalised, as in the old days of apartheid in South Africa and elsewhere, or as organised religious hostility. It might be informal, no more than a matter of preference.

Reading in the paper of a death which occurred some time before it was discovered, without the neighbours even noticing that the person was not around, may be less surprising than one might imagine. Yet being a good neighbour is one of the aspects of modern society which we like to value. It is typified for many English speakers by the much-loved covers of the *Saturday Evening Post* by the late Norman Rockwell (Guptil 1946).

In what we would probably describe as less developed society there is still in many places an interdependence which goes far beyond the lending of a cup of sugar, joining a car pool or sharing of garden tools which seem to symbolise suburban relationships. A group of people, adults and children together, work in a remote Balinese village to prepare and decorate the tower of wood which will be used at the cremation of a dead man, who lies temporarily buried nearby to await a propitious date for the final ceremonies to take place. The pieces of glass and the coloured decorations are put in place, the red cotton is wound around the structure (cotton because it is the funeral, we are told, of a humble man so that expensive materials cannot be used), and grief is dealt with communally.

In Bolivia, far into the countryside, a group of adults and teenagers kneel together at the river bank, washing the clothes of a dead woman, preparatory to these being burned as part of the ceremony of separation. The sadness of the mourners is helped by the sharing with others in this ritual of grief.

Where does all this fit into grieving and helping?

Neighbourliness in Response to Grief

In many places, illness of a neighbour may be met by informal rosters of helpers taking over cooking and cleaning, driving children to school. This is not possible in areas where both partners are working and, although the wish to help is there, it is impossible for a woman to give up her work in order to help her sick neighbour. Professional help or formalised neighbourliness must be provided, by a group such as LINC (Love In the Name of Christ, which operates in several places in the USAand in Australia on an interdenominational basis, or by some similar organisation. LINC, consisting mainly of retired persons, does the work which families used to be able to do, such as visiting and providing transport. Its members also go to local law courts to provide a listening and non-judgemental ear, especially to parents of young people facing the courts, and to provide simple meals and transport for those in need.

In a suburb of Sydney (where there is also a branch of LINC) a booklet was produced giving lists of resources for the local district. With brief paragraphs of information, this lists support groups for problems such as mastectomy, narcotics dependency, single parents, multiple sclerosis, potential child abusers, parents of children with epilepsy, and so on. This booklet was collated by me, typeset by a local church member, printed by local service clubs such as Rotary, and copies of it distributed to local medical practitioners, police, clergy, church members, pharmacies, community centres, and so on.

These examples provide a practical demonstration of neighbourliness, and, although it is at arm's length, this neighbourliness has proved of enormous value. Part of this value lies in empowering people to take the first steps in dealing with their own problems. There are times when we need first of all to turn to professionals for help. But there are also circumstances in which we have a strong need to take the first step for ourselves, making a decision as to what should be done, finding out where help is available. To have a booklet available with all the necessary lists of addresses, telephone numbers, times and places of meetings and a summary of the aims and objectives of each support group empowers us as we start to look for the right avenues of assistance in time of need.

The death of a neighbour may constitute an emotional crisis for a close-knit suburban group, especially if it is an untimely death of a relatively young person, such as the father of a young family. 'It could be me next!' is a (usually unspoken) response to such an event, and Sudden Infant Death Syndrome has similar effects upon all who hear of it, but is especially poignant when the neighbourhood is made up of young couples with children.

Marital break-up causes feelings of shock and distress to neighbours, and there is always some level of crisis, even if it has become a not unusual situation. Much depends upon the structure and life-patterns of the families.

Finding that the young adult son of a friend or neighbour is dying from AIDS or is HIV positive, finding that a neighbour is facing charges of grand larceny or child abuse, hearing on the grapevine that a neighbour is accused of violence against his wife; all these events are crises and sources of shock and grief for neighbours, which they may or may not be able to cope with. These events cause community grief, which can draw people closer together, but may separate them. The outcome may depend upon whether the prime reaction is that of shame, 'How could such a thing happen in our neighbour-hood!', or a wider acceptance that relationships can break down, and that even if one person can be labelled as perpetrator, the others of that group need support even more because of the allegedly shameful nature of the event.

How well do neighbours cope with tragedy and grief? Too often we are good at coping with practicalities such as bringing over a meal for the family, but we are not often so good at coping with emotional aspects of grief. And yet a young woman, coping with a painful marital collapse, spoke of the validation she experienced because of practical help she received from the mothers' club at the school and from other support groups. She described her response in these terms: 'If I am worth helping like this and people want to be with me, then the things my husband has been saying about me can't really be true. I am not really worthless and a failure.'

A major dilemma lies in our not knowing whether or not those affected want to talk about their loss or tragedy. Even if they do want to talk, we do not know what to say, and we either avoid conversation or we trot out the old useless platitudes:

> 'Try not to think about it.'
>
> 'Don't worry, I am sure it will all work out in the end.'
>
> 'You'll just have to get pregnant again as soon as you can.'
>
> 'Time is the great healer.'
>
> *After relationship breakdown:* 'Plenty of other fish in the sea.'
>
> *After a death:* 'God needed the baby more than you did.'
>
> 'He'd had a good life.'
>
> 'You did your best.'
>
> 'It was God's will.'

What do they believe about life after death? That the spirit goes on or that we go out like a light into total darkness? Religion might come up and we *never* talk about that in ordinary conversation! So do we dare risk talking at all? Our own spiritual beliefs alter the way we speak, and we might be able to offer comfort from our own spiritual depths and experience. However, it is often the pseudo-religious platitudes which are most unhelpful, followed closely by missionary zeal to achieve a conversion whilst people are vulnerable. There are words of comfort to be spoken, but, as sensitive clergy and lay believers know, the best comfort usually lies in simply being there, listening if people wish to talk, answering if they seek an answer, sitting quietly if they do not need words.

If all else fails, and the neighbours find no words to speak or, if they lack the capacity for silence, they ignore people! They even cross the road to avoid having to speak, which leaves the sufferer still more shattered by life's events and feeling that perhaps he or she should be carrying the leper's bell and calling out 'Unclean, unclean'.

Education is making inroads into our shyness and our ignorance but it would seem macabre to rehearse aloud in advance what we might say if a neighbour's wife died, had a miscarriage, lost a baby, got divorced. And yet that is what we need to do. We need to think, when we read or hear of a loss, how we would like people to speak to us, and then try to put it into effect.

Support Networks; Selection of Volunteers

It is from the recognition of our general ineptitude that the need has been identified for telephone and other support services. The Samaritans in the UK were perhaps the forerunners. Internationally their support services are known as Befrienders International but in the UK the original name is used. And there are numerous other services, all of them offering a listening ear and an understanding heart. Some are for telephone support only, but others, like Befrienders, also offer face-to-face listening, attending rock concerts and other major public events as well as having regular office hours in some centres. A few services actually offer concrete advice, solutions to problems, but most adopt the principle and philosophy of offering only reflective listening, believing that volunteers are not in a position to offer counselling or advice, and that there is danger in unqualified persons doing so, particularly when the only contact is by telephone.

Individuals are drawn to do voluntary work for a variety of reasons. Some are bored and want a positive activity and not mere time filling; some have been professionals and want a change; some are expiating guilt over some personal experience; some are trying to work through problems of one kind or another; some have received help and want to repay society for this, and so on. The selection of volunteers for hands-on work must therefore include some assessment of their motivation, lest people are selected who create more difficulties than they help to solve. Selection of volunteers should therefore be done by persons expert in assessment of trainees. Those who see telephone volunteering, for example, as an opportunity for proselytising are unsuitable, as are those who have judgemental views on such matters as abortion, alcohol use, etc.

Whilst not in any way colluding with destructive behaviour, it is not the task of the telephone volunteer, whatever one's personal views, to tell the caller where he or she has gone wrong, although enhanced insight does sometimes result from an empathic and non-judgemental conversation.

Training Programmes

The training of those who are accepted is also of vital importance, in order to give appropriate background information and understanding of human loss and the processes of grief, and for volunteers to work through any problems they themselves have experienced.

One aspect which one notices in the early days of training is the yearning of telephone volunteers to rescue, to make the person feel better. This can lead to the meaningless reassurance one may hear in training session role play: 'Don't worry, I'm sure that the test will show there's nothing terrible going on', 'I'm sure your son will come back to you when he has come to his senses.' Such comments are fairly typical of everyday comments in the street or shopping centre from would-be comforters.

All these are meaningless because they are without a basis of knowledge, and have their origin simply in a wish to take pain away. This is a laudable wish, but those who have been on the receiving end of such comments find them irritating or infuriating because it is clear that the reassurer has no knowledge of what could really take place!

Sufficient time must be allowed for the training of telephone volunteers. The service I know best has weekly training sessions of three hours each for a least three months with a further three months 'on probation', in itself a test of commitment! But this period also has the advantage that, during the training and group work, unsuitable people come to realise that this is not for them, or are gently helped to reach that decision. At the same time, all volunteers are able to grow inwardly at their own pace. Topics are various, depending in part on the nature of the services offered. For example, a support service for persons who know themselves to be at risk of harming their children would concentrate especially on this matter, another which specialised in suicide calls would specialise in suicide prevention and so on. But many general topics would be universally discussed, such as the following selection.

Theoretical matters

○ Understanding how unresolved grief affects people's lives and also understanding oneself, dealing with unresolved grief in one's own life.

○ Understanding and knowledge of the normal processes of grief.

○ Gaining knowledge and understanding of the unusual or abnormal griefs which may be presented by callers.

○ Learning how to impart self-esteem, so that the caller feels empowered, and changes can be made if necessary.

○ Examining one's own responses to problems which are presented, especially those with ethical or moral implications.

○ Allowing oneself to be less than perfect.

These would be supported by 'homework' with set books, videos, assigned tasks.

Practicalities

○ How to cope with a 2am call which wakes the volunteer from sleep, or a series of calls with little break between them.

○ How to terminate a call in which the person is going round in circles or replying 'Yes, but...' to any thoughts which are presented.

○ How to deal with nuisance calls, since all telephone services do receive a significant number of these.

○ How to help people unburden themselves without the listener asking over-challenging questions.

All these are expanded by role play with observers so that one gains new skills and self-confidence.

Books by Gerard Egan, such as *Interpersonal Living* (1976) provide a useful substratum for training in volunteer grief telephone support work. For face-to-face work, the only difference lies in coping with the more personal atmosphere of discussions under those conditions instead of the anonymity of the telephone.

A probationary period of work on the telephone, with the assistance of a mentor or supporter, is also valuable to give further opportunity for *reality testing*. No training can ever give the reality of a 4 a.m. call from a person trying to cope with the suicide of a partner, or the death of a child, nor show us whether or not we shall be able to remain outwardly calm while listening to descriptions of traumatic occurrences.

Opportunities for debriefing must be set up on a permanent basis because, even after training is complete, there is a continuing need for mutual support in discussion with other volunteers.

Reflective Listening

As with much professional work, reflective listening has associations with the approach of Carl Rogers (1951) – of unconditional acceptance and positive regard – and non-judgemental attitudes. The cartoonist's picture of such methods is the therapist sitting, bored into somnolence, uninterested in what is happening, saying nothing apart from an occasional 'Mmm?' whilst the client falls deeper into gloom as he describes his life problems. But this is not truly the reality of professional work (except perhaps in rare instances!) and neither is it the reality of reflective listening for volunteers and neighbours, which usually achieves something more positive.

Reflective listening consists of absolute concentration on what is being said, with enough comment to demonstrate that one is indeed still listening if the conversation is by phone, together with occasional comments or open-ended questions which help the person to understand more clearly what is actually going on for him or her. The nature of these comments will depend upon the nature of the problem, but may include comments such as the following.

> 'I can see why you needed to talk to someone not actually involved in things.' (*In any crisis situation, really only the equivalent of* 'Mmm?', *but also useful if the person feels guilty at talking to an anonymous volunteer rather than to mother, spouse or some other significant person.*)

> 'It was very difficult for you, wasn't it.' (*Useful when the caller is trying to prove that, despite sadness, he or she was in control, although the nature of the call makes it clear that this was not really so.*)

> 'It sounds as if it came as a real shock to you, that this could happen.' (*This may simply reflect back what the caller has said or it may help to clarify things if he or she has not realised the extent to which events have caused shock. To have this named helps the caller understand more clearly what has been happening.*)

'It is difficult to stay calm when we're very angry, isn't it!' (*This may be used to help reduce guilt over a response to an event or, as above, it may help the caller to identify personal emotions which have not been identified or are being denied.*)

These few examples do not provide a how-to-do-it set of instructions, but are instances of comments which have proved useful, whether for volunteers or for professionals, in clarifying grief issues for those who are suffering severe after-effects from loss.

Background Knowledge

It is important to provide volunteers with background knowledge of the processes of grief, awareness of the complexities of suffering, so that unusual descriptions by callers do not bewilder them. Volunteers need to know that grief can be mixed with a range of other emotions, some of which seem to have little to do with sadness as such. For example, after a woman died during 'routine' (not life-saving) surgery, her husband and children found that their sadness was made infinitely more complex by suspicions that the death could have been avoided and by their own consequent anger about the event. At times it seemed that the anger took over from sadness altogether, and, if they had sought help from a volunteer programme, it would have been unhelpful if the listener had not been aware of the normal nature of such a response.

Volunteers also need to know of the paradoxes of response to loss, the mixed feelings of relief and sadness which follow death or a separation of any kind. It is said that, even in the best relationship, there is some aspect which we dislike and, when the partner dies, we have a secret feeling of relief: 'Well, I shall not have to cope with that any more!' (dirty towels in a heap on the bathroom floor; the wayward family member whose life has caused constant anxiety but who has died in a car accident; the handicapped toddler whose care has placed a burden on the entire family and who has died from an illness; and so on).

Ordinary sadness is relatively simple to deal with, but the paradoxical response is more difficult. Yet these may well be the griefs presented to volunteers over the telephone, because the anonymity of the call makes it easier to talk freely than it is to talk in the same way to relatives or personal friends. Unless our training of volunteers has been adequate they may be unduly stressed by incoming calls, and their responses may fail to provide the empathic support which is needed.

Resource Lists

Trainers of volunteers normally provide the listeners with a handbook of resources, to which they can refer those who are suffering the effects of trauma and loss. These might include sexual assault counselling services, support groups for victims of crime, for survivors of suicide, for parents of children who have died, various child abuse advisory programmes, and so on. To have such information is part of putting people back into control of their own lives.

But whilst it is important that the telephone volunteer has the required addresses, phone numbers and so on, it is even more important that this information is not given too early in the conversation. If given immediately the problem is identified, the caller is often left feeling that the buck has been passed, that the listener does not want to hear of the emotional conflict or distress and is saying 'Don't bother me with how you *feel*, just get on and *do* something about it!'

If it seems possible or probable that the caller is planning suicide, it will be appropriate to ask questions, such as:

> 'Have you got anyone with you that you could talk to?'
>
> *or*
>
> 'Is there someone you trust who could come and spend time with you?'
>
> *or*
>
> 'When you are feeling desperate, it is OK to ask the local crisis team to come and be with you. I have the 'phone numbers here.'
>
> The last resort is to ask for the person's identification; the given name is enough, with the address.
>
> 'If you would give me your name and address I can arrange for someone to come and be with you?' (*police crisis team, local community mental health crisis team, or whatever is available locally*).

Although this may be seen as a breach of confidentiality it remains the decision of the caller whether or not to disclose this information. The Duty of Care and the Duty to Warn (Treadway 1990), to which all volunteers adhere, imposes on the support services the duty to save life if possible. Such decisions are often referred to as Tarassoff-type decisions, after the legal case in California which created a precedent, establishing the legal responsibility to warn.

At the same time it is essential for volunteers to know that they must not accept personal responsibility for or guilt over an individual's refusal to accept help. Generally, however, the fact that the person has called the telephone network is an indication that they are ready to be persuaded out of suicide, although there are a few who telephone as part of their anger with society, to punish someone by saying, 'I am about to kill myself and I just wanted you to know.' But for most people, either the telephone conversation itself is enough to defuse the situation so that suicide is no longer a risk, or the person is willing to allow a crisis team to call and assess the situation.

In all grief situations, one of the hardest experiences for the volunteer, and one which is almost unique to the telephone listener, is that of not knowing what happened next, knowing how to let go, both of one's questions and one's guilt at having possibly made a mistake in what one has said, failed the person at the other end of the line. It is a challenge to the telephone listener. It is a situation in which routine de-briefing is essential if the volunteer is to avoid burnout.

I am a professional support person for a group of telephone volunteers, and it seems unusual for professional guidance to be available in a formal way for telephone volunteers. The opportunity for regular, rather than *ad hoc* debriefing is of the utmost importance, whether the distressing call which leaves the volunteer shaken has occurred at midday or midnight. This service, *Grief Support*, based in a suburb of Sydney but open to telephone contact from anywhere in the state, also provides workshops on alternate weeks to which volunteers are committed, when they routinely bring to a meeting of their colleagues the difficult calls, the 'regulars', the once-only people in crisis, so that, by discussion, role play, in-service lectures or videos, and by input from the professional advisers, they deal with their own emotional responses and are better able to cope next time. Preliminary research suggests that the support system available to the telephone volunteers in this particular service is generally adequate (Bright 1994a).

The support services available today are not a substitute for, but an expansion of, personal involvement. Volunteers find that, as a consequence of their work on the phone, they bring greater empathy, greater interpersonal skills to their personal relationships, and it is probable that there is a wider effect so that the ripples spread.

Hospitals and Hospices

Hospitals and hospices commonly have rosters of volunteers. In time past, doing the flowers was all that volunteers were supposed to do, or perhaps a little shopping for those who had run out of soap and toothpaste. But they were certainly not expected to talk to patients, still less to encourage the patients to talk about their sadness or anxiety! Today, fortunately, such restrictive attitudes are over. It is still essential that people be selected for such intimate work. As with telephone volunteers, one's own agenda must not be allowed to dominate; we must not work through our own problems on the pretext of helping others. But, given appropriate selection and training, volunteers provide valuable support for patients and families. At one hospital in North America, where a world-class palliative care service is offered, there is a taped volunteers' handover so that, when coming on duty, volunteers can listen to the recorded account of the status of each patient they will meet, who has died, who is expected to live only a short time, how relatives are coping and so on.

Confidentiality is absolute. Volunteers are trained in ethical matters and are required to give assurance that they recognise the private and confidential nature of the information provided for them. The value of this information is great; it gives to the volunteer a sense of control, of knowing what is going on, of being involved and not merely sent blindfold into the wards without knowing what may happen next. Volunteers for this service are not accepted unless they themselves have suffered a major bereavement. Nor are they accepted until at least 12 months have passed since that bereavement took place.

It is therefore improbable that those who are accepted as volunteers are taking on that task as a way of working through problems associated with a death of a person significant to them which has taken place in the unit, or elsewhere. Gratitude immediately following the death may seem an adequate motive for volunteering at the time, but it seldom lasts the year unless it is *for real*.

Similar groups of volunteers work in general wards of hospitals, although in some places they tend to be doers of flowers or posters of letters rather than empathic listeners to those who grieve, because of the fears of professionals that the volunteers may say or do something which is unhelpful to the patient's progress or which conflicts with professional roles. Palliative care units seem to be more open than general hospitals to the gifts and skills offered by volunteers.

Community Groups for Support in Times of Grief

Volunteer groups are also organised in the community in many places, so that there is a register of people available, times and areas preferred, the skills they have to offer and the age group which they prefer. These tend to be regular commitments, sometimes to established charitable organisations, but can also include short-term crisis help offered to people in need. It is encouraging to find that community support groups are also available for families, such as families of children with a major handicap, whose grief is often submerged in the practicalities of everyday care, or where those practicalities are being used as a way of avoiding the processes of grief. Other services, such as Dial a Mum, are for children of any age who are worried or depressed at what is happening in their lives but who feel unable to talk with their own parents or other close relatives.

Even more encouraging is the fact that some telephone support services are provided for those whom the community as a whole would condemn, those parents who know themselves to be at risk of harming their children because of their own life experiences of violence, but who seek help to change their patterns of response. The anonymity of the telephone is of great value for such callers.

The examples given in this chapter are all from church or community groups, charities or situations personally known to me. This is not because these are necessarily any more effective than others but because personal knowledge gives a clearer picture of how such services can be provided and what the outcome can be.

The Needs of Volunteers in Rescue Work

Many people are involved in voluntary work in traumatic activities such as bush-fire fighting and surf rescue work or, on an *ad hoc* basis, in assisting when there has been a disaster such as a train smash or an earthquake. Because of the intermittent nature of even the formalised work of rescue and fire-fighting, the volunteer may not have access to the formalised debriefing and support services which are available to paid employees. Today the needs of police officers and others engaged in dangerous and difficult work are being met by the employment of trauma counsellors, and staff are encouraged to see this as filling a normal need and that to seek help is not an indication of cowardice.

Volunteers, however, may not have the same help given to them after a traumatic experience and there is a very real risk that post-traumatic stress disorder will follow. This has happened when a person rescued from the sea by a volunteer has drowned while being brought ashore, and the volunteer described the frightening and loathsome flashbacks he suffered of the victim's face as he died, struggling to free himself from the grasp of the rescuer. Post-traumatic stress disorder also affected many volunteers follow-ing a disaster in 1977 in the Sydney suburb of Granville when an overhead bridge was destroyed, falling onto the train beneath and thereby crushing and killing 83 passengers and seriously injuring a similar number. People nearby hurried to offer help and were totally unequipped to cope with the horrifying circumstances in which they found themselves, especially when cranes lifted the sections of the bridge off the train beneath and the full extent of the carnage was seen.

Some good did come from that tragedy in the establishment of the (Australian) National Association for Loss and Grief, and help was quickly mobilised for those volunteers as well as for professional workers similarly affected. Earthquakes and other natural disasters carry the same risk for volunteers. (Professional helpers too suffer from after-effects of trauma; their needs are discussed in Chapter 13.)

Debriefing Procedures

Originally used in military operations, when combatants and strategists discussed the outcome of an incident or a battle, this word is now more commonly used to describe the process of letting off steam, letting emotional responses be expressed so that they can be set aside or become less stressful, after a critical incident in a workplace or to a voluntary group. In telephone or face-to-face volunteer support groups, there is an especial need for debriefing because the helpers lack the mechanisms for offloading stress which are available to professionals. Not all services have a formalised process; some have only a debriefing mechanism on an as-desired basis. The disadvantage of the *ad hoc* system is that it can be perceived as a weakness to ask for help, whereas, when the mechanism is compulsory, no such risks arise.

In the telephone support service described earlier, there are four professional advisers who are available on a regular basis for debriefing and general support. Three mechanisms are available to volunteers, of which two are compulsory, and the third is compulsory under certain circumstances.

1. Each volunteer, at the end of the eight-hour shift, must debrief to the person next on roster, describing all calls in précis but in extended discussion when the calls have been stressful. There is no universally applicable classification of 'the stressful call', except for threats of suicide; responses are in part due to the personality of the volunteer.

2(a). Each volunteer has the option of contacting one of the professional advisers to the service, at any time of day or night, if (despite the debriefing described above) the volunteer is left with unfinished emotions such as anxiety, fear, anger or horror at what was disclosed in the call.

2(b). When the call involved threats of suicide, this call is compulsory and not optional.

3. All volunteers must attend three out of four of the workshops, held in alternate weeks, in which stressful calls are discussed and there is significant support from one volunteer to another. 'I can guess how you felt, I had the same man ring me up three times between 2 a.m. and 5 a.m. and I felt totally drained!' One or more of the professional advisers attend the workshop to facilitate the Calls Session which forms a major part of the workshop.

If a volunteer is unable to attend the Calls Sessions for several weeks, they must delay returning to telephone work until several such sessions have been attended, as a form of retraining. Other activities at the workshop include the checking of availability for phone rosters, special talks on aspects of grief and loss and so on.

All involved are volunteers, including those professionals who are concerned in the service. All assist in the training process although the training courses are run primarily by two trained professionals, who also give their services free of charge.

Summary

The possibilities for neighbourliness and volunteering are endless. But whether we do our own thing and just help out with neighbours in the street and the apartment block, or whether we give our time and energy in a formal commitment to volunteering in an organised group, being a good neighbour and being a volunteer helps us to gain increased self-esteem. More important, it also sets in place values which say that it is all right to grieve, it is OK to accept help, it takes time to adjust to loss and there is no shame in acknowledging that we cannot cope alone.

CHAPTER 11

Facilitating Change in Blocked Grief

It is common to discuss *normal* and *abnormal* grief, and, in considering approaches in facilitating the resolution of difficult grief, it is important to decide when professional help is needed and when it is not. The factors which influence this include the person's own nature and life experiences.

- Is the person dependent, co-dependent or independent?

- Is self-esteem high or low (and all the gradations in between!)?

- Has he or she dealt with loss before, and if so how?

- Are coping mechanisms damaged by past experiences?

- Are they damaged by alcohol or other chemical dependency?

- Is he or she suffering from psychiatric illness?

- Suffering from sub-clinical psychiatric problems such as dysthymia?

- Have there recently been other losses which have diminished coping strategies?

- What is the nature of the loss? (Does it alter the person's whole life? Has it elements of horror, as in post-traumatic stress disorder?)

- Is the grief a response to a death which is perceived as discreditable (death through drink-driving, drug abuse, gang-style murder, or, for many families, death by suicide)?

- Is the person left with guilt, whether logically or illogically (for example, over a discreditable death, as above)?

- Is family support available? Is the family functioning?

At one end of the spectrum we see grief dealt with, not painlessly, but with good outcome by a person who has achieved personal security of esteem, independence, has dealt with griefs and losses before, is not suffering from a psychiatric disorder, is not chemically dependent and for whom the loss did not alter the whole balance of existence, who feels no burden of guilt about the loss, and whose family functions adaptively so that difficulties are addressed and resolved. Such a person will probably not be in need of professional help. The sadness will be expressed normally, the pain will heal. Although there will be memories of loss and sadness, they will not spoil the rest of the person's life and relationships. A *normal grief*!

At the other end of the spectrum we see the grief for which professional help is needed to avoid a dire outcome for the person concerned. An example of such a person is one who has suffered rejection and childhood abuse, is highly dependent and exceptionally low in self-esteem, has dealt with previous losses in a manner which has proved destructive, is perhaps chemically dependent or suffering from a psychiatric illness, is burdened with guilty feelings over the loss, either because there was truly a fault or because the person has grown up believing that he or she will always be at fault if things go wrong.

Dealing with Blocked Grief

Like some other researchers, Pedder (1982), in an article given originally as a lecture at the Institute of Psychiatry in London, reviewed ideas about depression and mourning, from a psychodynamic point of view. Pedder quotes Freud as having, in 1917, drawn attention to the closeness of mourning and depression. He uses the term *morbid grief* to describe grief which remains unresolved, and which has deleterious effects on the sufferer's life, a concept similar if not identical to the term used here, *blocked grief*.

Lieberman emphasised the risks to the client of a marked separation between behavourist and psychoanalytical approaches (Lieberman 1983). The work described in this chapter, and in Chapter 12, supports a diverse approach in which both behaviourist and analytical approaches are used for the relief of blocked grief.

Family attitudes and support are also important; someone for whom family support is either non-existent or maladaptive, finds it difficult to deal with major losses (Kissane 1994). When someone already has an established way of life which is maladaptive, or has a known psychiatric illness, a loss will probably be expressed as a new episode of psychiatric illness, exacerbation of chemical dependency, further loss of self-esteem possibly to the extent of suicide attempts, increased dependency, anger and disruption to relationships, and so on. Unfortunately, unless such people are actually receiving treatment at the time of the loss, they are seldom identified before the maladaptive processes have begun and many people referred for music/grief therapy have already gone a long way down the road of chemical dependency, depression and self-destruction.

From time to time we see a manic response to grief, and this constitutes a major challenge for the therapist (Rosenman and Tayler 1986). Whether it is a form of blocking is not certain, but the person admitted to a psychiatric unit for manic behaviour following bereavement or other loss may require medication for amelioration of symptoms so that the grief itself can be dealt with by means of counselling or other methods. Superficially, the behaviour observed does not fit in with our usual ideas of grief response, but the underlying anger and stress (hidden beneath cheerful jokes and banter or excitement but emerging as unexpected flashes of anger or destructive comments) reveals to the therapist that the person is far from the happy person he appears to be (Bright 1994).

We also need to be aware of the risk that inappropriate medication can block normal grief work. A young woman became psychiatrically ill following the death of two of her young children and although this was partly due to the nature of the deaths, another significant factor was that she had been given large amounts of Valium because it would help her 'Not to break down during the funerals'. As a result she had been physically present at but emotionally absent from the ceremonies, and her illness was not finally resolved until she had been taken to the cemetery to cry (for over an hour), and write farewell notes to the children asking forgiveness for her actions which she felt had caused their deaths. Perhaps we should think about the implications of society's use of the words 'breaking down' to signify *normal* grief reponces but also for the *going wrong* of a motor vehicle?

The Difficult Griefs of Secret Sadness

There are some griefs which are difficult to resolve, and which might or might not become blocked, depending on the inner resources of the individual. These are the griefs and difficult emotions which one cannot acknowledge openly and for which one therefore receives no support. (See also comments in the Chapter 8 for the loss of rights to grieve often experienced by homosexual lovers of those who have contracted or died from AIDS.) Doka has called this experience 'disenfranchised grief' (Doka 1989), and there are many sources of such emotions, other than those mentioned above.

1.   There are various feelings of regret, loss, sadness, relief, anger at the life-threatening illness or death of the ex-spouse. Sometimes the person does not know that the illness and/or death have occurred,

so that there is a delay which complicates matters because it prevents any exploration of feelings at the time and creates additional regrets at not being there. Usually, however (although not invariably), the person who was once married to the deceased is excluded from any funeral arrangements, and yet there may be much unfinished business and even sadness to be dealt with.

One such man, whose marriage had ended when he became attached to a younger woman, suffered distress when he was told by the children of the marriage that his ex-wife was suffering from cancer, and he realised that he could not do anything to help her. A further cause of distress was his knowledge that stress has been discussed as a possible cause of malignant illness and he wondered whether the grief she had suffered at his change of allegiance had caused or contributed to her illness and death.

2. A person who has or is known to have had a love affair with the deceased would also usually be prevented from visiting the person during a terminal illness and from participating in the funeral. If nobody has known of the affair, the bereaved lover is left totally alone to cope with emotional unfinished business.

3. There is also the secret grief of (usually) an older woman who gave up a baby born out of wedlock for adoption, and who was not able to share her sadness because of shame at the circumstances of the death. (Condon 1986, p.119). One such woman, seen in her seventies when admitted to a psychiatric unit for depressive illness, was found to have had an episode of depression each year on the anniversary of the adoption of her illegitimate baby son. She needed strong reassurance and permission to grieve, which included singing the songs she would like to have sung to that baby had she been able to keep him. The outcome was encouraging, and suggests yet again that it is never too late to try to facilitate grief resolution.

Strategies for Facilitating Change

The process of change is complex and needs to be taken slowly enough for ideas to be processed at the client's own rate. Speedy resolution is not usually appropriate, although there are crises in which immediate help is vital. The case histories which follow illustrate approaches using music therapy strategies to facilitate grief counselling. (Further discussion of the actual method of using music is contained in Chapter 12.)

Improvised Music in the Management of Post-Traumatic Stress Disorder

Alan (not his real name), a 37-year old man, was admitted (after detoxification) for rehabilitation in a drug and alcohol service and was referred for
music/grief therapy because his drinking had escalated sharply following a
tragic car accident. Assessment supported a diagnosis of post-traumatic stress
Disorder (PTSD). The nature of the event and his symptoms matched at least
17 of the 19 criteria listed in *DSM IV* (American Psychiatric Association
1994). The features which did not match the DSM criteria were: hypervigi-
lance (definitely not present) and heightened startle responce (not observed
during the interview).

Alan had been driving a truck on a narrow mountain road with no
shoulders and had seen a car coming towards him at top speed on the wrong
side of the road, the driver evidently asleep at the wheel. Evading a collision
was impossible, and the driver was beheaded when his car went under the
front of the truck.

Initial discussion covered thoughts of:

- guilt at not being able to avoid the collision
- anger with the other driver for being asleep. Strong support was
  needed to allow Alan to express what he saw as *wicked* feelings of
  anger on this
- quasi-survivor guilt; Alan knew that he too had sometimes taken the
  risk of driving when overtired
- sadness that the driver had died
- horror at the memories which stayed with him as flashbacks, coming
  between him and everything he did, and spoiling relationships
- regret at his drinking (to try to blot out the flashbacks) so that the
  family was alienated.

After trust had been established through discussion of these thoughts, two
chairs were set in place, with explanation as to how *empty chair work* is done
and what it can achieve. Alan was not psychotic, nor did his flashbacks
constitute psychotic hallucinations, so the method was ethically acceptable.

Atonal music was improvised to elicit an atmosphere of fear, crisis,
agitation, trauma and despair. The music consisted of short chromatic upward
runs, increasing in tempo and volume, with discordant chords between the
runs and accompanying them, but without resolution, and finally loud
discordant crashing sounds, followed by silence. Whilst this was being
played, probably for only about a minute, Alan began to shake and sweat.

This may be seen as a regressive technique, and certainly the therapist was well aware of the powerful nature of the intervention.

Alan then spoke to the other driver, asking his forgiveness for not being able to avoid the collision, expressing his anger but also offering forgiveness and expressing sadness that the other man's life was cut short.

On changing chairs, Alan's voice changed and he spoke as the dead driver, asking forgiveness for having caused so much tragedy by going to sleep at the wheel. He then said, 'But God is looking after me and perhaps one day I'll see you and be able to say all this to you.'

Returning to his own role, Alan responded to this, saying that perhaps one day they would meet when they were both with God. After a few moment's silence, he then turned and said, 'I do not know what you've done for me, mate, but I feel different already!'

Music was then played to reflect ideas of peace and consolation, followed by hope for the future.

The session ended with de-roleing Alan, to put him back into his everyday self, with renewed reassurance that there had not been a ghost in the empty chair. Plans were made for the therapist to meet with his wife, who was expected for a family conference later in the day, and to meet again in a week's time.

In fact Alan made such dramatic changes immediately that the follow-up session consisted only of a separation interview. His posture changed, and, although his wife needed much reassurance that he was going to be different (so that Alan was discharged to a halfway house rather than directly home), there are hopes that the marriage will be rebuilt once confidence has been restored.

Discussion

Improvised atonal music had not been used precisely in this manner until the case in question, although improvised music is used

1. as a projection technique, so that clients 'hear' their own problems and needs in the unfamiliar music, and

2. as a means of reassuring a client that he or she has been understood.

Familiar music associated with the dead person has also been used to set the scene for empty chair work.

Feelings that 'nobody really understands how I feel' are so damaging to progress in therapy that improvised music is used routinely in convincing a client, as no words can do, that the therapist is trying to understand and has,

at least in part, succeeded! The sounds improvised here would have encom-
passed something of that need to be understood.

The occurrence of PTSD in everyday life is not as well discussed as that
condition in combat or in major disasters. But the case described here gives
a clear picture of the after-effects of a horrifying accident, in which the nature
of the event and the symptoms observed afterwards are clearly those of PTSD.

McFarlane (1990) has considered the frequent discussion of vulnerability
to PTSD. He points out that, by our discussions as to whether the condition
may occur chiefly in vulnerable individuals, we not only blame the victim
for his own problems but also reduce the likelihood that people will seek
help. Whilst we must of course investigate the role of earlier psychological
states in rendering individuals vulnerable to PTSD, we must also look
empathically at those who do suffer from the condition and do our best to
ameliorate it by every means possible.

The drinking which Alan used to blot out the horrifying flashbacks and
nightmares of the accident are a demonstration of the plight of the male
(especially the Australian male?) who sees it as 'wimpish' to look for help in
dealing with an event, however terrible.

A Young Adult Psychiatric Patient

Barbara, aged 23, was referred for music therapy by the clinical team of an
acute admission ward of a psychiatric hospital one week after she had been
admitted following two drug overdoses in 24 hours. The reasons given for
requesting music/grief therapy were:

○ unresolved 'grief' over suicide of her partner, and

○ grief over the fact that her baby had, for its own protection, been
   taken into care.

At admission Barbara was described as schizophrenic because she com-
plained of command hallucinations, the cause of her overdoses. It was noted
that she had a history of such 'voices', and that she was regarded as
cognitively impaired. She had shown suicidal ideation since age 15 and had
two admissions for suicide attempts in the last two years, one following the
adoption of her baby and one following the suicide of her partner. The
immediate cause of the current admission was uncertain.

It was significant that no name was listed as the person for notification,
so that Barbara was evidently without support. Further information was that
Barbara had been severely abused, sexually and otherwise, in childhood. She
had left home at age 15 to live in various women's refuges. Her relationship

with her male partner had been characterised by violence towards her, including frequent rape, which raised queries about the nature of the grief at his death described in the referral. Further, she had shown some capacity for violence towards her young baby, which had led to its being taken into care.

Treatment

Individual sessions took place on a weekly basis over the 12 weeks of Barbara's hospital stay. After discussion with nursing staff and the social worker, it was decided that the ultimate aim should be to enhance Barbara's self-esteem and capacity for emotional expression, but initially to establish a trust relationship, allowing Barbara to speak only as openly as she wished whilst providing an atmosphere of kindly support. It was fortunate that she enjoyed music and was able to play some simple tunes learned at school on the keyboard, the therapist providing an accompaniment, so that rapport was readily achieved. Information was disclosed gradually, as trust developed further, and as some music selected by the therapist contributed to reminiscence and discussion of life issues.

Information disclosed and the therapist's observations

With the exception of the provisional diagnosis of schizophrenia, made at admission, most of the information disclosed matched that given to the therapist at the time of referral.

- Barbara presented as mildly to moderately cognitively impaired, with some psychomotor retardation yet with occasional excitable (manic?) behaviour. It was known that she had thyroid dysfunction, which was treated after it had been identified at admission. This condition could have contributed to her (occasional) inappropriate affect. Some staff were uncertain as to how far her slowness was organic and how far it was a consequence of lifetime experiences of violence. The therapist was also aware that grief can manifest itself in manic behaviour, and this too was held in mind as the relationship developed (Rosenman and Tayler 1986).

- Barbara described severe systematic beatings by both parents because of her slowness, and she personally insisted (although not until later in the relationship) that she was not really impaired, saying, 'I was not born slow, it was beaten into me.' From later work in music therapy it did appear likely that this was at least partly true, that a mild degree of slowness had been exacerbated by beatings and fear of violence.

○ She was able to speak openly of sexual abuse (not by her father but by an uncle) in childhood. As a consequence, sexual relationships in the situation described below were not a source of happiness or emotional intimacy but something she endured.

○ She had been in a *de facto* relationship with a man who had brutalised her and had himself committed suicide after attempting to make her do the same. The alleged grief over the death of this boyfriend was complex: relief at his death mixed with guilt that perhaps she could have prevented it and an ethical principle that one should not rejoice over the death of anyone.

○ Because of her own difficulty in avoiding violence to her baby, the baby had been taken into care. This was an important topic for discussion during music therapy.

○ Barbara described voices telling her that she was worthless and would be better off dead, with commands to kill herself. The voice was sometimes that of her late partner. There was considerable controversy in case review meetings as to whether Barbara should therefore be diagnosed as suffering from paranoid schizophrenia (the opinion of the admitting medical officer) or whether these voices were over-vivid memories of things which had, it seemed, been said to her throughout her life – 'You'd be better off dead.' 'You're useless and stupid.' 'It is a pity you were ever born.' 'Why don't you just kill yourself and then we'll be rid of you.'

The belief that Barbara was not psychotic but only unhappy was held by nursing and social work staff as well as by the music therapist, and (following music therapy and other professional interventions) the voices were eventually categorised in her case notes as pseudo-hallucinations and non-psychotic. Heins and his colleagues had given accounts of hallucinations in persons who were sexually abused as children, and of the possibility of wrongly diagnosing psychosis in such people (Heins, Gray and Tennant 1990). These reports tended to confirm the rightness of the opinion that the patient had not been psychotic.

Music therapy included explanations to Barbara about the concept of 'tapes in one's head' (Harris 1969, p.32) and this she found helpful, gaining control over the 'tapes', so that she was usually able to ignore them. She also gained self-esteem in the success she had in playing the keyboard, a cause of admiration from fellow-patients. The weekly sessions usually consisted of playing music known to Barbara, including items in which she could participate.

It was interesting that the songs she chose were not recent pop favourites but from further back in her experience. It was probably significant that many of the songs which Barbara requested were nursery rhymes usually associated with very young children. At first it seemed that this preference might be linked with developmental disability, until Barbara explained (in answer to a question about her choice) that these songs were taught to her by a much-loved teacher. This teacher used to bring lunch to school for Barbara because her family provided her with none, nor gave her money to buy lunch.

Listening to the therapist's improvisation initially elicited anxiety because it aroused intense feelings but over a number of sessions Barbara felt safe to join the improvisation at the keyboard or with percussion instruments. Feelings such as fear, anxiety, anger and (later) hope and confidence were portrayed in the music. One receptive improvisation included visual images of herself as a seagull, floating on a thermal current and looking down at people on the beach below. She verbalised descriptions of what she could see and finally decided that it was safe to go down and join the group below. After this session Barbara, for the first time, hugged the therapist and said, 'Gee, that was great, thanks!' One matter for concern in that session was Barbara's comment that the only happiness she had ever known was in hospital, where she felt safe and accepted.

The implications of this were discussed with the community team, and with the social worker in charge of Barbara's care. Discharge planning centred upon the need to find an environment in which Barbara would feel safe and accepted. Otherwise she could well use another drug overdose as a way of getting back to the safety and acceptance of hospital, which appeared to have been her motivation for the overdose which had led to the present admission.

Song-writing was attempted but without success, probably because Barbara lacked confidence in her own use of words.

The matter of the violence in families was brought up by the therapist, but in a low-key manner, by commenting that it seems to go from one generation to another. The analogy of a row of dominoes was used (Barbara was familiar with the game), describing how, if a row of dominoes is standing on end, hitting the first one causes that one to hit the next domino and so on right down the line. The analogy ended with the remark: 'It takes a lot of understanding and guts to be the last domino!' Barbara said, 'I know. That is why I let my baby be taken for adoption!' This reply suggested that she had better insight than we had imagined.

Those who were sexually abused as children are recognised as having lost their childhood. The sexually abused child is thrown into pseudo-adulthood, in coping with the premature experiences of sex, the stresses of sexual exploitation and the secrecy which is always enjoined by the perpetrator, usually enforced by threats. This prevents the fun of a normal childhood, and this scenario became very clear in work with Barbara, who became playful and humorous as self-confidence increased and her slowness diminished.

At the final session, as part of the separation process, she was invited to choose a song which would help her remember the work achieved. Although she did finally ask for a serious song ('Climb Every Mountain' from *The Sound of Music*, which had already been used to symbolise the struggle to gain self-confidence), she asked first for a funny song, choosing 'Old Macdonald Had a Farm'. She was invited to choose an animal for each verse, which was then sung with appropriate sound effects, and Barbara chose not only ducks, pigs, cows, horses and chooks (Australian for hens) but also the tractor, with much laughter over shared attempts to make tractor noises!

> Her last request was 'A Dodo!'
>
> 'O.K., we can have a Dodo, but what sounds does it make?'
>
> 'Ha, we don't know, do we, because it is extinct!!' came the exultant reply! (Low intelligence?)

Barbara was finally discharged to a supervised group home, where proper support would be given. Extensive preparations were made for this discharge, and care was taken that Barbara left the unit feeling that she had graduated, not that she had been rejected or dismissed. These attitudes were strongly reinforced by all staff. Barbara has continued to do well in the group home, with regular support provided by the community health team. She is happy, is regarded as a trusted person, given responsibility in running the house, and has made a close friend in a young woman of the same age.

Discussion

Barbara made good progress during the time of her hospital stay, and it is probable that she will continue to lead a fairly stable life so long as she is given support at an individual level. The emotional scars caused by childhood experiences cannot be eradicated, but the enhanced insight and self-esteem which Barbara gained, partly from the therapeutic relationship in grief counselling, will permit her to deal adequately with the ordinary crises of life.

Bereavement in an Identical Twin

The emotional links between twins are discussed in everyday conversation and journalism (Maynard 1993, p.24), and in Australia a support group 'The Lonesome Doves' has about 60 members. A long-term study on twins, mentioned by Segal and Bouchard (1993), is in progress in Minnesota, but at the time of writing there has been no extended publication of the findings of that study.

All the people referred for grief therapy in a chemical dependency unit are characterised by low self-esteem and, probably, all have been dysthymic for varying numbers of years. Many of them, whilst not identified as being *cases*, have in fact suffered from actual depressive illness over varying periods. The life-histories of all patients include multiple losses, such as loss of relationships, the death of significant persons, loss of employment. Many also described sexual abuse and violence in the home, with alcoholic family members affecting their early experiences. Many such people can (like Barbara in the previous case history) be described as suffering the loss of their childhood, although this did not appear to be so for the man described below.

Charles, who was aged 39, had been assessed as suitable for rehabilitation in the alcohol-related brain damage unit. He was referred for music/grief therapy because he was known to have suffered the death of his twin, believed to have been identical, two years before the referral was made. He had at the time been in the unit for five weeks, after going through detoxification. He presented at assessment as a cheerful young man. His speech was somewhat slow but it was uncertain whether this was from alcohol damage or part of his family culture.

He described the relationship with his twin. Since no genetic studies had been done, there was no firm evidence as to whether they were monozygotic or dizygotic twins. The question 'Was your mother able to tell you apart when you were very young?' has been used in such situations, and the answer is usually a very clear-cut 'Oh yes, she didn't have any problems', or 'Oh no, she never knew which one of us was which!' Whilst this does not constitute scientific proof, it provides a working basis for therapy. Using this basis for assumptions, it seemed probable that Charles and his brother had been identical twins.

Assessment suggested that Charles had the (usual) male Australian presentation of a person using a tough, smiling exterior to mask any strong emotion, and (also common) he had used alcohol to block an experience of deep feelings. He saw himself as being at risk of death unless he could 'get a handle on' his drinking, and was able to acknowledge that the hazardous consumption of alcohol had started after the death of his twin. Before that death he had consumed alcohol occasionally but not to the extent which is classed as hazardous (four or more standard drinks, equal to 40g or more of alcohol per day).

Whilst we should not adopt stereotypic beliefs and assume that twins are necessarily devoted to one another, it seemed that there had indeed been a deep affection between Charles and his twin, and although not identical in pursuits, they had shared a strong bond. Charles described how his brother had saved his life when they were attacked by a street gang, to the extent of himself being injured and being unconscious in hospital for a few days, but without, it seemed, any lasting brain damage from this event.

The relationship had continued unchanged until the brother had slipped in the bathroom and hit his head on the tiled floor, with a few minutes of feeling 'off balance' and confused. He had, however, refused Charles' attempts to call an ambulance or take him to the casualty department of a hospital, insisting that he would be OK in the morning. In the morning, however, it was found that he had died, and post-mortem examination revealed that a sub-dural haematoma was the cause of death.

Charles' abuse of alcohol dated immediately from this event. He was willing to discuss events, and (by chance) had known another person who had been strongly affected by the death of a twin sibling. He was ready to consider ideas about bereavement as a source of substance dependency and especially for a bereaved twin, to the extent of asking whether anyone had done any special work on twins who lost a brother or sister.

A computer-based search of medical literature search for the ten years between 1983 and 1993 revealed only three articles (Chitkara Macdonald and Reveley 1988; Segal and Bouchard 1993; Woodward 1988), and all of these were obtained. Woodward's paper proved to be most helpful and was used in music therapy sessions with Charles over several weeks. Charles was given a copy of the paper. He found this greatly supportive, commenting frequently, 'So I was *normal* to feel like that!' Aspects of bereavement for which he found Woodward's paper comforting and reassuring included:

○   guilty feelings about survival; 'He saved my life but I couldn't save his!'

- the need to live out some of the twin's hopes for life
- a feeling that the twin was not really dead
- a sense that the twin lived on inside him.

Music was used which Charles recalled his brother enjoying, but no catharsis for the grief occurred until improvised atonal music was used to express conflict. Improvised music is used as a projection technique, after many years of observations that unfamiliar music, especially atonal or discordant music which contains unexpected surprising harmonic and rhythmic structures, elicits feelings which are otherwise unrecognised by the client, such as confusion, hopelessness, fear, guilt, etc. (This topic is dealt with in more detail in the next chapter.)

Clients initially listen to the music and describe what they think the music is describing. It has become clear that this constitutes projection and it has proved, perhaps surprisingly, easy to facilitate the patient's recognition that the feelings described may in fact be his or her own. Although it only occurs occasionally, they may later wish to participate, using percussion instruments or joining the therapist at the keyboard.

On hearing a series of clashing discords, Charles shouted, 'If he hadn't been so f...ing obstinate he'd be alive now!' He was then able to cry, partly with rage that his brother had rejected his efforts to get medical help, and partly sadness over the bereavement.

Because the brother's ashes were not interred, it was not possible to take Charles to the cemetery for a separation ritual, and in fact the disposal of the ashes is still not finalised. Charles and his brother hoped to regain possession of a small farm which had belonged in the family, and it is planned that eventually the ashes will be buried under a large eucalyptus tree which the brothers had loved. Meanwhile the ashes remain at home in a cupboard.

This is in some ways unsatisfactory, but in view of Charles's continued sobriety after 13 months, one must assume that there has been an essential separation even without disposal of the ashes. At the one-year follow-up interview, Charles volunteered the opinion that music/grief therapy saved his life. He spoke of the difficulty of saying that you are angry with someone who is dead, but that this acknowledgment was essential for him to continue living.

Other Techniques to Facilitate Grief Resolution

Every therapist or counsellor has his or her own particular methods of enhancing grief resolution. Those which follow have proved useful and although they are not the universal magic answer, they do often work!

1. It is often helpful to take the client to the cemetery to facilitate separation from the deceased. Whilst there, the person may be encouraged to write a note and set fire to it on the grave, to talk to the deceased, to rage, cry, seek forgiveness, give forgiveness, depending upon what the problem has been which has prevented resolution of grief. (I have found that, when the dead person has been a destructive influence or the cause of deep unhappiness in cruelty and violence, people are not able to put this behind by a facile forgiveness. There is a need first to acknowledge the hurt, that the anger is justifiable. Next comes – often – an understanding of why the person was like he or she was, and from this, eventually, comes some kind of forgiveness.

2. Whether the difficulties have arisen because of a bereavement by death or other loss, drawing sketches in the office for the client to work on before the next session is always useful. So also is encouraging the client to draw a *road map* of his or her life, marking in key events, bereavements, losses, etc., which help the client to understand why self-esteem has been lost, why substance dependency has developed, and so on. This can be done at leisure in the time before the next appointment, and then used as the basis for counselling. (One young woman used part of a roll of hospital continuous paper towel for this, and her 'road map' took up eight sheets of paper, so complex was her life story!)

3. Introducing the concept of 'putting the grief in the cupboard'. Many griefs cannot be forgotten. When there has been pain, cruelty, major life changes, it is probably impossible to put something completely behind one. But it is equally unhelpful either to attempt to repress the memory or to keep it too much in the front of the mind, where it can well become a justification for chemical dependency, failure to work at resolution and so on. To imagine oneself putting the grief in the cupboard, locking the door but keeping the key in a safe place, gives to the client a sense of control, of power over the painful past.

4. Similar to this is the drawing or writing of the problem on a piece of
    paper, scrunching it up and hurling it forcefully into a garbage bin
    as a symbol of getting rid of it, whilst recognising that it cannot be
    forgotten entirely but it can be removed from the active arena of
    one's life and relationships.

Summary

This chapter, with the case studies, illustrates something of the diversity of
grief and powerlessness. We have seen a strong adverse response to the
gruesome and horror-filled death of a person absolutely unknown to the
client, in Alan's accident, the terror of his powerlessness as he saw the car
careering towards a head-on collision, unable to avoid that collision because
of the narrowness of the mountain road; and we have seen his capacity to
benefit from treatment.

We have seen a web of loss and grief, with complete lack of power,
self-determination and self-esteem over many years in Barbara's circumstances, and her subsequent ability to grow.

We have seen the grief of the person who has lost someone highly
significant (both genetically and emotionally), in the death of Charles' twin.
We have seen Charles' anger with the twin for rejecting the offer of help in
calling an ambulance, and his anger with himself for not having gone ahead
anyway. Again we have seen his capacity to change when disclosure, reassurance and catharsis were complete.

Although not all causes of grief and powerlessness, and their treatment,
were included, enough has been described to make extrapolation to other
circumstances not too difficult.

CHAPTER 12

Music Therapy for Blocked Grief

One of the most obvious ways of using music therapy to assist in the resolution of blocked grief is by the use of familiar music. By this is meant music which is familiar to the client already and has either been directly involved in the lost relationship, such as songs from courtship or shared experiences, or which the client wishes had been part of the relationship, as in the vignettes below.

Vignette 1

John was a psychologist who attended a conference at which I spoke on music and communication, with strong emphasis upon music in grief resolution. At the end of the session he stayed behind to ask whether he could receive some personal help, saying that although he had worked in grief counselling for some time, he realised that he had never separated from his son, who had been stillborn many years before.

After a few minutes of quiet discussion, focusing upon his need to have done something for his son, perhaps in some way to have fulfilled his role as a father, he asked that Brahms' 'Lullaby' be played for him. As the music was played, he enfolded the baby symbolically in his arms, a technique which I find helpful for those who grieve over the death of a baby or a death through miscarriage or abortion, and sang the lullaby through his tears whilst looking down at the imagined child. When the music ended, silence followed for a few minutes and then John stood up, saying that at last he had said 'Goodbye' to his child, and was able to separate from him and move ahead, still remembering but no longer being tied to that tragic memory.

Vignette 2

Bill was a patient in a dementia unit of a major state hospital. He had developed Alzheimer's disease in middle age and his occasional aggression was sufficient to make nursing homes unwilling to accept his care, as was also true of several other patients in the unit.

Over several years, I spent time with his wife, helping her to deal with her anger that their plans for retirement had been destroyed by the disease, her guilty memories of being angry and irritable with him in the early phases before she realised why he was behaving so strangely, and also using music to help her communicate with Bill through their shared memories. It was explained to her that responses to music are, sadly, only temporary in those suffering from a dementing illness, but she was comforted to find that something of the 'Old Bill' was still there.

On one occasion, when Bill's wife, daughter and grandchild were all at the music group, he showed no recognition of any of the family. It was then suggested that he might like to dance with that lady over there, which he did, whilst their favourite courtship waltz, 'Fascination', was played. Bill danced well, with a good rhythm to his feet and correct waltz steps. The observers could see that, as they danced, the penny dropped for Bill and he had some recollection of who it was that was dancing with him. When the music had ended he left the circle of participants, and his wife, daughter and the new baby all sat together while Bill talked quite animatedly with them.

His understanding was still clouded. He seemed unworried by the meeting being in a large room with people around, but there was at least some restoration of his personality. There are, of course, private rooms for family visits but because of Bill's known responses to music, his family join him in the main room if they come at the time of the music group.

Bill has now deteriorated but he still dances sometimes, sits up straighter when his favourite tunes are played and smiles when people speak to him of his dancing skills.

Vignette 3

Music which was actually part of a relationship can be used to help someone separate from the memory of a difficult bereavement. Jean was a patient in a substance-dependency rehabilitation unit within a psychiatric hospital and the referral read: 'Please see Mrs So-and-so, she seems heartbroken over the death of her husband some years ago and has been drinking heavily ever since.'

Such a referral arouses suspicions that there is something hidden below the surface which the person has found difficulty in disclosing. Although sadness is not easy to cope with at the end of a relationship, it is usually the difficult relationships or the difficult circumstances surrounding the death which lead to substance abuse or psychiatric illness after a bereavement.

Jean settled into the conversation fairly well, and, when asked whether she and her husband shared any special music in their courtship days, responded quite eagerly with the name of the tune to which they had waltzed 'Charmaine', one of the songs from the 1930s whose popularity continued for many years. However, as the song was played on the electric keyboard in the consulting room, she became disturbed and angry, and it was important to give her permission to express whatever was troubling her.

As usual, I used a method which says 'People often tell me that they felt...'. The reason for this approach is that straight questions, if they concern matters which the client may well see as discreditable, are usually answered with a firm denial, but the suggestion that other people have felt the same gives release from the need to deny. If the therapist's guess is incorrect, the denial is quite different from the embarrassed denial which hides an affirmative answer!

This method allowed Jean to disclose that the song reminded her of her hopes for a happy marriage which had, however, not been fulfilled, and this was her first reason for distress. After many years of difficult marriage, her husband had suffered a heart attack and she had gone to the hospital only to find him not gravely ill and it was suggested by staff and by her husband that she should go home and come back next morning. She went home but had been there only a few minutes when the telephone rang to say that he had died.

Her feelings were mixed: guilt at having come home so that she was not there when he died; anger with those who had sent her home; feelings of relief that at last this difficult marriage was over; guilt at having such feelings. The funeral exacerbated these because so many people commented on what a wonderful man he had been, how much she must miss him and so on. She said 'What was wrong with me that I didn't find him like that?' She was reassured again that this was a normal sequence of events, first that people do not always show their whole personality to the neighbours and relatives, and second that, even if people had suspected that he was difficult, it was unlikely that they would have said to her at the funeral 'Your husband was sometimes nice but he could be a...'.

It was then suggested that Jean could express some of her feelings by playing a pair of Bongo drums whilst the therapist improvised some angry music. The Bongos were chosen for two reasons. They do not remind people of childhood, as some percussion instruments do, and are therefore acceptable for adults; and second, there is good tactile feedback to the skin and muscles, but none of the sense of using a weapon which a drumstick may give, and which is frightening for those who are only just learning to deal with their blocked anger.

Jean agreed to do this and as angry music was improvised, she drummed fiercely and shouted 'I hate you, I hate you!'. After this climax, the music was toned down so that she regained a feeling of being in control. After discussion it was decided that she would like to talk to her psychiatrist about the release of anger, and, fortunately, an immediate consultation could be arranged in the unit.

This intervention continued, but in a less dramatic atmosphere, for three more sessions, and culminated for Jean in greater understanding of her husband's own problems. He himself had come from a 'cold' and alcoholic family who did not make happy marriages, and she achieved both an improvement of her self-esteem and a sense of forgiveness of him. The outcome for Jean was good, she was able to maintain her improved self-esteem and insight, and remained alcohol-free following discharge.

Vignette 4

The following episode was included in my 1986 book *Grieving* but its timeless quality warrants its inclusion here too. The context was a music therapy session which provided the opportunity and the appropriate atmosphere for a counselling interaction. Even though the music itself was not part of this interaction, it formed the basis and the *raison d'être* for the conversation to take place.

The conversation took place in a nursing home with an elderly woman, Sue, who had been observed during a group music session, at first sitting sadly in her wheelchair looking at the ground but with a bright smile on her face when she was aware of anyone looking at her. As the music session had continued, she had become more involved in proceedings, and her facial expression seemed to change to a more genuine enjoyment. After the session was over she agreed to be recorded in an interview, since the whole programme was being prepared as part of an educational videotape. The observed losses were loss of hand function (shown by the position and loss of musculature of her hands, which lay limply on the book in front of her), loss of bladder control (shown by the catheter bag on the side of the chair), and loss of mobility, since she had to be wheeled in, unable to operate her chair independently.

Her speaking voice was that of an educated upper-class woman and from her participation it was also clear that she knew a good deal about music. The music sessions in this nursing home were at the time run not by a trained music therapist but by a person who could play just a few songs. The session which included the conversation was, unfortunately, a unique occasion.

SUE: 'You know, it's terrible. Sometimes I come down here and they have music, and they try to involve me (you know I was a good accompanist because I was a good sight-reader), and I think, "If only I could use my hands and sit at that piano!" But what's the good of it? There's some reason why I'm here, but what it is I don't know; I haven't found out yet.' (Laughs slightly.)

THERAPIST: 'You have times of feeling a bit useless...'

SUE: 'Oh, yes, many times. Many times I feel "Oh why am I here?" and I wish I were not. When I come down here and hear them fumbling... you know, trying to play the piano when they can't...'

The conversation continues in this vein for a minute or so, allowing the subject ample opportunity to express some of her sadness and frustration. She denied experiencing anger, and also spoke of her religious background, which may explain the predominance of frustration rather than anger.

THERAPIST: 'What actually went wrong, to make your hands...?' (*Gesture towards hands on lap.*)

SUE: 'O, something in my spine. The doctor operated but something just didn't go right with the operation.'

THERAPIST: 'It didn't go quite right...'(*Sensing that there is more to come.*)

SUE: 'I should have had another operation, but he said I'd've gone out to it...'*

THERAPIST: 'Yes... and how do you feel about that?'

SUE: (*Speaking very firmly here.*) 'I think they should have let me have it.'

THERAPIST: 'Yes...?'

SUE: 'And let me go out to it. Because he said it was either that or I'd become paralysed, the paralysis gradually creeping on.'

THERAPIST: 'Mmmmmmm?'

SUE: 'But you see, you don't know these things; this is hindsight.'

THERAPIST: 'Yes, it's easy to be wise after the event.'

SUE: 'I think they should have let me have it. The family, you
                know, and my husband, they didn't want it…'

THERAPIST: 'They hang on to life for other people… (*pause*)… You were
                saying before that sometimes you feel that you are crying on
                the inside but you keep happy on the outside?'

SUE: 'Yes, I was saying to my husband the other day, "You have no
                idea what it is like being here." He said, "Yes I have." And I
                said, "Not until you live here." My friends write to me and
                say, "You're so bright; you're an inspiration." But I say, "You
                don't realise what is going on inside; you put a bright face
                on it…"'(*Pause.*)

THERAPIST: 'We don't really understand what it is like, do we…?

SUE: 'Mrs X told me "It's as traumatic as losing a limb to have to
                come into a nursing home." And she has had three nursing
                homes so she knows what she is talking about.'

THERAPIST: 'Yes… because you have to put the past behind you… But you
                can't, because your past is you.'

SUE: (*In a triumphant tone of recognition.*) 'That's right… Because
                your past is you…'

Enough of this discussion has been given to bring out several points.

○ That it is important to interpret the words which are used (see phrase
  marked *, p.154). Those who speak of death do not always use the
  customary words but employ various euphemisms, as this patient did
  here; she used the words, 'Go out to it', as meaning 'die'. We must
  listen to what is said within the context of the whole conversation, so
  that we, through empathy, understand the precise meaning which
  each person assigns to the words spoken. If we cannot understand,
  then we must not hesitate to ask, 'What do those words mean to
  you?', or otherwise seek an explanation.

○ That the disabled person may have a failure of expectation when
  disability cuts short productive life and leads to dependency.

○ That the elderly disabled person will try to protect those close to
  them from being made unhappy and thus hides his or her own
  unhappiness in general; but not always, as conversation with the
  subject's husband revealed.

○ That death was seen as preferable to a life of total dependency.

- ◦ That adjustment is difficult, and it is probably impossible ever totally to put behind one the life of the past because this has become part of oneself.

- ◦ That decisions regarding life and death (in this instance relating to whether or not a risky operation should be undertaken) may be made on bases other than the sole wishes of the individual who is at risk.

One could in this case suggest that the reported wishes of the family were in fact a rationalisation of the subject's own wish not to risk death by having the second operation. However, this did not seem to be so; it appeared more likely that the decision was indeed made on the basis of not running the risk of guilt in the family if death did result.

But however we use familiar music, it is seen only as a tool and not an end in itself. I was present in a consultant capacity only so that, as no music therapist was employed at the facility, it was not possible for any long-term plans to be implemented in order to bring possibilities of musical participation for this lady in non-pianistic ways. Had there been an opportunity for ongoing work, efforts would have been made to involve the client in helping to plan the music session, as a way of assisting her to enjoy participation in music without the intensity of grief and frustration which she described.

Such an approach has been used successfully with several post-stroke patients, who have experienced major grief in loss of musical capabilities and who have therefore rejected participation in music therapy groups. To ask for help in planning a group programme has made use of their knowledge and, although they still may not wish to attend the sessions, this eventually changes and they attend, finally asking to play a percussion instrument with the hand which is still functional. This is not invariably successful in helping the person to learn a new dimension of enjoyment in music, but those who continue to resist have been found to suffer from a depressive illness as a consequence of the stroke, a common occurrence, or because depression has long been a feature of their mental state.

Familiar Music for 'Homework'

An approach nicknamed 'homework' makes use of familiar music. It consists of deciding, with the help of the client, which piece of known music best represents his or her goals for the series of music therapy interventions, or (on a smaller scale) for the week. Establishing such goals is, clearly, part of the therapeutic intervention; they must be chosen by common consent after discussion, and not imposed by the therapist! The music for this work must be so well-known to the client that he or she can recall it readily away from the session, either at home (hence the name 'homework') or as a resident of a hospital, nursing home, or hostel. Often a song is chosen because the verbal content is a key part of the work, so that 'Climb Every Mountain', with its theme of keeping on trying, is a frequent choice for those whose determination needs a boost!

Usually during the session when the homework is set there has been a visualisation symbolising effort and achievement, such as climbing a steep bush track and wondering whether one is making any progress. An actual place may be described or an imaginary one, depending on the preference of the client and other factors, and sketches are made for the client to take from the session. The choice is often the Bowen's Creek Track in the Blue Mountains outside Sydney, where the valley is so steep that the track has to zig-zag gradually up the sides in many stages, and it is only on looking back to the small river (creek) below that one has any recognition that progress has in fact been made.

Memories of the visualisation stay with the client and add to the effect of recalling the song in the week between sessions. The theme song 'Memories', from the film *The Way We Were*, which speaks of looking back at the past and asks whether in fact we would or could do the same things again, has proved helpful for those who are troubled by regrets and remorse, although this is usually only for a single week of preparation for the next session rather than (as for the previous item) a theme for a complete series of interactions.

For some people, however, an instrumental piece, such as the 'Dam Busters March', from the film of that name, has proved useful because it has connotations of determination and courage. The theme from 'Finlandia' is also useful, for those people who know the melody well. It too symbolises determination to overcome difficulties. Since the melody lends itself also to song-writing, in which words of the client's choice are allied with the existing melody, the effects of the homework are enhanced. One client chose to sing 'I won't give in, I'm going to keep on trying!' to the first part of the melody.

If song-writing has been a part of the music therapy session, in which both words and music are new, composed either by the client or (more commonly) as a shared project, this too is useful in reinforcing the work done in the office, provided that the song has become sufficiently familiar to the client to be recalled without anxiety. The client is asked to think of the song as often as is reasonable, remembering the conversation or the visualisation which took place, and to try to see how the ideas embodied might be put into practice in everyday life and thought.

Self-talk can be either productive or destructive. Many clients have, perhaps for years, concentrated on thoughts of failure and anger, and the use of music to strengthen positive self-talk, because it reminds the client of the content of the therapy session, is valuable. The client may also carry strong memories of improvised music, but, although one can recall the feelings which accompanied such work, it is rare indeed for a client to be able to sing to himself the themes which emerged.

Song-Writing

A variant of song-writing is for the client to write a poem, not necessarily strictly poetical in form but with some theme expressed in an imaginative way. This is then spoken by the client with music improvised by the therapist to reflect the mood of the words. The client may also play an instrument such as a drum to emphasise the rhythm and feeling of the verse.

One teenager, suffering from depression following her father's gender-reassignment surgery and trying to cope with the complex changes of relationship resulting from this reassignment from male to female in her parent, wrote words for which she selected a 'rap' rhythm from an electric keyboard to accompany the words. While she read her verses, she played (thumped, to the extent of making a hole in the skin) a drum as she spoke. Although at the time she denied being angry, this pseudo-catharsis proved useful in moving the therapy along (Bright 1995).

One young man, abused in childhood and drug-dependent for a significant period of his life, wrote two poems which he read to the accompaniment of two types of musical background. The first described his early life, in which he looked back to see himself as a child crying in a cot, reaching out through the bars and longing for love, but nobody came. The second, describing his rehabilitation, spoke of himself as a small plant pushing its way through the hard roadway, leaving behind the darkness, dankness and smells of the life below to reach up to the clean air. The achievement of writing the verse and the ideas contained therein were significant in his progress towards freedom from chemical dependency.

Song-writing is useful in palliative care, when the person has sufficient energy to create a verbal picture of the chosen subject. Whilst one cannot totally equate palliative care with grief therapy, there are substantial areas of overlap: sadness, anger, loss for the person who is soon to die and similar emotions for the family and friends, and music therapy in palliative care has been valued for several years (Munro and Mount 1978).

Techniques such as song-writing can be used in very similar ways whether one is looking at grief counselling for bereavement and other losses of health and happiness, or the anticipatory grief and grief over the losses already sustained which we see in palliative care (Bailey 1984). Songs composed can become a valued legacy for those who are left, whether they are written down or recorded on tape.

Improvised Music

I use improvised music in three different ways, of which the first is the most important in grief resolution. The three methods are:

○ Improvised music to reflect back to the client and to validate the life-story which has been told, whether it has been disclosed to the therapist through conversation, in poetry or in sketches such as the life road-map, depicting in stick-figure form the points of decision, the events which proved life-changing, for good or for harm, and so on. (This task is commonly set as homework.)

○ Use of improvised music as a projection technique in which the client *hears* and *sees* in the music a symbolic representation of his or her own life-story and problems, often with new personal insights, giving the therapist additional information through which to work.

○ Use of improvised music through which the client comes to some resolution of his or her problems, symbolically working these out through the playing of improvised music.

Improvised music has several advantages in grief resolution therapy. No matter what item of pre-composed music is played, one cannot be totally certain that the client has not already built up personal associations with the music, whether of happiness or sadness and anger. As noted above, specific associations can be of vital importance in counselling and resolution, but there are times when one needs to have greater freedom of emotion, especially when memory has been blocked and some strategy is needed to remove the blockage.

Some workers have attempted to build up lists of music of particular moods (Wedin 1972), presumably for use by those who are not practising musicians, but recorded music is necessarily a poor substitute for live improvised music in that it lacks flexibility. One cannot have every recording available at the time of the interview, and also because of the associations mentioned above.

Even if almost all of the population perceive the mood of an item as *happy*, and respond to it by an uplifting of mood, for the one person who is our client the music may have such associations of tragedy that there is a paradoxical response. Such responses are useful in achieving progress, but it must be a planned intervention and not a 'wrong' response to a particular piece of music.

Improvised music, on the other hand, is totally flexible. One can change the mood in a matter of seconds if the client's responses make this useful and necessary, and one does not depend on repertoire to find the right thing to play (Bright 1994). Furthermore, pre-composed music is strongly affected by cultural factors, and one must question whether a person whose musical and other cultural experiences and knowledge are totally different from those of the therapist can benefit from pre-composed music which comes from the therapist's cultural background! (Bright 1993). Improved music can, however, usually be adjusted culturally by the sensitive therapist.

In my clinical practice, improvised music follows assessment, so that it is introduced only after one has built up a good picture of the client's experiences, grief, loss, anger, guilts and so on, and, a vital factor, the extent of his or her vulnerability.

Many of the matters brought to mind by improvised music are seen by the client as being discreditable, and it is indeed usually this aura of discreditableness which has previously prevented their disclosure and which has in turn led to substance dependence, depression, etc. We can therefore not expect to complete assessment and move on into improvisation until trust has been developed.

One can be too clever! If, by the music played, one elicits without any preparation such an emotional storm that the patient is overwhelmed and suicidal, the therapeutic benefit is questionable. Assessment as a first step is vital, but this is only rarely achieved at the initial interview. It has, however, been known to occur, as is described in the section on post-traumatic stress disorder, and the use of improvised music to enhance the Gestalt technique of empty chair work.

The technique of the therapist in improvising varies from one person to another, and is also determined by the client's needs. In Western culture, there are certain features of music which are commonly interpreted in similar ways by different listeners and it is useful to bear these in mind although one may decide to discard many of them.

Although individual sessions have much variation, the general methods are as follows. Major and minor keys do not carry the stereotypical moods of happy and sad which are popularly ascribed to them. As the late Paul

Nordoff (1974) pointed out, some of the saddest tunes written are in a major key – 'Danny Boy' (or the 'Londonderry Air') from Ireland, and 'Way Down upon the Swanee River' from the USA! The converse is also true; many happy tunes in the past, like the seventeenth century Christmas carol 'Patapan' (Dearmer Williams and Shaw 1964) were written in the Dorian mode, or an approximation of the present-day minor. In the twentieth century, too, cheerful songs, such as the popular comic song 'Donald Where's Your Trousers?!' are written in a minor key.

Suggestions about Improvised Music

The ideas and comments which follow must only be seen as the fruit of my experience and observation, working with clients whose background is conventional diatonic harmony in classical or popular music of a Western style. There is no suggestion that these approaches will work for everyone nor that they are represent universal truth! Although the author has worked with persons from Indochina and other places of non-Western culture, their responses are undoubtedly different and there has been greater reliance upon recorded music, despite its disadvantages, in order to provide a valid cultural base for work in grief counselling. Jointly improvised music has also proved useful in this area of work.

Slow block chords moving downwards, with occasional *wrong notes* in the chords, are usually perceived as meaning *deterioration, descent into tragedy with some conflict*. It seems likely that it is the close-knit nature of a chord (so that it has a heavy feel to it) and the low speed at which the progression is played, together with a gradual downward shift of pitch, which produces these emotions or a sense of *solemnity and sadness*.

Delayed resolution of harmonies as accented passing notes, or a slow mordant to embellish the final note of a phrase, are also effective as symbolising hope deferred or other similar feelings such as nostalgia or loss.

Tension can be symbolised by repeated single notes, escalating to minor 2nds, C and C# played together, with increasing rapidity and volume. Note that this can produce intolerable feelings of tension, fear and anxiety and should be used with great care. For one client, whose description of his recent life showed that he had made repeated efforts to change but achieved nothing, the cluster of three black notes was used, played repeatedly up and down, on a discordant bass. At the end he pointed to that cluster of notes on the keyboard and said excitedly, 'When you played those notes it was exactly like my life, I've been going round and round getting nowhere!'; this was a new insight for him.

Feelings about change, whether for better or for worse, can be evoked by playing unfamiliar but conventionally diatonic music, and abruptly changing key every few bars, changing without any of the usual devices to attain a smooth transition from one key to another. This could be called a crash modulation, a sudden and aesthetically shocking change to a distant key, one which is harmonically unrelated. For example, one might play a few bars in D major and suddenly move to A♭ minor, then to C# minor, next to F# major, adding also changes of dynamics.

Apprehension, hesitation about decision-making can be symbolised by delayed resolution of harmonic progression, and, even more effectively, by a one or two second break of total silence in the middle of a lyrical melody or in an otherwise simple chord progression. The feeling of shock which the sudden break evokes gives a powerful impetus to imagery.

Feelings of *resolution and determination* can be represented by progressions of moderately-heavy chords, a total of six to eight notes shared between two hands and spread across the centre of a piano keyboard, usually in a major and with a sense of upward progress achieved by modulation into the dominant key (rather than the downwards sensation of modulating into the subdominant key).

No matter what we improvise we can give only a general emotional picture; however, the client will interpret the details according to his or her own life experiences and emotional state. This was demonstrated in work with a young man who had gender uncertainty as the result of sexual abuse in childhood. He had strong suicidal ideation and great fear as to what his life in the chemical dependency unit would be like if his fellow-residents realised the true nature of his underlying problems. Improvised music was played for him as a projection approach in order to enhance his own insight and also the therapist's understanding of him.

As always, the improvisation was prefaced by saying, 'I'd like to reflect back to you something of what you have been describing of your life by improvising music; would you tell me how it seems for you?' The improvisation included conflict, alternating hope and despair, but with an overall sadness. As it drew to a close, the client shouted 'It's two men knocking at the door, one is saying "let me *in*!" and the other is shouting "let me *out*!"'.

This was not an appropriate interpretation, on the surface, of what had been played, but it provided a startlingly vivid representation of his feelings. In the discussion which followed he was able to identify the way in which the improvisation represented his inability to feel any personal sense of gender and a tragic failure of belonging. He felt that he belonged neither to men nor to women. Certainly no such clear picture had been in the mind of the therapist, although there was an awareness of his ambiguity on gender.

Clients' Own Improvisations

Some, but not all, people do gain benefit from improvising their own music on tuned or untuned percussion instruments. Those who do try it are usually middle-class people who have good memories of school music, intellectual people who recognise that things are worth trying, or those who are so simple of heart and mind that they feel no self-consciousness. Those who reject such work appear to the author to be those whose self-esteem is so low that they fear people try to humiliate them, or they have bad memories of music at school which was seen as childish or as the wimp's alternative to real life. Bongo drums seem immune from this reaction, perhaps because they are seldom or never found in kindergarten classes. Improvisation seems best begun with a structure, a theme to start the process off rather than the totally free improvisation which experienced musicians can enjoy.

The author does not interpret the client's own improvisation for a number of reasons:

1. People vary in how they express emotions in music, especially if, for example, they regard anger as shameful and forbidden.

2. There are micro-cultural influences in musical expression: whether, for example, the person has grown up with Bach and Brahms, with Rogers and Hammerstein, or is familiar only with this week's Top 40 chart of favourites.

3. One's own background may influence interpretation, both culturally and as regards transference and counter-transference issues.

We recognise all these but they can still influence interpretation. It is therefore ethically correct and professionally responsible to *check things out*, although we may have made an inward guess as to the meaning, and even if we have doubts as to the veracity of the interpretation presented by the client! We may do this either by asking directly, 'I wonder how you were feeling as you played that?', perhaps describing particular features if these are clearly delineated, or by saying, 'I felt you were pretty stirred up when you did so-and-so...?'

On one occasion a girl who was clearly extremely angry (about her father's gender reassignment surgery) denied this, saying cheerfully 'I'm all right. No, I'm not angry', and yet some months later, at a separation interview, she said, 'Do you remember that time I was so angry I went through the top of your Bongo drum?' In this instance, the therapist's interpretation of anger was in fact correct, but it might not have been!

Mention has already been made of song-writing, the writing of poetry and the drawing of a life road-map. One client, who had been asked at the previous session to bring such a road-map, brought to the session a roll of paper towel about two metres long on which she had drawn illustrations or symbols of all the tragic events of her life. This formed the basis both for counselling and for improvised music to validate the trauma of what she had described.

Music therapists vary in their professional practice and the ways of using music which were described here are those which I have used over many years, those which have *worked* for a wide range of clients. But there is no suggestion that other ways may not work equally well. Much depends upon the approach of the therapist and the need of the client, and it would be rare to find the same situation twice!

The suggestions in this chapter have been for those who are professional music therapists, but those from other professions may find the insights useful. They might indicate the extent to which truth is hidden and the challenge to the therapist of helping the client towards disclosure. This disclosure is not so much to give information to the therapist as for the client to learn it for himself or herself, in the hope that the client's life may change.

CHAPTER 13

The Challenges and Griefs
of the Helper

The first practical step in dealing with our own griefs as helpers is to acknowledge their existence! From there we can go on to deal with them in some way, so that we can, if possible, avoid burnout. It is in fact one of the risks of being a helper that we do tend to deny our own grief, our stress, our emotional investment in those we care for. But these stresses are very real, whether we deal strictly with the physical (if indeed anyone today does thus separate body from mind!), or work in matters of the mind and the emotions (Beszterczey 1977).

We tend to feel guilty if we cannot cope with any given situation, if our skills are not adequate to reach resolution of all problems, if our clients fail to get better, fail to appreciate what is being done for them, deny that they need help, and instead get worse or fail to improve, are angry with us for not being able to fix things, insist that they can manage perfectly well without us.

The trouble is that sometimes they are right. We do make mistakes. Some people actually do improve more by working on their own. Sometimes we are meeting our own agendas rather than those of our clients. And to realise this is humiliating! But there are many occasions on which we have done the right thing, have dealt with matters on the client's terms and not our own, and still the outcome is disappointing.

What are the special challenges for the therapist or counsellor who works with people who are grieving, or whose grief over a significant loss has been blocked? What are the causes of our responses? The challenges include:

- ○ the overload of experiencing one loss after another, of working continually with those whose lives have been disappointing, horrifying, stressful

- working with someone whose problems or behaviour 'presses buttons' for us, so that it is hard to remain objective because we are constantly reminded of things in our own lives which, perhaps, we prefer to put aside

- trying to help someone to cope with a loss which resembles a personal experience of our own, especially if our loss has remained partly unresolved, and we find that our own grief gets in the way

- working with someone whose condition causes us particular ethical problems; for example, being consulted about termination of pregnancy when the professional is a person whose religious views forbid the intervention

- trying to cope with difficult processes of transference and counter-transference; when the client reacts unexpectedly towards us, or we to the client, not because of anything that has happened in the interaction, but because there is a transference of unacknowledged emotions which really belong to someone else or to another relationship

- trying to help someone cope with a grief which is so far outside our own experience that it sounds unreal, almost unbelievable, or is emotionally difficult to bear, and we find it difficult to respond in a helpful way

- letting go at the end of a period of therapy, whether the end has come through normal separation at the completion of therapy or by the client's choice

- letting go after a client dies, especially if we are left with unfinished business, as often occurs in suicide

- not feeling unduly guilty when a chemically-dependent client 'busts', and our work seems to have been a waste of time

- trying to work productively with someone who has the characteristic of sabotaging any moves towards change for the better

- not feeling guilty when we are (privately) angry or irritated by the destructive behaviour of a client who seems unable to perceive how this is wrecking his or her life, and the lives of others

- working with a client whose spiritual outlook differs strongly from our own

- not feeling guilty over our irritation or anger when someone refuses to take medication, or ceases medication on leaving hospital and all the work of the clinical team appears to 'go down the drain'

- recognising our own inadequacies, allowing ourselves to be human and, in ordinary terms, to *fail*!

- accepting that it is not always possible to facilitate change, that sometimes – despite our best efforts and for reasons outside our control – matters do not improve

- feeling OK about referring a client on to someone else when it becomes obvious that what we are doing is not quite enough

- trying to cope with colleagues who are actually difficult or who 'press buttons' for us

- allowing ourselves to take holidays without being so stressed that people have to tell us to take time off!

All of these difficulties are fairly common challenges for any experienced therapist or counsellor, and no less so if we work in grief resolution through music therapy, and they must be addressed.

There is significant stress in working constantly with those who are dying (Mount 1986), or with those whose illness or disability proves ineradicable so that no treatment can effect any significant change. We experience powerlessness and it can be difficult to maintain our level of care and concern in the face of such events and our own responses.

There is also a grief associated with powerlessness for those whose work necessitates the imposition of suffering in the interests of successful treatment. For example:

- The stress suffered by the venipuncture nurse or technician who has to draw blood from a distressed young child or frightened older person to assist in diagnosis or assessment of progress in a disease such as leukaemia.

- Staff involved in debridement of dead tissue in those recovering from severe burns suffer distress, especially when children are involved, knowing that the technique is essential to recovery but that the pain they have to inflict in the process is severe.

Staff are powerless to prevent the distress of the patients and yet know that the treatment is essential and must be done.

Powerlesness and grief at one remove

We are stressed by working constantly with those whose lives have been so distressing that simply to listen to the accounts of their experiences disturbs our equanimity. The lives of professional people have often been relatively sheltered in terms of upbringing and family relationships, and to hear graphic descriptions of violence, sexual abuse, trauma and torture is demanding.

We grieve when we are involved in the treatment and care of a child who has been physically abused, and imagine only too clearly the helplessness of that child. We suffer a sense of powerlessness in trying to heal not merely the physical injuries (which can sometimes be rectified) but – more importantly – in trying to heal the emotional damage caused by the abuse, especially if it has been a long-sustained pattern of experience for the child.

Stress and powerlessness, often mingled with grief, are experienced by those professionals who work with abused women; the women are often powerless to extricate themselves from an abusive relationship because their own low self-esteem, coupled with 'brainwashing' by the abuser, leads them to believe that the abuse is their own fault and well deserved.

Some women are able to leave an abusive relationship but many are not, and those who work with them suffer stress from their own inability to facilitate change in the situation.

Other Stressors

Various conditions cause particular difficulties for professionals. The disease of AIDS, with all its psychosocial and other implications, provides a clear example (Hurley Grossman and McGriff 1990). To be involved with someone who suffers the extremes of pain and discomfort, of anxiety and fear, of loss of dignity in a distressing and disfiguring disease, all have their effect upon the helper, whatever disease the person suffers from, and our sense of powerlessness is a feature of our distress.

The Client or Patient Whom We Find Difficult

Even more stressful, as being usually more difficult to discuss with colleagues, is to work with a difficult patient or client. Usually this occurs in counselling or various forms of psychotherapy, but can arise in any other form of treatment also. This brings its own sense of powerlessness and fatigue, and we experience grief because we are powerless.

In 1978, an article entitled 'Taking Care of the Hateful Patient' (Groves 1978) was published. This aroused controversy in the correspondence columns of subsequent issues of the New England Journal of Medicine and elsewhere, because some people denied that any patient should rightly be called *hateful* whereas others found comfort in knowing that professional people might find a patient difficult! But what Groves's actually wrote about was not hating our patients but recognising that the difficulties which arise may not have their origin in personality clashes, but out of particular characteristics of the patient, as a consequence of our counter-transference.

Transference and Counter-Transference

Even without being a fully committed disciple of Freud, we recognise that people often react to each other not on the basis of reality (the behaviour which actually occurs), but on the basis of what or who that person reminds them of. Such responses are not, of course, planned, but are usually at an unconscious or subconscious level.

Someone's name can put us off before we have ever met, if that name also belongs to a person who humiliated us. We can be introduced to someone and feel an instant qualm as to whether or not the person is to be trusted, because they look like someone who let us down badly at some time. We may feel a strong urge to placate someone without really knowing why; but there is a reason way back in our past which tells us to do so. We do not always recognise these reactions, and may even grace them with the descriptor *instinctive like or dislike* when what we really mean is that they pressed some button for us which we cannot or do not wish to identify!

The client is similarly affected by the therapist. The position of the therapist as a person in authority may arouse old feelings about authority figures. Someone who is older may elicit unresolved feelings about a parent; a young therapist may bring out feelings associated with rejection by a younger person such as a son or daughter, and so on.

There are several consequences of unresolved transference. The client may become, or seek to become, highly dependent upon the therapist, manipulating the relationship so as to make it personal rather than professional. And then, sometimes, the client might reject the therapist as a way of punishing those who have previously been the rejecters. The hidden needs transferred to the therapist by the client can lead to:

1. a clinging dependency which exhausts the therapist

2. the client saying 'Yes, but...' to every suggested avenue for change

3. the client courting failure when any positive outcome seems likely

4. the client being highly manipulative in order to fulfil some personal agenda, and so on.

There are two common responses to such people. We may become self-punishers out of guilt at our own powerlessness to facilitate change or because of our irritability. Or we may blame the patient because the person who does not improve is an insult to our powers of healing, and we prefer not to blame ourselves!

Even if we manage to analyse why the patient behaves like this, finding a cause, for example, in childhood abuse and powerlessness, in a sub-clinical personality disorder or whatever diagnosis we can produce, it is still true that such people leave us drained at the end of a session. What we are experiencing, as Groves pointed out, is our counter-transference process to a difficult client in response to the client's transference to us.

This opposite process, counter-transference, is of importance. We may respond to a client's behaviour to us in ways which are not explicable in terms of that client's behaviour or personality, but are based upon our own old experiences and relationships. Such responses may be positive or negative, but if we can recognise them for what they are, they are useful to us in the therapeutic relationship, and are not harmful.

The processes described, if remaining unacknowledged, contribute to fatigue and, ultimately, to our having to leave the particular area of work. It is thus of utmost importance that we arm ourselves with self-knowledge and with knowledge of the processes. Further, we must be willing to talk to our colleagues without embarrassment when difficult relationships arise as a consequence of transference and counter-transference (Malan 1979).

We must, nevertheless, recognise also that not all hostility, not all admiration and liking are consequences of transference. Our client may be angry with us, not because we remind her of a difficult parent but because we are consistently late for sessions, accept phone calls in the middle of interactions, and in general behave as if the client is of secondary importance (Wilson and Kneish 1988, pp.728–9).

Conversely, the client may like us and approve of the work we do, not because we remind him of a favourite school teacher but because he has found, perhaps for the first time, that he is able to let his defences down and discuss inner feelings without feeling stupid.

We too can find a client irritating not because of any obscure personal reaction of our own but because the client really is an irritating person.

'Burnout' the 'What's the Use!' Syndrome

To work with grieving people causes stress but this does not necessarily cause burnout because there are ways of dealing with stress: by professional supervision, peer support groups and informal opportunities to debrief

(Scully 1983), by professional knowledge and our own attitudes and self-esteem.

What does cause burnout is a loss of meaning in our work, with feelings of helplessness that – whatever we do and however hard we try – we shall not be able to facilitate change (Farber 1983), so that we feel as powerless as our clients. (Hence the heading above, the 'What's the use!' syndrome.) This is seen in the mid-1990's in some members of peace-keeping forces in the former Jugoslavia when Cease-fire agreements fail, in workers who try to establish health and prosperity in places such as Rwanda where tribal factions lead to massacres, and so on around the world.

We cannot plan for the continuation of meaning in our work, but we can ensure that our goals are realistic and that our self-esteem permits us to meet failure with some degree of equanimity.

Those who encounter horrifying circumstances in their work (firemen, rescue workers, ambulance staff, police and others) may suffer from post-traumatic stress disorder but this should not be entirely equated with burnout, even though the end results have much in common.

Spiritual Diversity

One of the more difficult challenges is to work with someone whose religious and spiritual outlook is very different from our own. How does an atheist, for example, work with someone who sees the hand of God in every event, good or bad? How does a Christian cope with agnostic views about death if he or she works in a palliative care unit? (Mount 1974). How does the committed Christian cope with a Muslim extremist who sees the world in very different ways, and who may respond poorly to a female therapist because of learned attitudes towards women as being inferior? How does a therapist who is strongly humanist, perceiving strength in the individual without supernatural intervention, or who is a sincere New Age follower, having confidence in one's inner power and in vibrations from crystals or from the stars, cope with a client who is conventionally and strongly Christian and who sees all power as having its origin in God? Or vice versa?

One hopes that natural empathy and professional training will enable the therapist to cope with such challenges. But it is a mistake to think it will always be easy, especially when one works with those who face the possibility of death because of a life-threatening illness, those who have been bereaved of a child or suffered similar losses, and when their responses to those losses lead to spiritual questioning, anger and rejection.

Yancey's writings have proved provocative and useful for some such situations, especially for Christians who feel let down by God when tragedies spoil their lives (Yancey 1988).

Gender of the Therapist

How important is the gender of the therapist? This was mentioned above, in the context of a woman professional and a male client who, for cultural reasons, sees women as inferior. Is it more productive of progress to work with a same-sex or an opposite-sex client? (Mogul 1982). In some situations it may seem infinitely easier to work with a same-sex client, as when a woman therapist works with a woman who fears men because of sexual assault in the past. Yet it may be more productive of insight and resolution for the client to work (for at least some of the time) with a male therapist, despite the difficulties in building trust, in order that conflicts may be acknowledged and perhaps, to a workable degree, resolved.

Difficulties can arise for a woman when working with a homosexual man for whom fear or distrust of women has been significant in the formation of his sexual preference. One needs to be aware of transference issues in such a situation.

Matters of sexual conduct between therapists and clients are frequently under discussion, and it is clear that different boundaries are perceived by different people. Even when seduction as such is excluded, there are still areas of sexuality between client and therapist which may affect the therapeutic alliance and thereby affect the outcome of the therapy itself. Does a woman therapist, for example, touch a male client or a lesbian client on the arm? Will this be perceived as a minor empathic gesture or could it be misinterpreted as seduction?

The age difference may be seen as an important factor in the building of a therapeutic alliance. One young man was referred to me because of difficulties in relationship with his mother, and it was thought that it could be helpful to have as a therapist a woman who was of a similar age to his mother, so that he could work through his difficulties. But transference is not necessarily restricted by age. A mother may transfer to her young son the antagonism she feels to her father, not because of her son's age but because of his gender or because he bears the same name.

Awareness that gender and age can be factors in therapy is probably the best method of dealing with difficulties or potential difficulties, rather than restricting one's practice to clients of particular age or gender. It is also important, as a practical measure, to discuss any such dilemmas with our colleagues. Their opinions may well help to solve the problem or reduce the therapist's anxiety.

The promotion of a sense of alliance between client and therapist may well be of crucial importance in determining the outcome of any intervention. For example, the client's perception of the therapist's concern for his or her well-being and the warmth of that concern are of major importance in establishing a good working relationship. We may find it valuable to have ways of assessing the progress and predicting the outcome of the therapeutic alliance (Allen *et al.* 1984; Luborsky *et al.* 1983).

Letting Go

Although there are a few clients whose departure through the door we view with relief, separation from the client is often a therapeutic challenge. The difficulties of letting go are magnified when the decision is that of the client and when it is made *against medical advice*. This is true whether we think of work in psychiatry or in general medicine. The psychiatric patient may leave because the intervention is too close to home, changes are in the air, and the whole business is too frightening for the client to continue.

But physical medicine too brings difficult challenges to the patient which may lead to his or her leaving treatment. In a renal dialysis unit, for example, there will be some who decide to cease treatment and stop coming for dialysis because they have had enough, believing that the quality of their life is not sufficient to justify continuing. Others sabotage their dialysis treatment by going on eating binges of foods forbidden to the person with compromised renal function.

Such responses may be perceived by staff as tantamount to suicide and they experience many emotional difficulties, such as anger that their treatment methods are being rejected. It is important that these difficulties are kept in the open rather than being hidden (Cramond Fraenkel and Barratt 1990).

In counselling for psychosocial difficulties following a major loss, there are similar difficulties when the client opts out. We then have to deal with our own responses:

- relief that a difficult client has gone
- regret that difficulties were not worked through and the person is likely to relapse or to continue on a downhill course of behaviour and relationships

- disappointment, irritation or frank anger that our care was not
  accepted as potentially useful.

There may be no formal separation; the client cancels future appointments
or walks out of the door vowing never to return. However, it can happen
that someone has to cease appointments for personal, family or financial
reasons so that there is some warning of separation. There is then an
opportunity for a last assessment, with discussion as to how griefs were dealt
with, whether the client has learned new strategies of coping in the future,
whether the past losses are still troublesome. If this can be done, even a
premature termination can leave a sense of achievement for the client and for
the therapist too. If there is the opportunity to return in the future, should
the need arise, the premature separation can still have been useful.

When a series of interviews has had a good outcome, separation is simple.
The client is more confident of the capacity to work through problems, and
past griefs and guilts have been identified and come under some kind of
control. We feel that we have done a good job and there is mutual satisfaction.
It is helpful to have a definite task of separation. We might ask the client,
without seeming to ask for thanks or congratulations, to assess how much
change has taken place during the sessions, whether memories from the past
still affect everyday functioning, how far he or she feels better able to cope
in the future.

The self-assessment that I have used at intervals through a series of
sessions is useful. It shows ten steps with a scene of peace and happiness at
the top. The client is asked which step he or she is on at the time, perhaps
one foot on the next step? A flag to hold with key words written on it
provides another measure of progress, or lack of it, and this is usefully
included in a separation interview (Bright 1986).

Griefs of the Helper

Challenges are a potential source of disappointment and grief to the therapist,
and some of the challenges listed above overlap with the griefs of our work.
There are others as well:

- grief over the death of a client at the end of a period of interactions,
  especially if the end has come suddenly (even if it has not been death
  by suicide) and we have not been able to say 'goodbye'
- feelings of sadness and revulsion when clients describe to us lives of
  such unremitting cruelty, rejection and loss, or of a series of

(otherwise normal) losses which are abnormal by their frequency and severity, that we feel overwhelmed

- ○ grief, mingled with anger, when family members are destructive or simply unhelpful to the client's welfare

- ○ sadness when a period of remission, as can occur in leukaemia, ends and we know that the outlook is poor

- ○ sadness when we are not able to help, and the person either leaves treatment or commits suicide

- ○ sadness when tests reveal malignancy or some other condition with a poor prognosis for a person whom we have been supporting in the waiting time

- ○ stress mingled with grief, if our work involves trauma and horror-filled circumstances such as are found in rescue work, fire-fighting, police work, ambulance work and so on.

In all of these challenges, all of these griefs, we must acknowledge our own needs if we are to continue to work effectively.

Coping with Our Own Griefs

Usually the training for grief counselling has included exercises to improve and enhance self-knowledge, helping us to work through old partly-unre-solved griefs so that they do not obstruct the work we do with others. But the grief and losses of life do not stop when training begins and we must hope that the self-awareness and skills of resolution learned in training will permit us to resolve new losses, perhaps with the help of a counsellor for ourselves, so that they do not diminish our usefulness to others.

We need to continue with in-service training and learning of skills, not to follow slavishly every new fad or trend, but at least to find out what new ideas are being promulgated, and decide whether or not these are useful for us. Most of the helping professions include in a code of ethics and profes-sional conduct a requirement that the professional continues to study and develop new skills by attending seminars and so on. Such study is a preventive measure in preserving our sense of balance.

The requirement for in-service study is almost impossible to police, but to have it in writing does remind new professionals of their responsibilities to remain in touch with new ideas and with innovative work of colleagues, so as to decide which is or is not useful for their own work.

Stress is no less for personnel involved in rescue, fire, ambulance and police work because the occurrences happen frequently! There is a danger that, because it is part of the job, personnel will tend to deny their own emotional needs in response to the trauma, and post-traumatic stress disorder is a very real risk. Raphael and Singh have written of the (sometimes unrecognised) need to care for the rescuers who are involved in disaster recovery work (Raphael and Singh 1983/4).

One man described the flashbacks and suicidal depression (characterised by guilt) that he suffered because of a life-changing incident when fighting a bush-fire. The fire appliance on which he served was at the edge of a conflagration which had got out of control and the other truck of the team, which was a distance away and nearer the heart of the fire, became engulfed by the fire when its engine failed, so that all the men on board were killed. His flashbacks focused on his inability to get to his mates and save them from death, with horrifying knowledge, born of his own experience, of what their death would have been. His flashbacks included smelling smoke, visual images of walls of fire, and the sound of the siren of the stalled fire truck.

Today the emotional needs of such people are better recognised than in the past and the services normally employ trauma counsellors, so that counselling is perceived as routine and not a sign of weakness.

Signs of Possible Risk

Various things will warn us of possible difficulties ahead. The therapist may need the client to improve, to boost his or her own self-esteem. He or she may need the client to become dependent as part of a need to rescue. Clients may remind us of someone with whom we had a difficult personal relationship, people for whom our professional interventions were not successful and we feel we must succeed this time. And so on.

Several types of responses or incidents will alert us to possible risks, for example:

° finding ourselves unreasonably impatient, irritable or even angry with a client

° blaming the client for failing to improve, and yet recognising that this is unreasonable

° being manipulated, willingly or unwillingly, into the role of 'the good mother', 'the reliable friend', 'the loving partner', instead of remaining a therapist

○ feeling unduly cast down when a client decides to leave therapy, or feeling totally despairing when a suicide occurs

○ seeking the client's approval or admiration for what we are doing;

○ being frightened lest we fail in a therapeutic relationship

○ feeling dismayed or feeling a failure when colleagues do not approve of the way we work with a particular client.

All of these may happen from time to time, when we are over-tired, stressed, have other things on our mind. Forgiving ourselves for being human is important, but if they happen often then we need to take note.

Our Responses to Suicide

Suicide of a client is perhaps the most difficult event we have to cope with in professional work. However much we try to convince ourselves that we bear no burden of guilt, we are usually left with feelings of 'If only I had done this or that...', 'If only I had not been away on leave just at that time...', 'If only they had tried this or that medication...' and so on. It is vital that we already have debriefing systems in place as a normal part of the way the workplace operates, to follow suicide or any other traumatic incident.

Summary

The risk of *being a rescuer* is often mentioned today, and we must recognise the need for emotional investment without emotional involvement. We must care what happens to our clients; otherwise our objectivity may become insensitivity and withdrawal. But we must avoid involving ourselves in their emotional experiences and trauma.

Only by acknowledging our own humanity can helpers cope with personal responses. Despite all our successes that help to keep us going, we are often in the midst of sad and stressful situations, and we need to be able to accept help to cope with success and with what seems like failure. We must be honest with ourselves, sharing difficult feelings with others (a common source of reassurance, especially when another staff member says 'Join the club!') and in general allowing ourselves to be human.

Whitfield wrote a helpful article on stresses of the psychotherapist, much of which is entirely applicable to the grief counsellor. She compared the therapist to an athlete who undertakes increasing challenges but must prepare and train for these. She emphasised the need to recognise our own limits and the need to build up our own emotional support resources and to maintain our physical health (Whitfield 1980).

Our stresses all need to be addressed if we are to avoid burnout. We can do so by group debriefing, by individual debriefing and supervision, by additional training for particular crises, by adequate holidays and changes of activity, by maintaining our own relationships at a satisfying level, by all or any of these. If we acknowledge the need for self-care, we shall be able to continue!

CHAPTER 14

Summary

Grief and Loss

As we have seen, people respond differently to changes and loss. Some are able to deal with change in life, seeing it as a challenge or as a normal part of living which does not engender any extraordinary fear or anxiety. Some are able to cope with loss over a period of time, by accepting and coming to terms with the loss as a reality, adjusting to life after loss, and moving on. They do not need nor do they seek counselling or other professional help, and those who from time to time are sarcastic about there being a *counselling industry* fail to differentiate between the majority of the population, who cope with their pain and grief following a normal loss, and those who are not able to do so.

Many people cannot cope with losses, and there are many reasons for this.

The loss itself may be outside normal expectation, as in the death of a child or a young adult; it may have overtones of horror, as in post-traumatic stress disorders, and leave such painful memories that professional help is usually needed. The loss may concern someone or something which had previously caused difficulties, as when a difficult parent dies, when the ex-spouse dies, when a violent and abusive person dies, when a divorce occurs and one has doubts as to whether the relationship should end or should continue, when we are robbed of our self-esteem and feel ourselves to be worthless, and so on.

Guilt is also the cause of ongoing, unresolved loss, as when we feel responsible in some way for the death – not calling the ambulance in time, not realising someone was on the verge of suicide, not being there at the time of a crisis, and other situations which can lead to self-blame. Guilt is especially complex because it is not necessarily governed by logic. We may have guilty feelings about something, whether it was something done or not done, when there is no logical basis for those feelings.

Suicide generally leaves scars in the survivors, and although some people are able to deal with these, others are not.

There is frequent discussion as to the similarities and differences between grief and depression, whether those who become depressed following loss were or were not specially vulnerable. Certainly there are aspects in common and those who are depressed or who have a history of depression are particularly susceptible to depression as a response to loss. The pre-existence of psychiatric illness leads to major difficulties in resolving loss, whether bereavement by death or an all-pervasive loss of self-esteem.

But all of these difficulties may be helped by appropriate intervention, whether, as we saw in Chapter 10, by empathic neighbours and volunteers, or by trained specialists in grief counselling.

Empowering our Clients

It is tempting and seductively easy to be constantly rescuing, always taking over things for our clients rather than letting them try things out for themselves. 'I'll do that for you, don't you worry about it!' Clearly it takes sensitivity to decide when help is needed and when people are better left to do things for themselves. In the first stages of shock and powerlessness which characterise grief, there is difficulty in organising one's actions. People forget to do things, drive the wrong way to even familiar shopping centres and they do need support.

But as that first period of powerlessness and disorganisation recedes, it is more helpful to give some responsibility for actions. Otherwise people think 'I must really be pretty hopeless if they won't even let me do this or that!', naming some relatively trivial task.

Powerlessness is both a consequence and a cause of grieving. When we grieve we lose control, and losing control causes us grief.

We cannot consider grief in a vacuum without also considering, in the widest of terms, its effects upon the lives of those who mourn.

Neither can we examine the human condition without realising the extent to which powerlessness is a primary cause for grief, especially in countries which we often label as *third world* or *under-developed*. Rights of the individual often seem to be the privilege of an affluent society, but it need not remain that way if enough of us seek to promote change.

Grief counsellors are unlikely to be numbered among the power-brokers of the world, but even if all we can do is work in our own area of the world, to recognise and in some way deal with the need of the individual for self-determination, the right to struggle through his or her own grief and loss, the right to live life without fear of violence and abuse, we shall have achieved something and our attitudes may spread further than our own particular cabbage-patch!

Being a Therapist; a Personal View

What do we need to be a grief counsellor and therapist?

- Willingness to set aside other concerns (phone calls, interruptions, one's own private agenda) in order to concentrate on the client.

- Background knowledge of the diversity of grief, especially of unresolved grief, and the effects this has on a person's self-esteem, achievements and relationships.

- A listening ear, which picks up cues of speech intonation, the choice of phraseology and even the changes in respiration.

- An observant eye which picks up cues of changes in body language such as the whitening of knuckles, the sudden loss of eye contact, the jerk of the head as a difficult memory is evoked.

- Insight, to understand the implications of those cues.

- Capacity to communicate a non-judgemental attitude which, over a period of time, allows everything to be told.

- Empathy to convince the client of one's genuine interest in the person and not merely in the history.

- Willingness to allow the individual to disclose things at his or her own pace.

- A capacity to reflect back what the client has told, in emotional as well as factual terms, so that the sadness and trauma are validated.

- Skills of assisting clients to achieve catharsis whilst giving them a sense of control, so that the experience is neither terrifying nor overwhelming.

- The ability to convince the clients of their own worthwhileness, their own capacity to change and to sustain that change.

- The insight to know when to leave the client to work it out alone and when to outline ideas for the future.

- Patience to persevere but also wisdom to know when to stop!

- Personal self-esteem to be able to cope with one's own failure to facilitate change.

- Understanding of the processes of transference and counter-transference as these affect the therapeutic relationship.

This is what I believe it means to be a therapist.

In summary, the clinical skills which one needs if one is to be involved in grief resolution, in helping our clients to resume power over their own lives, include both knowledge and skills, personally and professionally:

- to understand oneself and one's life responses
- to have background knowledge and understanding of what the illness or disability means to client and family: emotionally, spiritually, cognitively, physically and socially
- to have appropriate knowledge of the grieving process and of the problems which people of all ages experience, and how they respond to those losses
- to have knowledge and understanding of the work of other disciplines, and to be willing to work in the context of a co-operative team
- to be non-judgemental about other people's life and experiences
- to have profound respect for people's resilience and capacity for change
- to avoid being a perfectionist and to be able to forgive oneself for making mistakes.

Those who work in grief counselling combined with music therapy will need additional special skills and methods of working:

- providing colleagues with information on music therapy, in order to enhance overall teamwork in hospital, day centre, special school, etc., and to ensure that referrals are appropriate
- developing appropriate music skills for different populations
- applying music to therapy – a repertoire to suit any given population, methods of improvisation as a projection technique and to achieve catharsis as a positive experience, and so on.

Being a therapist or counsellor who works in grief resolution will not bring acclaim on the world scene, nor will it bring universal success in the tasks we undertake. But it will provide a means of communication with those in need which brings to them some degree of control and self-esteem with personal dignity.

Ideas for Reading

Introductory Thoughts

The early seventeenthth century philosopher Bacon said *Nam et ipsa scientia potestas est*, 'Knowledge itself is power'. Whilst this may be too broad a generalisation, there are instances in which it stands firm. Knowledge of cardio-pulmonary resuscitation techniques can save lives; knowledge of where help is available in support groups is useful; knowledge that what seems to be abnormal behaviour is actually a normal response to trauma is comforting. All these help to empower us, whatever our role.

It is, however, worth thinking about the powerlessness experienced by those who, for one reason or another, are unable to read and who do not seek help because of embarrassment or shame. 'Please could you read this form for me? I seem to have left my glasses at home.' said the young woman at the counter of the government office, the look on her face suggesting that this was her way of hiding the fact that she was unable to read it for herself.

Migrants, too, have similar difficulties and, in multi-cultural countries, leaflets are commonly available in all migrant languages and placed in public places such as post offices to provide information about a wide range of needs, such as psychiatric illnesses, epilepsy, diabetes, single-parent families, pensions and so on. (In Australia, free interpreter services are also available face-to-face or by telephone.)

Such measures do not, however, address the needs of those who are unable to read in any language, and who cannot even read the multilingual posters that advertise the availability of interpreter services. In such circumstances, neighbourliness seems the only answer!

Books can help to empower us by giving us knowledge, ideas for dealing with problems, the comfort of feeling less alone. The title of one book recommended below speaks to us of this: *I thought I was the only one.*

Books are listed in several categories:

° books for professionals, who wish to gain deeper understanding of their work or to meet their own needs

° books for adults who want to gain understanding of their own problems in grief, with or without professional help

° books for adolescents, who want to understand more about problems they observe or situations in which they are personally involved

° books for parents and others to use, giving them greater skill in helping children to cope with grief, or actually to share with children.

There are no lists of resources for specific disabilities because support groups normally provide their members with lists of appropriate material. People with special needs, therefore, in conditions such as autism, Down's syndrome, epilepsy, mastectomy, ileostomy, Alzheimer's disease and so on should look in their telephone directories or in local information services provided by libraries or community centres for details of special interest or support groups.

I have scrutinised all the books which are listed, but not every book which appealed to me will appeal equally to others! Reading a book as an outsider is very different from using it as a resource when one is living through the actual crisis.

Parents who wish to point their children in the best direction, or professionals who wish to direct the reading of their clients, can suggest that the almost universal Dewey system of library classification can be used with advantage to find the topics one seeks.

Books on grief and loss will be numbered on the shelves around 155 (point something-or-other), various numbers following the decimal point depending upon the type of grief under discussion, and normally followed by the first few letters of the author's name as a clue if one needs to find a specific book amongst a number of others on the same topic. A case in point is Rosemary Wells's book *Helping Children Cope with Grief*, which is classified as 155.937. WELL. Libraries may vary in the details of the figures after the decimal point, depending upon the aspect of the book which is assessed by the classifying librarian as the most significant, but the numbers before the decimal point will not vary for the same topic.

Books on the consequences of marital breakdown will be classified with the numbers 306.8 something, so that Mavis McLean's book on women's resources in surviving divorce is 306.89 MACL, whereas a book by Ambrose on men surviving divorce is 306.86 AMBR. (Not listed because I was unable to find a copy to read, but the book does exist; it was published in 1982 by Wheatsheaf books in Melbourne, Victoria, Australia, and may be available in some libraries.)

Books on euthanasia will be classified under 179.7, and (as in other sections) the first letters of the author's name will appear on the label on the spine of the book so as to separate on the shelves the various books on that topic.

Books on psychotherapy will be classified under 615 and those on specific medical conditions will have the prefix 618. There is an International Books and an International Serials classification also, ISBN and ISSN, the number for which appears on the back cover of all books and journals. But this is not helpful to the ordinary library-user; the Dewey system is that normally in use.

Books for Professionals: Death, Dying and Other Losses

Background information on human relationships

The Child, the Family and the Outside World by D.W. Winnicott. Published in 1964 by Penguin, Harmondsworth.

A classic text in helping us to understand children's development in relation to parents and other adults, events and circumstances.

Attachment and Loss by John Bowlby. Three volumes: Volume 1: *Attachment*, Volume 2: *Separation. Anxiety and Anger*, Volume 3: *Loss: Sadness and depression*. Originally published by the Tavistock Institute of Human Relations and the Institute of Psycho-analysis but subsequently available from Penguin books, Harmondsworth.

Three major works on human responses to relationships and losses, which form essential reading for all who work with grieving people, no matter what their losses are.

More specific topics:

Dying by John Hinton. First published in 1967 and reprinted since then by Penguin, Harmondsworth.

The forerunner of many books on death and dying by different authors, this is the pioneering study of the dying process and of bereavement. John Hinton covers a wide range of topics, including religious beliefs as influencing the fear of death for better or for worse, fear of the cost of treatment as influencing attitudes towards death, and so on. I was privileged to have a conversation with John Hinton some years ago and remember his belief that we should never assume people are too old to change, that we must retain a sense of hope; this is encouraging for all who are concerned with human emotions.

On Death and Dying by Elisabeth Kubler Ross. Published in 1970 by Tavistock, London, and reprinted since then.

One of Kubler Ross's many books on death and dying, all of which will provide information and empathic coverage of these topics. Useful both for the professional and for the person living in the grieving process, some of her books are to share with children.

Bereavement: Studies of Grief in Adult Life by Colin Murray Parkes. Published in 1975 by Penguin, Harmondsworth, and reprinted several times since then. One of the most important books about bereavement by death, this publication includes research and case studies as well as general discussion. Although written in terms of 'professional' and 'patient', all who work with grieving people, whether in hospital or in the community, will find information and help in this work.

The Anatomy of Bereavement by Beverley Raphael. Published in 1984 by Basic Books, New York.

An overview of responses to loss, including those other than death and dying. Professor Raphael has been involved in direct work with people grieving over loss in bush-fires and other disasters as well as in difficult bereavements by death. Her writing bears the stamp of first-hand experience as well as profound professional knowledge.

Grief in Children: A Handbook for Adults by Atle Dyregrov. Published in 1990 by Jessica Kingsley Publishers, London.

A small book with excellent coverage of responses in children of all ages to life-threatening illness and death. There is no index but the modest size of the book and the detailed chapter headings and subheadings make it easy to find any particular topic. Children's fears are well described and include such practical matters as a child's fear that he may be expected to pay off his father's mortgage and bank loans. The author also discusses deaths which are especially traumatic, like the effects on a child who finds the body of a parent who has committed suicide. The needs of teachers and other helpers are also addressed.

Helping children cope with grief. Facing a death in the family by Rosemary Wells. Published in 1988 by Sheldon Press, London.

This is a small book, but (as well as dealing with general aspects of grief in bereavement) it points the reader to many situations which are not always discussed, for example:

o   the trauma of the public tragedy and disaster, with all the resulting media intrusion, and the fact that the public nature of the grief means that everyone knows about it, and people ask questions which are not usually asked in the private tragedy

o   the death of a handicapped child and the complex responses to this

o   responses of children to the suicide of a sibling.

The author also brings into the open the problems associated with relief following the death of a domineering and cruel mother, or after the death of an incestuous father, which to one child brings relief but for another child a quasi-widowhood. This occurs when the incestuous behavior was without violenc or cruelty, with apparent affection, so that the child has not recognised its inherent abnormality.

The author emphasises that, after some deaths, children may need professional help from a psychiatrist and points out that parents may be alerted to this need not by obvious grief but by anxiety and misbehaviour.

Although this book is listed as being for professionals, it could also be useful for clients, although the condensed coverage of the various topics means that each client would probably require more detailed information on his or her particular need.

A Voice for Children by M.G. Flekkøy. Published in 1991 by Jessica Kingsley Publishers, London.

Although this book is about work in Norway, the information and discussion are helpful to anyone who wishes to know about and become involved in the championship of children, who otherwise are generally powerless in society.

The author was the first-ever ombudsman appointed to represent children, and in the course of fulfilling that task dealt with such diverse matters as: the vulnerability of children and parents to advertising and the dangers of commercial pressures which say, 'If you do not buy this or that you are not doing the best for your child'; the rights of children to education; the impossible dilemma of the parent who needs to stay with a sick child at home yet needs to go to work to maintain employment and income; the needs of young people who are inappropriately imprisoned, when what was truly required was psychiatric help and extended opportunities for education; and so on.

A book which challenges the rest of the world to follow Norway's lead!

I thought I was the only one by Hazel Edwards. Published in 1992 by Collins-Dove, Melbourne.

This book is to help teachers to cope with grief in the school, on a 'whole school' preventative basis rather than to cope with an individual crisis. The author is a playwright and has included several suitable scenarios for helping to develop children's ideas on loss, and for guiding children's writing and presentation of dramatic work which will deal with other situations.

The ideas in the book are useful for guiding children into a gradual understanding of the permanency of death; some of the aphorisms have profound meaning for all of us: 'When we lose someone older we lose the past; when we lose someone younger, we lose the future.'

Play Therapy with Abused Children by A. Cattanach. Published in 1992 by Jessica Kingsley Publishers, London.

This is not a how-to-do-it book but contains information about the value of play therapy in helping children who have abused, and ideas on how help may be obtained. Cattanach discusses the broad issues of abuse including the rights of the child not to be exploited, coerced, violated, not to be videoed in pornographic material, and so on. There is no index but the detailed table of contents is good.

Psychiatric Clinics of North America: Psychiatric Manifestations of HIV Disease edited by L. Zegans and T.J. Coates. Published in 1994; one of a large series under the general title *Psychiatric Clinics of North America* by W.B. Saunders, Orlando.

Although the title of this book suggests that it is strictly about psychiatry, the chapters (by various authors, some of whom have already been cited in the body of the text in this book) provide excellent coverage of the whole psycho-social implications and effects of HIV infection.

In addition to discussing the functional and organic consequences of the infection for the sufferer in psychological impairment and in dementing and psychiatric conditions, the authors consider the grief and powerlessness of the sufferer, of friend, of relative and of lover.

Strongly recommended for professionals who work with grieving people, of any of the categories listed above.

Stress and Burnout in the Human Service Professions edited by B.A. Farber. Published in 1983 by Pergamon, New York.

This book consists of 17 chapters by various authors, and includes in its scope the difficulties experienced by a wide range of 'helpers', such as police, teachers and psychologists, as well as the medical and allied health professions.

It suggests that burnout may be a form of learned helplessness, and the whole book is a useful resource for all who work in stressful therapeutic relationships.

Books for Adult Clients: Various Topics

My Daddy died by Heather Teakle. Published in 1992 by Collins-Dove, Melbourne.

This is a first-hand account of a young woman whose husband was killed when one of her children was two years and the other five months old. She acknowledges that she had not been highly maternal and describes with great clarity the changes in her life, the way she herself coped with the bereavement and how she supported her children in their development. An honest and moving book which offers help to bereaved mothers.

I couldn't cry when Daddy died by Iris Galey (acknowledged as being a pseudonym because of the nature of the book). Published in 1988 by Benton Ross, Auckland New Zealand, and in the USA by Mother Courage Press, Racine, WI.

An adult's account of her experiences of powerlessness and horror in prolonged incest, but also of her survival and growth, culminating in sadness for her father's inability to experience truly loving relationships. This is written as a story rather than as a clinical study, but has much to recommend it both for a professional's raising of consciousness and for an adult with similar traumatic memories.

No Time for Good-byes. Coping with Sorrow, Anger and Injustice after a Tragic Death by Janice H. Lord. Published in 1987 in Australia by 'Millennium', Newtown, NSW, and in the USA by Pathfinder Publishing, Ventura, CA.

I found this an informative and useful book, it deals with all kinds of sudden death and with the difficulties which commonly follow – not simply because of the suddenness of the death itself and the sudden ending of relationships, but also because sudden death is often difficult by its very nature.

Sudden death may well have been caused by suicide, murder, motor vehicle accidents, drug overdose, and when police and criminal justice departments are concerned with the circumstances of the death, it is still more difficult to cope with one's own emotions.

Janice Lord discusses the difficulties experienced by children after sudden death, gives helpful information and ideas, and reassures parents that quarrels and jealousy are common amongst surviving children after the death of a sibling.

The uniqueness of each person's grief is acknowledged and the author's work as counsellor for victims and survivors of crime, motor accidents and other trauma enables her to write with directness, genuineness and empathy.

Suitable for people working through their difficulties without professional help, but also for professionals, who may wish to recommend the book to clients.

Loss of a Baby: Understanding Maternal Grief by Margaret Nicol. Published in 1989 by Bantam, Sydney, NSW.

This helpful book covers neo-natal death, stillbirth, and miscarriage as well as the termination of pregnancy due to foetal abnormality. Importantly, this book is written not only for the grieving mother, but also for the father of the child, in order to understand his own grief and also to understand the responses of his wife to the tragedy.

Last Touch: Preparing for a Parent's Death by M.R. Baker. Published in 1992 by New Harbinger Publications, Oakland, CA.

Useful for adult clients, to help them to understand their own reactions to impending death.

On the Death of a Parent edited by Jane McLoughlin. Published in 1994 by Virago Press, London.

This book consists of personal stories about the death of a parent, and is particularly helpful in that it includes accounts of dealing with the death of a parent whom one found difficult or whom one disliked.

When Your Partner Dies by Mary Mortimer. Published in 1991 by Hale & Iremonger, Sydney, NSW.

A useful book, which includes open discussion of problems which can arise with children when the parent becomes emotionally interested and/or involved with someone else.

Information about loss in old age

Music in Geriatric Care: A Second Look by Ruth Bright. Published in 1991 by Music Therapy Enterprises, Sydney, NSW.

This book includes discussion on loss in old age and how this affects others; provides insight for relatives and professionals on responses to frailty and disability.

Music Therapy in the Dementias: Improving the Quality of Life by Ruth Bright. Published in 1988 by MMB, St Louis, MO.

Certain sections provide information and enhance insight into grieving associated with dementing conditions, useful for relatives and professionals.

Your Best is Good Enough by V.E. Greenberg. Published in 1989 by Lexington Books, Lexington, MA.

A helpful and reassuring book for the adult children of older parents, which openly discusses the conflict of loyalties and feelings of powerlessness which are experienced by those who are torn between their children, their spouse and their parents. Special emphasis is given to the demanding nature of some older adults, and the grief of coping with accusations of not doing enough. Hence the title of the book!

The Thirty-six Hour Day. A Family Guide to Caring for Persons with Alzheimer's Disease, Related Dementing Illness and Memory Loss in Later Life by Nancy Mace and Peter Rabins. Published in 1981 by Johns Hopkins University Press, Baltimore, MD, USA. Revised edition 1991.

A practical source of ideas and support for those who care at home for a person with a progressive dementing illness. The title of the book alone speaks of empathy and comfort! (Usefully combined with study of the preceding book.)

Divorce and Separation

Helping Your Child Through Separation and Divorce by Glenda Banks. Published 1981 (reprinted 1988) by Collins-Dove, Melbourne.

Useful in alerting the reader to their own feelings when the marriage ends, with separate sections on the role of the 'custodial' parent, the role of the 'access' parent, and the difficulties which may arise for the children when the parent becomes emotionally interested in or involved with someone else.

This is a self-help book which would be useful for any parent trying to cope with marriage breakdown, especially when there are children.

Must Divorce Hurt the Children? by Ruth Inglis. Published in 1982 by Temple Smith, London.

The author emphasises that there are no perfect solutions, that there will always be problems and that one should hope for a 'less bad' rather than a 'good' situation. In some ways the book seems a little dated, at least for the Australian reader, because single-parent families are less stigmatised today than the author's comments suggest, but there are still areas in which the lone parent is greatly disadvantaged, despite the formation of support groups such as Parents Without Partners.

Ruth Inglis discusses some matters which are not always openly discussed such as the risks of the 'access' parent kidnapping the child(ren) during permitted visiting. She describes the book as a 'child-centred study of divorce' and the way in which the material is presented lives up to this claim. *Surviving Divorce: Women's Resources after Divorce* by Mavis McLean. Published in 1991 by Macmillan, London.

Although useful for those who are living through the aftermath of marital breakdown, this reads as more of a study than a 'how to' book. But it has helpful discussion of women's resources after the end of a marriage.

Just Me and the Kids by Diana Kupke. Published in 1987 by Penguin, Melbourne. Now, regrettably, out of print, but still to be found in libraries.

Although the resource lists of names, addresses, telephone numbers of organisations and support groups make this book useful mainly for Australian readers, there is much other material included to make it worth reading anyway.

Step-family Realities by Margaret Newman. Published in 1992 by Doubleday, Sydney, NSW.

This deals in thoroughly practical terms with the challenges facing the combination of two families through marriage of one parent of each family. Such families are often described as 'blended', but the author points out that 'curdled families' is often a more accurate description, so many and so varied are the difficulties encountered! (Throughout the book there are amusing illustrations which drive home a point through humour without trivialising the matter in question.)

The author looks courageously at matters often 'swept under the carpet', such as: sexual relationships between step-siblings and the risk that the need for love may lead to manipulation and exploitation of a younger child by an older one; the risks that a child's search for love may permit incestuous abuse from a step-parent to a child from the spouse's own family, and that this can be heterosexual or homosexual exploitation; jealousy and quarrels between the two parts of the step-family.

A valuable resource for those who are coping with the realities of bringing two families together after divorce or death.

Euthanasia

The Challenge of Euthanasia by Brian Pollard. Published in 1994 by Little Hills Press, Sydney, NSW.

Dr Pollard is a leader in palliative care and writes convincingly of the risks of so-called voluntary euthanasia, expressing fears that we may move from death as the consequence of stated wishes of the sufferer to the presumption of a wish for death and from thence to death to suit the convenience of others, whether personally or by society, to avoid financial burden on the community. He also points out that many cases described as being 'Euthanasia' are in fact death as a result of withdrawing extraordinary measures to preserve existence rather than 'true' euthanasia, which involves active measures to kill.

Willing to Listen, Willing to Die edited by Helga Kuhse. Published in 1994 by Penguin, Melbourne.

A series of articles and essays on euthanasia, emphasising the right to die. Some of the sections, however, are not about active measures to induce death but the withdrawal of support measures to maintain life artificially. The risks of manipulation to produce a request for death are not discussed.

Books for parents or others to share with children.

Talking with Children about Death. A Dialogue between Parent and Child by Earl Grollman. Published in 1991 by Beacon Press, Boston, MA.

Grollman has produced a small book (this is the third edition which covers both theoretical needs and practical ideas for talking with children. It covers death of a pet, phrases *not* to use such as 'God loved him so much he needed him', which leads the child to think 'Well, God loves me too – am I next?', and so on.

The book includes illustrations to support the interactions and ideas to encourage free conversation, but the book cannot truly be described as a child's picture book.

Daddy's New Baby by Judith Vigna. Published in 1982 by Albert Whitman, New York.

A picture book for young children to help them cope with a parent's new relationship and the birth of a step-sibling.

Sam's Sunday Dad by Margaret Wild. Published in 1992 by Hodder and Stoughton, Sydney, NSW.

A book to help children cope with spending some time with the access parent and the emotional mixture which can result from this.

Poppy's Chair by Karen Hesse, illustrated by Kay Life. Published in 1993 by Macmillan, New York.

A picture book for adults to share with young children; the 'Poppy' of the title is the child's grandfather (parents may wish to add to the name if the book is used for a real-life situation so that the child recognises 'Poppy' as being a grandparent). The book deals with the issues of bewilderment, avoidance and grieving, and an adult will probably find help for himself or herself whilst reading this with a child! After the book has been read several times together and the child feels comfortable with the topic, even the non-reading young child will probably benefit from looking at the book alone.

The Tenth Best Thing about Barney by J. Viorst. Published in 1980 by Atheneum Books, New York.
    Useful for children to cope with grief and loss, includes humourous touches!
How Does it Feel to be Old? by N. Farber. A picture book for children to share with parents. Published in 1979 by E.P. Dutton, New York.
    This book consists of poetry and illustrations to help children understand about the processes of ageing; useful for a child who has fears about old age for their grandparents or parents.

Books for older children and adolescents to read for themselves.

Learning to Grieve. Life Skills for Coping with Loss by Geoff Glassock and Louise Rowling. Published in 1992 by Millennium Books, Sydney, NSW.
    A study and work book to support adolescents as they develop their own coping skills in dealing with grief. The authors' wide experience makes this book very true-to-life.

The Kids' Book of Divorce: By, For and About Kids edited by Eric Rofes, published in 1982 by Vintage Books, Random House, New York.
    This book was written by a group of school children aged 11 to 14 years, at a school in Boston. The book is delightfully illustrated and written in a racy style which makes it appealing to all ages. The children describe their feelings of anger, fear and helplessness, their shame when their friends see their parents fighting, their dread lest they themselves are the cause of the fighting and ultimately of the separation, and other realistic matters.
    The after-effects on parents of marital breakdown are described – parents may be grouchy, paranoid and broke! The children themselves will probably be lonelier, will also gain a greater sense of responsibility, will grow up more quickly (the professional might say 'Too quickly!') and have a better understanding of family finances than in the traditional family where finances are dealt with only by parents.
    The book includes a very helpful practical section which tells other children how to reach the resources they need. Instructions are given on how to use the Yellow (classified) sections of the telephone directory to find counsellors, and suggests headings under which such people will be listed (social worker, psychotherapist, and so on); suggestions are given for finding free clinics for counselling.
    Finally the children writing the book assure those who read it that the divorce is not their fault: parents often seek to make the children take sides in arguments but do not actually hate them even when the children are used in the arguments.

Let's Talk about Divorce by A. Grunsell. Published in 1989 by Gloucester Press, London.
    A practical discussion geared to a child's needs.

Nothing To Be Ashamed Of by S.H. Dinner. Published by Outhrop Lee and Shepherd Books, New York.
    This concerns the challenges to the young person when growing up with mental illness in the family, and helps to overcome loss of self-esteem through stigmatisation.

Mental Retardation by L. Dolce. Published by Chelsea House, New York.
    Although there is today a bewildering variety of fashionable descriptive names for the condition, the frank use of 'mental retardation' is probably helpful and certainly enables a child in a library to locate the book which is needed, in order to find out about these potentially handicapping conditions.

Understanding Cancer by S.N. Terkel and M. Lupiloff-Brazz. Published in 1993 by Franklin Watts, New York; London, and Sydney, NSW.
    This book has humorous illustrations but in no way trivialises the issues. It discusses cancer as it affects children, either from the disease in themselves and friends or in adults, and examines the possibility of death but without dealing with the after-effects of death from cancer on friends and family. Well indexed.

Alzheimer's Disease by E. Landau. Published in 1987 by Franklin Watts, New York, London and Sydney, NSW.

Includes photographs and discusses the topics in a down-to-earth manner but probably without being harrowing to the young adult reader.

Teenagers Face-to-face with Cancer by K. Gravele and B.A. John. Published in 1986 by Julian Messner, New York.

In this book, 15 teenagers describe their own experiences with cancer. No topics are hidden, they describe their fears, emotional responses, the possibility of death and their chances of recovery. This book stands as a positive contribution to the available literature for young adults. Well indexed.

How it Feels when a Parent Dies by Jill Krementz. Published in 1983 by Gollancz, London.

This book is especially helpful because it contains 18 very personal and even intimate accounts by different children, aged between 7 and 16 years, of how they felt when a parent died.

The book is illustrated with photographs of the children who wrote the book, which adds to its real-life feeling. There is considerable variety in the experiences and responses described, so that any bereaved young person who reads it is likely to find some relevance to his or her own situation.

Everything You Need to Know about... This is the generic title of a series of very useful books written for adolescents, all of them published by the Rosen publishing group in New York.

The books mentioned here are especially relevant to issues of grief and powerlessness but all of the books in the series will hold interest at one time or another for the adolescent who maintains awareness of what happens in society.

Everything You Need to Know about AIDS by Barbara Taylor. Published in 1988.

Helpful information and although the book perhaps need up-dating (perhaps already is in the process of re-issue?) it covers the questions commonly asked by young adults, and others.

Everything You ever Wanted to Know about your Parents' Divorce by L.C. Johnson, published in 1989.

Helpful information, giving answers to the questions adolescents may or may not ask but need to know about, for example about arrangements for living accommodation and visits to parents, together with emotional needs.

Everything You ever Wanted to Know about Grieving by K.S. Spies, published in 1993.

This book considers diverse effects of grief, a useful book for adolescents.

Everything You ever Wanted to Know about When a Parent Dies by Fred Bratman, published in 1992.

This book includes discussion of terminal illness and how this affects the teenager, for example when the parent comes home temporarily from a Hospice, returns to hospital, etc.

Fiction for older children

The mysterious world of Marcus Leadbeater by Ivan Southall. Published in 1991 by Mammoth, Melbourne.

A book for adolescents about the death of a grandfather. Like all Southall's books, this is true to life without being unduly harrowing.

References

Allen, J., Newsom, G.E., Gabbard, G. and Coyne, L. (1984) Scales to assess the therapeutic alliance from a psychoanalytic perspective. *Bulletin of the Menninger Clinic 48*, 5, 383–400.

American Psychiatric Association (1987) *Diagnostic and Statistical Manual (DSM III R)*. Washington DC: American Psychiatric Association.

American Psychiatric Association (1994) *Diagnostic and Statistical Manual (DSM IV)*. Washington DC: American Psychiatric Association.

American Psychiatric Association (1994a) Age-related cognitive decline. In APA *Diagnostic and Statistical Manual, DSM IV*. Washington DC: American Psychiatric Association.

Atkinson, J.H. and Grant, I. (1994) Natural History of Neuropsychiatric Manifestations of HIV Disease. *Psychiatric Clinics of North America 17*, 1, 17–33.

Australian Broadcasting Corporation (1995) Drive (segment on AIDS in Australian Aboriginal population) National Radio Network, 24 April.

Australian Bureau of Statistics (1993) I. Castles (^d) *Disability, Ageing and Carers*. Australia. Summary of findings (Catalogue No: 4430.0). Canberra: Alan Law, Government Printers.

Bailey, L.M. (1984) The use of songs in music therapy with cancer patients and their families. *Journal of Music Therapy 4*, 1, 5–17.

Barker, R.G., Wright, B.A. and Gonick. M.H. (1946) *Adjustment to Physical Handicap. Illness and Disability. Social Science Research Council Bulletin 55* (New York).

Bartels, S.J. (1987) The aftermath of suicide on the psychiatric in-patient unit. *General and Hospital Psychiatry 9*, 189–197

Bartrop, R.W., Luckhurst, E., Lazarus, L., Kiloh L.G. and Penny, R. (1977) Depressed lymphocyte function after bereavement. *Lancet* 16 April, 834–836.

Basoglu, M. and Marks, I. (1988) Post-torture syndrome. *British Medical Journal 297*, 1423–1424

Beauvoir, S. de (1972) *Old Age*. London: Andre Deutsch.

Beck, A.T., Steer, R.A., Kovacs, M. and Garrison, B.S. (1985) Hopelessness and eventual suicide: a ten-year prospective study of patients hospitalized with suicidal ideation. *American Journal of Psychiatry 142*, 559–563.

Beszterczey, A. (1977) Staff stress on a newly-developed palliative care service: a psychiatrist's role. *Canadian Psychiatry Association Journal 22*, 347–353.

Birchwood, M. (1992) Early intervention in schizophrenia: theoretical background and clinical strategies. *British Journal Clinical Psychology 31*, 3, 257–278

Boccelari, A. and Zeifert, P. (1994) Management of Neurobehavioral Impairment in HIV-I infection. *Psychiatric Clinics of North America 17*, 1, 183–203.

Bowlby, J. (1971) Attachment. In Volume 1 of J. Bowlby *Attachment and Loss*. Harmondsworth: Penguin.

Bowlby, J. (1975) Separation: anxiety and anger. In Volume 3 of J. Bowlby *Attachment and Loss*. Harmondsworth: Penguin.

Bowlby, J. (1981) Loss: sadness and depression. In Volume 2 of J. Bowlby *Attachment and Loss*. Harmondsworth: Penguin.

Bright, R. (1986) *Grieving: A Handbook for Those Who Care*. St. Louis MMB.

Bright, R. (1991) *Grieving*. St Louis: MMB Music Inc..

Bright, R. (1993) Cultural aspects of music in therapy. In M. Heal and T. Wigram (eds) *Music in Health and Education*. London: Jessica Kingsley Publishers, 193–207.

Bright, R. (1994) *Music Therapy for Grief Counselling* (video). Sydney: Music Therapy Enterprises.

Bright, R. (1994) Music therapy. In E. Chiu and D. Ames (eds) *Functional Psychiatric Disorder of the Elderly*. Cambridge: Cambridge University Press 580–593.

Bright, R. (1994a) Results of Research Questionnaire on stresses and satisfactions of telephone volunteers. Grief Support, Sydney, Australia (unpublished).

Bright, R. (1995) Music Therapy as a Facilitator in Grief Counselling. In T. Wigram, B. Saperston and R. West (eds) *The Art and Science of Music Therapy*. Chur, Switzerland: Harwood Academic, 309–323.

Brody, E. (1981) Women in the middle. *Gerontologist 21*, 5, 471-80.

Broome, R. (1982) *Aboriginal Australia*. Sydney: Allen and Unwin

Bryson, Y.J., Shen, P., Wei, W.S., Wei Lian, S., Dickover, R., Diagne, A., and Chen, I.S.Y. (1995) Clearance of HIV infection from a perinatally infected infant. *New England Journal of Medicine 332*, 833–838.

Cain, A.C. (1964) Children's disturbed reactions to the death of a sibling. *American Journal of Psychiatry 34*, 741.

Carroll, L. (1933) *Through the Looking Glass*. London: McMillan.

Cassell, E.J. (1972) Being and becoming dead. *Social Research 39*, 528–542.

Chadwick, P. and Birchwood, M. (1994) The omnipotence of voices: a cognitive approach to auditory hallucinations. *British Journal Psychiatry 164*, 190–201.

Chesney, M.C. and Folkman, S. (1994) Psychological impact of HIV disease and implications for intervention. *Psychiatric Clinics of North America 17*, 1, 163–182.

Chitkara, B., Macdonald, R. and Reveley, R.M. (1988) Twin birth and adult psychiatric disorder: an examination of the case records of the Maudsley Hospital. *British Journal of Psychiatry 152*, 391-8.

Chochinov, H.M., Wilson, K.G., Enns, M., Mowchun, N., Lander, S., Levitt, M., Clinch, J. (1995) Desire for death in the terminally ill. *American Journal of Psychiatry 152*, 8, 1185–1191.

Condon, J.T. (1986) Psychological disability in women who relinquish a baby for adoption. *Mededical Journal of Australia 144*, 3, 117–9.

Cotton, P.G., Drake, R.E. (Jr), Whitaker A., and Potter J. (1983) Dealing with suicide on a psychiatric in-patient unit. *Hospital and Community Psychiatry 34*, 1, 55–59.

Cramond, W., Fraenkel, M. and Barratt, L. (1990) On Letting Go; the Patient, Dialysis and Opting Out. *Australia and New Zealand Journal of Psychiatry 24*, 268–275.

Danziger R. (1994) The social impact of HIV/AIDS in developing countries. *Social Science and Medicine 39*, 7, 905–917.

Dearmer, P., Williams R.V. and Shaw M. (1964) *Patapan. Oxford Book of Carols* (no.82). London: Oxford University Press.

Diggory, J.C. and Rothman, D.Z. (1961) Values destroyed by death. *Journal of Normal and Abnormal Psychology 63*, 205-10.

Dilley, J.W. (1994) The University of California AIDS Health Project. *Psychiatric Clinics of North America 17*, 1, 205–225.

Doka, K.J. (1989) *Disenfranchised Grief*. Lexington, MA: Lexington Books.

Easterbrook, P.J. (1994) Non-progression in HIV infection. Editorial comment. *AIDS 8*, 8, 1179–82

Ebmeier, K.P., Calder, S.A., Crawford, J.R., Stewart, L., Besson. J.A. and Mutch, W.J. (1990) Clinical features predicting dementia in idiopathic Parkinson's disease. *Neurology 140*, 149–153.

Egan, G. (1976) *Interpersonal Living*. Monterey, CA: Brooks/Cole Publishing.

Einfeld, S.L. (1992) Clinical Assessment of Psychiatric Symptoms in Mentally Retarded Individuals. *Australia and New Zealand Journal of Psychiatry 26*, 1, 48–63.

Eisenbruch, M. (1984a) Cross-cultural aspects of bereavement. 1: A conceptual framework for comparative analysis. *Culture, Medicine and Psychiatry 8*, 283–309.

Eisenbruch, M. (1984b) Cross-cultural aspects of bereavement. 2: Ethnic and cultural variations in the development of bereavement practices. *Culture, Medicine and Psychiatry 8*, 315–347.

Ellard, J. (1968) Emotional reactions to death. *Medical Journal of Australia 1*, 23, 979–983.

Farber, B.A. (1983) Dysfunctioal aspects in of the therapeutic role. In B.A. Farber (ed) Stress and Burnout in the Human Services Professions. New York: Pergamon, 97–118.

Folkman, S., Chesney, M. and Christopher-Richards, A. (1994) Stress and coping in caregiving partners of men with AIDS. *Psychiatric Clinics of North America 17*, 1, 35–53.

Gilmore, N. and Somerville, M.A. (1994) Stigmatization, scapegoating and discrimination in sexually-transmitted diseases: overcoming 'Them and Us'. *Social Science and Medicine 39*, 9, 1339–1358.

Glaser B and Strauss A. (1967) *Discovery of Grounded Theory. Strategies for Qualitative Research.* Chicago, IL: Aldine Publishing.

Gosling, P. (1980) Mourners without a death. *British Journal of Psychiatry 137*, 397–398.

Grotjahn, M. (1955) Analytic Psychotherapy with the Elderly. *Psychoanalytic Review 42*, 419-27.

Groves, J.E. (1978) Taking care of the hateful patient. *New England Journal of Medicine 298*, 16, 883–887.

Guisewhite, C. (1995) *Sydney Morning Herald,* March 4.

Guptil, A.L. (1946) *Norman Rockwell: Illustrator.* New York: Watson-Guptil.

Harris, T.A. (1969) *I'm OK, You're OK.* New York: Harper and Rowe.

Health Commission of New South Wales (1981) *Cultural Diversity in Health Care.* Sydney: Health Commission of New South Wales, Migrant Health Unit.

Heins, T., Gray, A. and Tennant, M. (1990) Persisting hallucinations following childhood sexual abuse. *Australia and New Zealand Journal of Psychiatry 24*, 4, 561–565.

Hill, P. (1993) *Confronting the Avioded Spot.* Lecture given at 10th Annual Kings College Conference on Death and Bereavement, London, Ontario, Canada.

Hinton, J. (1967) *Dying.* Harmondsworth: Penguin.

Holland, L.K. and Whalley, M.J. (1981) The work of the psychiatrist in a rehabilitation hospital. *British Journal of Psychiatry 138*, 222–229.

Hurley, P.M., Grossman, A.H. and McGriff, E.P. (1990) Who supports the nurse when the patient has AIDS? *RN* July, 39–42.

Ingham, J.G., Kreitman, P., Miller, P. McC., Sashidharan, S.P. and Surtees P.G. (1986) Self-esteem, Vulnerability and Psychiatric Disorder in the Community. *British Journal Psychiatry 148*, 375–385.

Jamrozik, W. and Hobbs. M. (1989) Migrants and medicine: many challenges. *Medical Journal of Australia 150* 17 April, 415–417.

Kastenbaum, A. and Aisenburg, A. (1972) *The Psychology of Death.* New York: Springer. 6–26.

Kayton, L. and Freed, H. (1967) Effects of a suicide in a psychiatric hospital' *Archives of General Psychiatry 17*, 187–194.

Kennedy, E. (1977) *On Becoming a Counsellor.* Melbourne: Dove Communications.

Kertesz, A, (1985) Aphasia. In P.J. Vinken, G.W. Bruyn, H.L. Klawans (eds) *Handbook of Clinical Neurology 45* (volume 1 of new series). Amsterdam: Elsevier, 287–332.

Khin-Maung-Zaw (1981) A Suicidal Family. *British Journal of Psychiatry 139*, 68–69.

Kissane, D.W. (1994). Family-based grief counselling. *Australian Family Physician 23*, 4, 678–680.

Kohen, D. (1991) Psychological sequellae of torture (letter). *British Journal of Psychiatry 158*, 287.

Lewis C S. (1964) *A Grief Observed* (2nd impression). London: Faber.

Lezak, M. (1982) Coping with head injury in the family. In G.A. Broe and R.L. Tate (ed) *Brain Impairment* University of Sydney: Post-graduate committee, Medicine, 5–15.

Lieberman, S. (1983) Mourning and Melancholia. *British Journal of Psychiatry 142*, 100.

Lippman, S.B., James, W.A. and Frierson, R.L. (1993) AIDS and the family; implications for counselling. *AIDS-CARE 5*, 1, 71–78

Lord, R. (compiler) (1976) *Inscriptions in Stone. St David's Burial Ground.* St George's Church, Battery Point publication. (Reference to public outcry on second, unnumbered page.)

Low, S.M. (1985) Culturally interpreted symptoms or culture-bound syndromes: a cross-cultural review of nerves. *Social Science and Medicine 21*, 2, 187–196.

Luborsky, L., Crits-Christoph, P., Alexander, L., Margolis, M. and Cohen, M. (1983) Two helping alliance methods for predicting outcome of psychotherapy. *Journal of Nervous and Mental Diseases 171*, 8, 480–91.

Malan, D.H. (1979) *Individual Psychotherapy and the Science of Psychodynamics.* London: Butterworth, 64–73.

Maynard, R. (1993) Losing a Twin. *The New Idea Magazine 4*, 24.

McFarlane, A. (1990) Vulnerability to post-traumatic stress disorder. In M.E. Wolf and A.D. Mosnaim (eds) *Posttraumatic Stress Disorder. Etiology, Phenomenonology and Treatment.* Washington, DC: American Psychiatric Press, 2–20.

McNamara, L. and Morrison, J. (1982) *Separation, Divorce and After.* Brisbane, Queensland: University of Queensland Press.

Mogul, K. (1982) The sex of the therapist: an overview. *American Journal of Psychiatry 139*, 1, 1–11

Mount, B.M. (1974) Christian and agnostic attitudes towards death. *Ontario Medical Review*, January issue, 11–14.

Mount, B.M. (1986) Dealing with our losses. *Journal of Clinical Oncology 4*, 7, 1127–1134.

Mount, B.M. (1990) *Meaning in Dying* (video). Montreal: Royal Victoria Hospital Palliative Care Services.

Moyle, A. (1980) *Waiting for Harry* (video). Canberra: Australian Institute of Aboriginal Studies.

Munro, S. and Mount B. (1978) Music Therapy in Palliative Care. *Canadian Journal of Psychiatry 119*, 9, 3–8.

Murphy, M. (1977) Migration, culture and mental health. *Psychological Medicine 7*, 677–684.

Nordoff, P. (1974) Lecture on Music Therapy given at State Conservatorium of Music, Sydney, Australia.

Olson, D.H., Russell, C.S., and Sprenkle, D.H., (1983) A circumplex model of marital and family systems: theoretical up-date. *Family Process 22*, 1, 67–83.

Parkes, C.M. (1975) *Bereavement.* Harmondsworth: Penguin.

Paykel E.S., Myers, J.K., Dienelt, M.N., Klerman, G.L., Lindenthal, J.J., and Pepper, M. (1969) Life events and depression. *Archives of General Psychiatry* 21 Dec., 753–760.

Pedder, J.R. (1982) Failure to mourn and melancholia. *British Journal of Psychiatry 141*, 329–337.

Petrie, K., Chamberlain, K. and Clarke, D. (1988) Psychological predictors of future suicidal behaviour of hospitalised suicide attempters. *British Journal of Clinical Psychology 27*, 3, 247–257.

Proctor, H (1973). Head injuries. *Physiotherapy 59*, 12, 380–382.

Rabins, P.V. (1982) Psychopathology of Parkinson's disease. *Comparative Psychiatry 23*, 5, 421–429

Raphael, B. (1983) Australians in Disaster. In proceedings of the *Third National Conference of the National Association for Loss and Grief.* Sydney: Association for Loss and Grief pp.4–12

Raphael, B. and Singh, B.S. (1983/4) Who helps the helpers? *Omega 14*, 9–20.

Reid, J. and Strong, T. (1988) Rehabilitation of refugee victims of torture and trauma: principles and service provisions in New South Wales. *Medical Journal of Australia 148*, 340–346.

Reid, J., Siloh, D. and Tarn, R. (1990) Development of New South Wales services for treatment and rehabilitation of torture and trauma survivors. *Australia and New Zealand Journal of Psychiatry 24*, 4, 486–95.

Robertson, J. and Robertson, J. (1967) *Young Children in Brief Separation* (film) London: Tavistock.

Robinson, R.G., Book Starr, L., Lipsey, J.R., Rao, K. and Price, T.R. (1985). A two-year longitudinal study of mood disorder following stroke: prevalence and duration at six-months follow-up. *British Journal of Psychiatry 144*, 252–262.

Rogers, C. (1951) *Client-centred Therapy. Its Current Practice, Implications and Theory.* London: Constable.

Ron, M.A. and Feinstein, A. (1992) M.S. and the mind. J. Neurol Neurosurg and Psychiatry 55, 1, 1-3.

Rosenman, S.J. and Tayler, H. (1986) Mania following bereavement: a case report. *British Journal of Psychiatry 148*, 468–470.

Ross, O. and Kreitman, N. (1975) A further investigation of differences in the suicide rates of England, Wales and Scotland. *British Journal of Psychiatry 127*, 575–582.

Rowling, L. (1994) *Loss and Grief in the Context of the Health-promoting School* Unpublished PhD thesis, Faculty of Education, University of Southampton.

Russell, C. (1981) *The Ageing Experience.* London: Allen and Unwin.

Russell, C. (1995) Old people's constructs and dependency; some implications of aged care policy. In S. Graham (ed) *Dependency, the Life Course and Social Policy SPRC Reports on Proceedings 118*, (Social; Policy and Research Centre, University of New South Wales, Jan 1995) 85–100.

Rutter, M. (1985) Resilience in the face of adversity. *British Journal of Psychiatry 147*, 598–611.

Sacks, O. (1990) *Seeing Voices.* London: Picador.

Scully, R. (1983) The worksetting support group: a means of preventing burnout. In B.A. Farber (ed) *Stress and Burnout in the Human Services Professions. New York: Pergamon, 188–197.*

Segal, N. and Bouchard, T.J.(Jr) (1993). Grief intensity following the loss of a twin and other relatives: test of kinship genetic hypotheses. *Human Biology 65*, 1, 87–105.

Selye, H. (1975) *Stress without distress.* London: Hodder and Stoughton.

Siegel, K. (1982) Rational suicide: considerations for the clinician. *Psychiatric Quarterly 54*, 2, 77–84

Siegel, K. and Gorey, E. (1994) Childhood bereavement due to parental death from acquired immunodeficiency syndrome. *Journal of Developmental and Behavioural Pediatrics 15*, 3 (supplement), 66–70.

Sigal, J.J., Weinfeld, M. and Eaton, W.W. (1985) Stability of coping style 33 years after prolonged exposure to extreme stress. *Acta Psychiatrica Scandinavica 71*, 559–66.

Singer, M. (1994) The politics of AIDS (introduction to a set of papers). *Social Science and Medicine 38*, 10, 1321–1324.

Sloman, L., Springer, S. and Vachon, M. (1993) Disordered communication and grieving in deaf-member families. *Family Process 32*, 171-183.

Solomon, G.F. and Moors, R.H. (1965) Rheumatoid arthritis and personality. *General Practitioner 32*, 113.

Stackhouse, J. (1981) Threat to important site. *The Bulletin* (Sydney) 13 October, 43–50.

Stedeford, A. and Bloch, S. (1979) The psychiatrist in the terminal care unit. *British Journal of Psychiatry 135*, 1-6.

Stevens, J.M. (1982) Some psychological problems of acquired deafness. *British Journal of Psychiatry 140*, 455–456.

Sydney Morning Herald. (1995) Vietnam wrong: verdict divides US. 15 April. Sydney, Australia: John Fairfax Ltd.

Tarassoff v Regents of University of California (1976) *131 CAL Repts. 14*, October (Reference quoted in Wulsin, Burztajn and Gutheil 1983).

Tate, R.L., Lulham, J.M. and Strettles, B. (1982) Severe head injury: outcome impact and adjustment. In G.A. Broe and R.L. Tate (ed) *Brain Impairment*, University of Sydney: Post-graduate committee, Medicine, 81-91.

Treadway, J. (1990) Tarassoff in the therapeutic setting. *Hospital and Community Psychiatry 41*, 1, 80–81.

Twycross, R.G. (1980) The relief of pain. In C. Saunders (ed) *The Management of Terminal Illness.* London: Arnold. 65–92.

Twycross, R.G. (1988) Optimal pharmacological control of chronic cancer pain. *Recent Results in Cancer Research 108*, 9–17.

Waechter, E. (1971) Children's awareness of fatal illness *American Journal of Nursing 7*, 1168–1172.

Wahl, C.W. (1971) The psychodynamics of suicide. *Annals of International Medicine 75*, 441–458.

Wedin, L. (1972) A multidimensional study of perceptual-emotional qualities in music. *Scandinavian Journal of Psychology 13*, 241–257.

Whitfield, M. (1980) Emotional stresses on the psychotherapist. *Canadian Journal of Psychiatry 25*, 292–296.

Wilson, H.S. and Kneish, C.P. (1988) Transference and counter-transference. In *Psychiatric Nursing.* Menlo Pk CA: Addison Wesley.

Winnicott, D.W. (1974) *Playing and Reality.* Harmondsworth: Penguin. pp.76–100.

Wolff, S., McCrae, W.M. and Forfar, J. (1973) In J. Forfar and G. Arneil (ed) *Textbook of Paediatrics.* London: Churchill-Livingstone. p.1753.

Woodward, J. (1988) The bereaved twin. *Acta Geneticae Medicae et Gemmellologiae 37*, 2, 173–180.

Woolley, F.R. (1983) Ethical issues in the implantation of the total artificial heart. *New England Journal of Medicine 310*, 5, 292–296.

Worden, W. (1982) *Grief Counselling and Grief Therapy.* London: Tavistock. (Opening chapters.)

World Health Organisation (1980) *Changing Patterns of Suicide Behaviour* Copenhagen: WHO European Office.

World Health Organisation (1981) *Classification of Disease and Disability.* Geneva: World Health Oranisation.

World Health Organisation (1992) *ICD-10, Classification of Mental and Behavioural Disorders 10.* Geneva: World Health Organisation.

Wright, B. (1960) *Physical Disability: a Psychological Approach.* New York: Harper.

Wulsin, L.R., Burztajn, H. and Gutheil, T.G. (1983) Unexpected clinical features of the Tarassoff decision: the therapeutic alliance and the Duty to Warn. *American Journal of Psychiatry 140*, 5, 601–603.

Yancey, P. (1988) *Where is God when it Hurts?* New York: HarperCollins.

Subject Index

Author Index